So, You Want to be an RVer?

Published by

John and Kathy Huggins

FORWARD

This book is and will continue to be a work in progress. We have put down as much of our experience and knowledge as we can remember and research, as well as material from others who have permitted us to use their work. There is still so much about the RV lifestyle to tell. We wrote the most about the things we know and have experienced. We have said many times, "We are experienced, but not experts".

We want to especially thank the loyal listeners of our podcast, "Living the RV Dream". The "you should write a book" talk started in 2011. At that time, writing a book was the farthest thing from our minds. We were working and travelling as well as keeping up a weekly one-hour radio show. Then in 2012 we received a flurry of e-mails asking us again to publish the stuff we talk about on the show. It is now 2015, and much material has changed. We have also put a great deal of new material in this revised edition. We have also decided that the print and electronic versions should have the same title. So here you are folks. We give you the much revised and double the size edition of our labor of love. We believe you will think it was worth the wait.

We want to thank our son Steve who first asked us to do an RV radio show. To Jim Bathurst, author of "Cat on a Leash" and very thorough editor and proofreader, go our sincere thanks. To our daughter in law Dr. Shelley Huggins who helped with proofreading, thank you for taking time away from our grandchildren to do this for us. We give a special thank you to Nick and Terry Russell. Nick is the author and editor of "The Gypsy Journal" and bestselling author of the "Big Lake" series of books. Nick, you gave us the encouragement to do this project and shared your knowledge of e-publishing. You also took time out of your busy schedule to be one of our proofreaders.

To our Lord and Savior Jesus Christ go all the thanks and all the glory.

TABLE OF CONTENTS

SECTION I
ALL ABOUT THE TYPES OF RVS

SECTION II
RV SYSTEMS

SECTION III
ALL ABOUT TOWING

SECTION IV
FULL-TIME RVING

SECTION V
PART-TIME, WEEKEND, AND FULL-TIME RVING

SECTION VI
RV TIPS

ALL ABOUT THE TYPES OF RVs

Choosing from the many types of RVs can be a lot of fun if you approach it with a plan you both agree on. We have met folks who are camping seasonally in a short 18-foot-long travel trailer. Others have to have the largest rig available. You both have to agree on the lifestyle you want to live. Some folks are into ATVs and other motorized "toys" and a good fit for them would be a toy hauler. Maybe you want to travel around our beautiful country and see as much of it as possible? Others may want to settle in for a season and move with the changing seasons. Can you say "Snowbird"? While there is no ideal rig for a particular lifestyle, the decision is up to you. Unless you can figure out how to live full-time in a class B conversion van, you will probably need to tow something. You might tow a fifth wheel trailer behind a truck or tow a car or truck behind a motorhome, but you will most likely be towing. This, too, factors into the decision of what RV to buy. In order to avoid a major financial mistake, make sure the rig you choose is the right unit for the lifestyle you have chosen. You won't know the magnitude of your mistake until you go to trade the rig in.

This whole decision process over types of RVs is both subjective and emotional. Debates rage over Motorhome or Fifth wheel trailer. Do you prefer a Class A Motorhome, a Class C Motorhome, or a Class B Motorhome? Perhaps you are interested in converted bus. What about Towable RVs? Do you like the Fifth wheel trailer, the bumper pull or Travel Trailer? Another constant debate is Gasoline power vs. diesel. New versus used types of RVs is always a lively discussion. There is no right answer. You must decide what will work best for you. We will give our opinions about these and other issues involving types of RVs, but they are our opinions based on what we thought we would need and what we could afford. We also will look at rigs that easily lend themselves to full time RVing. We'll also discuss Truck Campers, Pop-up Tent Campers, and Teardrop Trailers.

CHAPTER 1

MOTORHOME OR FIFTH WHEEL TRAILER?

The debate about Motorhome or Fifth wheel trailer rages on in America at campfires, on the internet, and wherever RVers gather. It is especially contentious between folks living full-time in their RVs. I have to admit I may be a little slanted towards Motorhomes because that is the only rig we have owned. I have looked at this issue very closely on many Facebook groups and internet forums over the last several years. Neither one comes out as a clear winner or loser wherever I have looked. It is with a fair amount of trepidation that I undertake this study of both sides of the ongoing great debate. My hope is that it may help someone make up their mind about which fits their needs better. No matter which you have, you will be towing something, be it towed car or trailer.

■ Fifth wheel trailer Pros

Without a doubt, the Fifth wheel trailer provides the most homelike living experience of any RV. Equipped with as many as 5 slideouts, they open up to as much as 400 square feet or more. Island kitchens are commonplace and appeal to folks who like to cook with lots of countertop preparation space. Living room space with residential recliners and sofas look like a cozy cottage complete with fireplace and large entertainment system. Desks with computer storage are commonplace.

Classic Fifth Wheel styling places the bedroom up front over the hitch with center galley amidships and rear living room. Lately, there are models with the living room up front with a rear master bedroom. Opposing slideouts accommodate facing sofas or recliners. With the bathroom moved to the rear, there is plenty of space for large screen TVs.

With no engine, transmission, or cockpit area, all the space in a towable rig is useable for living and storage. The area below the front space is utilized as bulk storage as well as storage for batteries and LP gas tanks. It is a large space accessible from street or curb side. More storage is available in the bed of the truck towing the Fifth Wheel.

Usually, the total cost of a trailer and suitable truck are less than a Motorhome with a towed car. I say usually because there are so many different rigs that it is difficult to make an absolute statement. Insurance will also be less expensive for a Fifth wheel trailer and truck.

■ Fifth wheel trailer Cons

The first issue that should face a Fifth wheel trailer owner is matching it to a suitable truck. Or, if you already own a truck, obtaining a trailer that matches the capabilities of the truck. This involves matching specifications of the truck with the weights of the trailer. Unfortunately, dealers are usually no help here. The very best place I have found for help is http://www.fifthwheelst.com. Fill in the blanks formulas there will help you match up truck and trailer.

For folks just getting into RVing, maneuvering a truck and trailer is a new and often intimidating skill set. Backing any type of trailer into a campsite requires a lot of practice.

The tires that come standard on the majority of Fifth wheel trailers are cheap China sourced ones that are bought in large quantities. There are many horror stories about multiple failures on the same trip. Those failures often result in damage to the trailer. These tires have the absolute lowest load rating for the dry weight of the trailer. Many folks end up replacing all the trailer tires with higher load rated tires early into the owning experience.

While many new top line Fifth wheel trailers have automatic leveling systems, the majority have manual jacks that must be lowered individually. Jacks at all four corners must be lowered and the trailer leveled. Then the truck must be unhooked and driven forward. Usually, this truck is your only vehicle to tour and get groceries. Mileage unhooked is better, but not great either.

Hooking back up requires some pretty precise backing up to the trailer. Once the pin is engaged, it must be locked in the hitch. Otherwise, when you drive forward with the trailer, the pin separates from the hitch and the trailer slams down on the bed of the truck. This will leave some fairly serious dents in the sidewalls of the truck bed. I have seen many trucks bearing this mark of shame, so it must happen occasionally. I'm sure there is some damage to the trailer as well.

If the tow truck breaks down, what do you drive? Will a tow company tow your Fifth wheel trailer to a campground? Check with your roadside service plan to be sure. Not all will.

■ Motorhome Pros

The most widely publicized advantage to the Motorhome is the ability of the passenger to get up, use the toilet, get food and drinks from the refrigerator, and return to the cockpit while the rig motors down the road. While not the only advantage, it is a big one.

Most modern Motorhomes are built on heavy duty truck chassis's. That allows for basement storage compartments down both sides and sometimes all the way across from side to side. This makes for a lot of storage capacity before getting inside the rig. The heavy duty frame also allows for the towing of a vehicle, also known as the toad. The toad can be a smaller high mileage vehicle for touring and shopping. If the Motorhome breaks down, you still have a car to drive.

The Motorhome driver sits almost on top of the front wheels. That makes for easy maneuvering. Most have at least a 50-degree wheel cut that makes it easy to back into campsites.

Most larger Motorhomes have either manual or automatic leveling jacks that are deployed from the driver's seat. On a rainy night, a Motorhome owner drives into his campsite, lowers his leveling jacks, and goes to bed. He can hook up in the morning. The Fifth wheel trailer driver is going to get wet no matter what. This is a security issue as well. The motorhome owner can leave an unsafe area without leaving the safety of his rig. The trailer driver must leave the safe zone of his trailer to go to the truck to leave.

As many as four slide-out rooms make the Motorhome almost as roomy as the Fifth wheel trailer. Almost. Most newer Motorhomes also have built-in generators in case of loss of campground power or for boondocking.

■ Motorhome Cons

The first big downside to me is initial cost of a Motorhome. You are paying for both an RV and a motor vehicle rolled into one.

Maintenance costs on a Motorhome are much higher than a pickup truck as well. The heavy duty chassis maintenance is the same as a commercial truck. Make it a diesel powered rig and the scheduled maintenance costs triple. 22-quart oil changes are at least $300 now. However, the frequency of required services like oil changes is much longer as well. Wheel bearings, brakes, compressed air systems, hydraulic systems, all require maintenance.

Now add in the cost of another engine in the toad and another whole set of maintenance costs. Vehicle insurance is higher for a Motorhome as well as adding insurance on the towed car.

Upgrading to a bigger or better Motorhome will cost much more than upgrading a Fifth wheel trailer which can be towed by the truck you already have. It is also probably easier to sell a used Fifth wheel trailer than a used Motorhome.

■ Motorhome or Fifth wheel trailer?

I'm sure there are more pros and cons for both types, but I am trying to put together a relatively brief synopsis of the controversy and possibly clear up some misconceptions. One big one is that when your Motorhome breaks down you have to stay in a hotel. This is absolutely not true. In our years on the road, we have only had one hotel stay, and that was due to very cold weather and the fact that the repair shop only had a 20 amp drop for us. We opted for a 2-night hotel stay and then were right back in our rig. Most shops have at least power so you can stay the night in your rig. It will be in a service bay during the day and back outside at night. This has been our experience.

CHAPTER 2

GAS VS. DIESEL POWER

The gas vs. diesel debate will rage on as long as we have a choice of engines in trucks and motorhomes. When we were looking at motorhomes (having already heard the Motorhome vs. Fifth wheel trailer debate), we found the choice pretty easy as soon as someone mentioned air ride and air brakes. There is a lot more to this discussion than that though.

■ Diesel Pro's

Diesel engines are designed to last a long time, usually in the one-million-mile range. We will never drive that many miles, but it's great peace of mind to know that we can. Diesel engines are large and heavy, so a very robust chassis is required. This means you will have much more cargo carrying capacity in a diesel rig. The motorhome chassis are also capable of towing between 5 and 10 thousand pounds and even more in some very heavy duty applications.

As I mentioned before, most diesel motorhomes have air brakes, usually with front disc brakes and rear drum brakes. These air actuated brakes will give you the stopping power for such a heavy rig. Almost all will have either an exhaust brake or a mechanical engine retarder (Jake Brake) to help bring the coach speed down without having to use the service brakes. This is almost an essential on long downgrades. Most also have air bags at each corner to cushion the ride. Some higher end units use this feature to level the coach both when on the road and in a campsite. An exhaust brake is an accessory that can be fitted to most diesel pickup trucks.

A diesel engine is designed to have substantially more torque at lower engine speeds which allows a diesel powered coach to climb mountain grades more easily that its gas counterpart. This power at lower RPM allows for increased fuel economy as well.

■ Diesel Downsides

Maintenance on a diesel engine is much more involved as well as more expensive. Oil changes in motorhome can require 20 quarts or more. There will be 2 or more fuel filters, one of which is a fuel/water separator filter. It must be changed each oil change. These intervals are every 5000 miles or annually. On a motorhome, there are air dryer cartridges in each air brake can which must be changed periodically. Cooling system fluid has critical additives for a diesel engine. The heavy duty transmission must have fluid and filter changes on a periodic basis. All of these required services can be quite expensive. Most service and virtually all engine and chassis repairs must be made in either manufacturer's shops or authorized truck repair facilities. Diesel pickups can be serviced at the truck dealer. This maintenance issue is a major stumbling point for diesel in the gas engine vs. diesel engine debate.

At this point in time, diesel fuel is substantially more expensive than gasoline, partially negating mileage gains.

■ Gasoline Pro's

First and foremost is the fact that gasoline powered coaches are typically 40 to 50 thousand dollars less expensive than a diesel coach. Gas pickup trucks are at least $15,000 less. They also can usually be repaired at either a Ford, Chevrolet, or Dodge dealer depending on engine type. Oil changes can be done by the owner and require much less oil. There are standard power assisted brakes and usually no air bags and their associated compressors. Almost all run on standard grade unleaded gasoline available everywhere and less expensive than diesel fuel. This lower cost issue leans toward gas in the gas vs. diesel argument.

■ Gasoline Con's

Although gasoline engines can produce more horsepower than a diesel engine, they do not produce anywhere near the torque. Horsepower may get you to go faster, but it's torque that gets you up the hills and mountain grades. Gasoline rigs typically have lighter duty chassis than a diesel rig, so the gas rig will not have the cargo carrying capacity of the diesel. For this reason, I cannot in good conscience recommend a gas powered pickup truck for towing trailers over 12,000 pounds. This alone should shift the diesel vs. gas towards diesel power.

■ The Gas vs. Diesel Debate Rages On

It should be obvious by now that I am a diesel motorhome owner. I do tend to go back to my first impressions of "air brakes" and "air ride." I have no prejudice against gas rigs however. Both have their place in the RVing community. Someday we may downsize to a gas rig. I'm convinced this whole gas vs. diesel debate boils down to finances.

CHAPTER 3

NEW VS. USED RVs

When we were in the homework phase of deciding what rig to buy, we got a lot of advice, sometimes conflicting, about whether to buy a new or a used RV. We'll look at both sides of the issue. A new rig of any type will have warranties on the chassis, drive train for motorized units, and appliances such as refrigerators, air conditioners, stove and hot water heater and furnace(s). This is great peace of mind for many folks. Another issue is that you will be the first to use the unit so everything will be pristine. There won't be bedbugs in the mattress or stains on the carpet. Obviously, this is appealing to many people. The big ugly cloud over any RV purchase is depreciation. No RV will increase in value. Drive-off depreciation on any new rig will be at least twenty percent. On the more expensive units, it will be more. As each year passes, the depreciation continues in smaller increments. To quote from Bob Randall; Mark Polk (2011-09-29). RV Buyers Survival Guide (Kindle Locations 684-685). RV Education 101. Kindle Edition. "Depreciation is only a major problem if you pay full MSRP (Manufacturer's Suggested Retail Price). Depreciation is figured based on what the unit should have sold for, not what you paid for it." We bought this book prior to our RV purchase; it should be an essential part of every future RV purchase you make.

A maddening problem common to all types of RVs is that almost all new rigs have "issues". These can be drawers that don't fit properly, appliances that don't work as they should, small leaks around windows and roof mounted items, and other such annoying things that fall under the warranty. Axel misalignment is a common issue with towable RVs that manifests itself with premature tire wear and even blow-outs. Even though covered, the RV must be returned to the dealer for service and repairs, thus robbing you of the use of your rig. In extreme cases, this can go on and on for months. Even the most thorough pre-delivery inspection can miss some things.

A two to three-year-old RV will have had most if not all of those "new rig bugs" fixed and/or resolved. The first two or three years are the largest chunk of depreciation as well. A two to three-year-old motorhome will probably have some warranty left on the drive train. We spent a lot of time doing the math and we calculated cost of a new motorhome to still be more expensive versus a two-year-old unit with better specifications. At the end of the day, we decided on a one-year-old rig with much more equipment than what we were originally considering. This fell right in line with another bit of advice we had heard which was, no matter what types of RVs you consider, "Buy your third rig first". An entry level unit will have a more acceptable price, but you will probably be looking for a better one in a year or two. Now you will have two sets of depreciation to deal with as well as sales commissions. We have heard of folks buying three or four RVs within five years. What an expensive hassle! On the other hand, unless you are an experienced handyman, buying a fifteen-year-old rig might end up being more expensive than a five-year-old one.

CHAPTER 4

MOTORIZED RVs

■ Class A Motorhomes

The Class A Motorhome is the top of the food chain for RVs. They cost more, they're bigger than other RVs, and they are just macho cool. The amenities in a class "A" make it a condo on wheels. Multiple large screen televisions with surround sound systems are common. Combination washer/dryers are available as well as a separate stacked washer and dryer. Electric residential refrigerators are available on many newer coaches. Almost all have combination convection and microwave ovens. Slide-out rooms provide more square footage for living aboard. Built-in central vacuum systems are common options. How about an electric fireplace under that large flat-screen? Basement storage is an advantage common to both gas and diesel motorhomes. There are doors along both sides that open into storage compartments to hold gear you don't need inside the coach. Depending on the chassis, there may be pass-thru storage accessible from either side. Almost all class "A" coaches will have either hydraulic or electric jacks for leveling the coach.

■ Diesel Class A Motorhomes (Pro's)

OK, I'll start at the top. The Class "A" diesel pusher motorhome was our choice when we started and we haven't changed our minds. A key point is lots of storage and basement space. We have almost four thousand pounds of available cargo carrying capacity. That's a lot of grills and lawn chairs. The diesel chassis provides air brakes and air bag assisted suspension. This makes for both safe and comfortable driving. A side benefit to this is an air chuck tied to the on-board air compressor for airing up tires. It also has the ability to handle four slide-out rooms. I've even seen five on one rig. I was told by the tour guide at the Winnebago plant that each slide room can add as much as one thousand pounds of extra weight to the coach. That big motor provides plenty of torque to move all that weight up hills. An exhaust brake or a mechanical engine retarder is provided to help save the service brakes going down those same hills. Another benefit with the engine in the back is very low noise when driving, although there are some front engine diesel entry level motorhomes on the market today. Typically, a diesel coach will get a little better mileage than a gasoline engine Class "A", but the currently higher price of diesel fuel may offset this. An exciting new development in diesel motorhomes is the introduction of shorter wheel base, aero-dynamic shaped designs that get better fuel mileage. Time will tell about the popularity of these smaller coaches.

■ Diesel Motorhomes (Con's)

On the down side, diesel engine maintenance is more expensive and complicated than a gasoline engine motorhome. Oil changes require about 20 plus quarts of oil plus replacement of a fuel/water separator filter. The recommendation is that this two hundred and fifty-dollar service be performed annually. The heavy-duty transmission in the pusher requires fluid and filter changes to the tune of about three hundred dollars every several years. There are driers in the air brake system that will need replacement every few years as well. Most diesels, and now the larger gas coaches, have 22.5 inch wheels with tires in the five hundred dollar plus each range that must be replaced every five to seven years. The cost of this maintenance must be figured into your budget.

■ Gasoline Powered Class A Motorhomes (pro's)

Next up is the Gasoline engine motorhome. In recent years, these coaches can have up to a twenty-six-thousand-pound gross vehicle weight chassis. This is the same as many lower end diesel coaches. They can have as many as four slide rooms and boast most of the amenities of a diesel coach. These are front engine designs using mostly Ford large displacement truck based motors. A big advantage is that they can be serviced at most Ford dealerships. Periodic oil changes are much less expensive than on a diesel coach. They are typically about forty thousand dollars less expensive than a diesel coach of similar size.

■ Gasoline Powered Motorhomes (Con's)

Virtually all currently produced gasoline engine coaches are riding on the Ford F-53 chassis. This is derived from a truck chassis and as such, has all the comfort and handling characteristics of a bread truck. The redoubtable Ford V-10 engine powers these coaches and is mounted between driver and passenger. The engine noise is tolerable under normal conditions, but hill climbing causes it to scream like a banshee. Without much extra insulation, engine heat escapes into the cabin as well. There are aftermarket kits to improve the ride and handling, but at an additional $1500 to $2000 to add front and rear sway bars and a steering stabilizer.

Other negatives about gas coaches are poor hill climbing ability compared to the high torque diesel coach. Fuel mileage is also typically several miles per gallon less. Both the last statements are magnified when towing the extra weight of a car. Cargo carrying capacity, or the stuff you want to put into the coach, is typically less in a gasoline chassis. I haven't seen any gas rigs with air suspension or air brakes either. At the end of the day, your choice of Class A Motorhome is largely subjective.

■ Class B Motorhome

Class B Motorhomes have been called camper vans or van campers. I guess Kathy and I started RVing back in 1970 when we purchased a used VW camper bus. We took it to Italy when I was stationed there and it was camped in plenty. We even bought another when we returned. I'm not sure this was the forerunner to the Class B Motorhome, but it did seem so.

Of the three types of motorized RVs, Class B motorhomes are the smallest. Commonly, a minivan or a full size van will be specially customized and turned into a mini RV. There are many professional conversion companies that do an excellent job of converting mini vans and full size vans into RVs. After their conversion, they don't look much different on the outside other than the "bubble top" extension they now have which allows people to walk upright in the interior of the van, and some vans also have a lowered floor to make even more headroom.

Many new Class Bs have slide rooms built in them. In the last several years, the Mercedes Benz "Sprinter" cargo van has been introduced in this country. With its diesel power and eighteen to twenty miles per gallon fuel economy, it was a natural to be turned into a class B motorhome. There are at least seven or eight companies producing these including Winnebago with a Class B and a beautifully engineered twenty-five-foot Class A on a Sprinter chassis. Recently, the Ram ProMaster chassis has been introduced. It is the North American version of the Fiat Ducato. This is a gas chassis that can accommodate both Class C and Class B Motorhomes. While the Class B may boast most of the amenities of larger coaches, the sheer small size and lack of storage makes them mostly unsuitable for full-time living. The holding tanks are quite a bit smaller than even a small Class C rig, and the fuel and propane tanks are also smaller. Pricing on Class B Motorhomes is rapidly rising above the one hundred-thousand-dollar mark as well.

The Class B Motorhome is gaining popularity with current RVers who want to downsize and even full-time RVers who are coming off the road and want to travel occasionally.

■ Class C Motorhome

The Class C motorhome, or mini motorhome, is an RV built on a cut-away van or truck chassis, including the cab. Many Class C motorhomes are roughly the size and shape of rental moving trucks. It differs from the Class A motorhome in that the Class C chassis comes with the cab from the manufacturer. Another distinguishing feature of the Class C is the bed compartment over the cab. Although that sleeping bunk area in a Class C is typically used for sleeping, not everyone wants to have a bunk bed that they have to climb up in to. In response to this, some manufacturers have made it optional to turn this area into an entertainment system area or storage area. Other manufacturers are building very large Class C motorhomes on a diesel powered stretched semi truck chassis. These units are every bit as large, luxurious, and expensive as Class A's. These are known as Super C's.

Class C motorhomes come with both gasoline and diesel engines depending on manufacturer and model. The same pro's and con's apply here as in Class A motorhomes. The typically lower cost of a Class C Motorhome makes it quite appealing to first time RV buyers, especially in the twenty-five to thirty-two foot models. Most Class C Motorhomes have sleeping arrangements for 6 to 8 people, more than a Class A unit. Generally, Class C motorhomes cannot carry as much load as a Class A because they are usually built on a light truck chassis. They also have smaller fuel and holding tanks as well as very limited basement storage areas.

If you are considering a used Class C, be especially mindful of the area above the cab as it is a prime place for cracks and subsequent leaks to form. Check this area very closely before purchasing.

This is a Super C class Motorhome from Renegade

■ RV Bus Conversions

RV Bus Conversions are among the least populous of the RV types. They can be multimillion dollar Prevost factory conversions, to re-purposed passenger buses, to even the lowly school bus. All are included in the RV Bus Conversions group. My friend Nick Russell, who with his wife Terry converted a MCI bus and toured in it for many years, wrote a piece that will give you a flavor of it.

Millenium Coach Corporation commercial Prevost bus shell conversion

MCI passenger bus conversion done by Nick and Terry Russell of the Gypsy Journal

A school bus converted to an RV

Is an RV Bus Conversion Right for You?
by Nick Russell used by permission

New RV shoppers have a lot of choices when it comes to finding the perfect RV for their needs, and the search can be frustrating because, as any experienced full-time RVer can tell you, there is no such animal. Every type of RV, from truck campers to fifth wheel trailers to diesel motorhomes have their advantages and disadvantages, and there is no one size fits all.

One often overlooked choice is a bus conversion. Built on commercial bus shells, buses offer certain major advantages over most production motorhomes. They are designed to go a million miles or more with regular maintenance, they are built to carry passengers in commercial service, so many safety features are built in to them, and their payload capacity is much more than standard motorhomes, which are often close to being overweight by the time you fuel them and fill the fresh water holding tank. The diesel engines on these buses, designed to carry 40 or 50 passengers and all of their baggage, are more than capable of hauling two people and their traveling home with no strain at all.

But who can afford one? Don't buses cost a small fortune? Not necessarily. There are a couple of options if you decide a bus is right for you; you can purchase a professionally converted bus, which are usually built on a Prevost chassis. These are almost always the choice of professional entertainers who must travel tens of thousands of miles a year. A new one can easily set you back $500,000 but prices drop steeply on the used market after a few years.

Many RVers choose to convert their own buses, using everything from a high end Prevost chassis to older GM, Eagle, or MCI shells. These are usually former charter or Greyhound buses that have been replaced when the fleet was upgraded. By shopping carefully, one can find a good bus that will still render many, many years of service for about what you would expect to pay for the down payment on a new gasoline powered motorhome. When we began looking at buses seriously, we were surprised to learn that there are a lot of very good running, structurally sound older buses on the market that can be had for very reasonable prices.

While a 25-year-old motorhome would be long past ready for the scrap yard, we have seen many bus conversions dating from the early 1960s and even the 1950s still going strong. These machines are built to last forever it seems.

Converting a bus can be an intimidating project, and having a place to work on it and some basic carpentry, electrical, and plumbing skills is necessary. But the end result can be very rewarding – a coach specifically designed for *your* needs, not a cookie cutter unit full of compromises to satisfying the general public.

This article was reproduced here by permission of Nick Russell.

Here is a detailed link to Nick's Bus Conversion project.
▶ http://gypsyjournal.net/bus_conversion_page_1.htm

Here is a link to the Bus Nut Online website with a wealth of information for anyone interested in converting a bus.
▶ http://www.busnut.com/home.html

■ Truck Campers

The slide-in Truck Camper is one type of RV that is neither motorhome or towable. It is essentially a box that slides into the truck bed and serves as living and sleeping quarters. These rigs make awesome hunting vehicles paired up with a four-wheel drive truck. Some folks are able to live in their larger models as full-timers. Even with a camper on board, most trucks will still have some towing capacity, so this versatile rig can also tow a utility trailer or even a small car.

Truck Campers are available for almost all sizes of pick-up truck. Some of these units slide into the bed right up to where the tail gate was. Many of the larger units extend out past the end of the bed and down to the bumper. Some of the newer high end units can have as many as 3 slide outs. With a side door, one comes out the back. These units come equipped with all the convenience and luxury items that are found on motorhomes, but scaled down to fit the size of the box.

■ Weight is Critical

Weight is a critical issue with these units. The camper shell can weigh as much as 4000 pounds without cargo and filled water and propane tanks. Those units will require at least a very heavy duty truck. You may already have a truck and want a camper for it. You must research what campers will work with your truck's weight limitations. Ideally, you shop for the truck camper you want and then find the truck that can handle the weight. If you pick out a camper with slide outs, then you're looking at a 1 ton or better dual rear wheels long bed truck.

These campers can be equipped with hydraulic jacks that extend to the ground and lift the camper shell off the truck bed. Then you drive the truck away and the camper is useable without the truck.

■ Truck Camper Configurations

You can choose from hard sided units or a popup roof model. The popup roof extends the interior height so you can stand up inside. When lowered, the overall height is lowered and the rig can traverse some wooded terrain not possible in a hard sided rig. You should take a good look at both pop-up and hard-side models. Consider what you will be using the camper for. Off-road use will favor the lower clearance and lighter weight of a pop-up. If you want a more domestic feel, like to camp in colder environments, or are considering living full-time in your camper, the qualities of a hard-side model is likely to be a better option.

You might also decide whether you want a rear bath or a mid-bath. The mid-bath separates the rig into living and sleeping areas that some folks find desirable. You also must look at the type of bath. The wet bath uses the entire bathroom as a shower. The dry bath has a conventional but small shower.

Two major manufacturers of truck campers are Lance Camper at http://www.lancecamper.com/ and Northwood Manufacturing which makes the popular Arctic Fox models. Their website is http://northwoodmfg.com/ . Below is a Pop-up Truck Camper

CHAPTER 5

TOWABLE RVs

■ Fifth wheel trailers

The fifth wheel trailer, affectionately known as the "Fiver", is very popular and is probably the most common towable for full time RVers. The trailer connects to the tow vehicle directly over the bed with a special fifth wheel hitch, similar to that on a semi tractor's hitch to its trailer. This causes several feet of the connected trailer to hang over the tow truck, placing about eighteen to twenty percent of the trailer's weight on the rear axle of the truck. Usually the bedroom is located in this raised forward section, but some newer fivers have the living room there.

A main advantages of a fifth wheel trailer is that it's easier and safer to tow than travel trailers, but requires more caution and skill than motorhomes. They also tend to be easier to back up than travel trailers. Their spacious, open floor plans are quite suitable for full time RVers. Numerous slide-outs provide an almost residential space. They have the most living space of all trailer type RVs, and provide more interior space per foot than a motorhome because it does not contain driving and engine compartments. The tow vehicle doubles as local transportation, but large trucks aren't much fun in crowded grocery store parking lots.

On the downside, a fiver doesn't have nearly the storage capacity of a motorhome. They may not have the cargo carrying capacity to carry a lot of excess "stuff". The tow truck requires a fifth wheel hitch in the truck bed which is removable. Larger three axle trailers can require a medium duty truck to provide the power to get them up hills and mountains and be able to stop on the way down. The living area is largely inaccessible while moving because the slide out rooms are in. I have seen folks towing cars, boats, motorcycles and ATV's behind fifth wheel trailers. This "triple tow" is illegal in many states, and provides some interesting handling issues. The larger models can be difficult to maneuver in tight spaces. On tall models, top clearance can be a problem under low branches and structures. It gets worse if there are items on the roof such as canoes.

■ Toy Hauler Fifth wheel trailers

The term toy hauler is applied mostly to fifth wheel trailers, and it describes an RV designed to carry toys—small cars, dune buggies, four wheelers, motorcycles, etc. A distinguishing feature of a toy hauler is the large door in the back which opens down to create a ramp. The dedicated garage area or fold-away furniture is typically stored in the main living compartment, and usually a third axle to support the heavy toys. That garage space can also be used as a second bedroom with beds dropping from the ceiling on rails. They also make a great office, craft room, and workshop. Younger RVers with children often convert this space to a home school room. There are a few travel trailers and motorhomes set up as toy haulers also.

■ Travel Trailers

Travel trailers, in one of their many forms, are probably the first RV most folks will buy. Early rigs were mainly small and resembled a canned ham, a term used today to identify trailers of that era. Most of them were quite light and were on a single axle frame that could be pulled by many cars of the day. Currently, the pickup truck is the tow vehicle of choice. Today's trailer comes in lengths from 15 feet up to almost 40 feet with the larger models having triple axles. There are Teardrop styles as well as popups, park model trailers and even a hybrid trailer and popup trailer. Many have slide rooms that make them feel almost residential inside. Included in this group are the ever popular Airstream models.

■ Small Travel Trailers

Smaller Trailers are extremely popular with young families camping mostly on weekends. This is largely due to their lower cost. Some features on the newer models include an outside kitchen with built-in gas grill and small refrigerator. This allows the sleeping areas inside to spread out without a galley taking up space. Outside built-in televisions are another popular option on these units.

■ Teardrop Trailers

The teardrop style trailer was made extremely popular by the R-Pod branded models. They are very low and aerodynamic and their single axle configuration can be towed by many SUV's. There is room inside for a bed and little else. Sometimes. a compartment opens up in the back and turns into a camping kitchen.

■ Popup Trailers

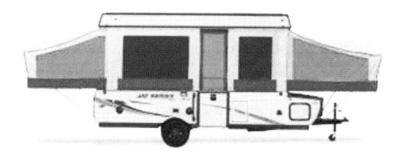

Popup Trailers are the ideal entry level unit for folks wanting to try the RV lifestyle. The very first rig we ever owned was a canvas sided aluminum framed popup with a wooden box for a body. We had a lot of fun with it. Nowadays, pop ups have come of age with rigid fiberglass or aluminum tops, often with air conditioners, skylights, and batwing TV antennas. The side wall material is often waterproof acrylic material. Once the roof is cranked up (or electrically raised) the sides fold down to form 2 large sleeping areas. Some of the larger ones even have a side slide-out room. Most of these are light enough to be towed with a Jeep or SUV. This is a great way for a young family to get into RVing.

■ **Hybrid Trailers**

Hybrid Trailers combine the best features of a conventional small travel trailer with the extra sleeping features provided by fabric sided drop out sleeping platforms of a popup trailer.

■ **Park Model Trailers**

Park Model Trailers are a specialized type of trailer made to be set on a campsite for an extended period of time. Most do not have holding tanks as they will be hooked up when in use. They might have large double sliding doors as in a home.

■ **Hitches for Travel Trailers**

Almost all the pro's and con's associated with fifth wheel trailers apply to the larger travel trailer except for the method of hitching to the tow vehicle. The travel trailer connects to a hitch ball attached to the frame of the tow vehicle. In years gone by, small trailers would be hitched to a ball attached to the vehicle's bumper. Thus the term "bumper pull" still in use today to describe trailers using a ball type hitch.

Inherently, this type of trailer is not as stable on the road or as easy to maneuver and park as the fifth wheel trailer. Almost all of them should use special weight equalizing hitches. This will help to eliminate trailer sway, or the "tail wagging the dog" effect. In technical terms, sway is the fishtailing action of the trailer caused by external forces that set the trailer's mass into a lateral (side-to-side) motion. The trailer's wheels serve as the axis or pivot point. This is also known as "yaw." The weight equalizing hitch is designed to damp the swaying action of a trailer, either through a friction system or a "cam action" system that slows and absorbs the pivotal articulating action between tow vehicle and trailer. We will cover trailer hitches in great detail in the section on towing.

CHAPTER 6

RV WEIGHTS AND MEASURES

■ Weigh Your RV

It makes good sense to weigh your RV as soon as possible, perhaps before you complete the purchase. There are many different weight ratings and no single one can tell you if you are under the maximum. It is also important to weigh all wheel positions to know if your rig is overloaded on one side or front to back. There are several ways to do this.

■ How to Weigh Your RV

The RV Safety and Education Foundation has an excellent program for weighing RVs. They have been doing this for many years and have developed an excellent way to quickly and accurately weigh each wheel position of your RV and towed vehicle (for a motorhome) or tow vehicle (for towable RVs). This paid service is available at most major RV rallies and some RV shows across the country. Go to their website for a schedule at http://rvsafety.com/weighing/weighing-schedule. The first thing done is to record the weight data on the plate inside the RV. Then they place a scale device with a load cell under each front tire, and under each of the rear tires or, if equipped, the set of dual tires. If the rig has a tag axle, a scale is placed under each tire of the tag axle. Once these weights are recorded, they place the scales under the tires of your towed vehicle (for motorhome) or towing vehicle (for trailers.)

At this point, the actual weights are calculated and compared against the inside data plate to determine any overweight conditions. They will also indicate the side to side weight differences. All this is given to you on a sheet indicating all weights recorded. You should have a tire pressure chart from the tire manufacturer indicating maximum suggested pressure for a range of axle weights. This will give you an indication of the proper tire pressure for the actual weight of your rig.

The Escapees RV Club also has a program called SMARTWEIGH that is quite similar to the RVSEF program. Escapees offer the service at 3 of their RV parks – in Bushnell, Florida, Livingston, Texas, and Congress, Arizona. They also offer it at their annual Escapade national rally and several other events. Check the link above.

Those are the only services I know about that will weigh individual wheel positions. You can use a commercial truck stop scale, but they will only weigh axle positions. That is still good information and you can determine all the measures posted inside your RV. You will not be able to determine your side to side weight differential. Here is a link to use a CAT scale at a truck stop.

To determine tongue and pin weights for travel trailers and fifth wheel trailers, first weigh the tow vehicle. Then hook up and drive on the scale truck only. Subtract the total you got with the truck alone and you have the tongue or pin weight. Those weights should be approximately 10 to 12% of total RV weight for travel trailers and approximately 20% for fifth wheel trailers. Then drive the trailer up on the scale one axle at a time to get the axle weights and the total. That will give you a pretty good idea if you are overweight on any of the primary measures.

■ RV Weights and Measures

It is absolutely essential that an RVer have an understanding of RV Weights and Measures. Trailers and their towing vehicles must be matched so the tow vehicle can handle the weight on the rear axle or bumper. The tow vehicle must be capable of towing the loaded weight of the trailer on the road that will be encountered. The towing vehicle must also be capable of stopping in a safe distance with the trailer attached. Motorhomes must not be loaded beyond published weight specifications. All of this is about safety of both the RVer and passengers, as well as others on the road nearby.

RVs that are overweight can experience premature tire failure as well as severe handling problems. Weight distribution is also an important issue. Too much weight on one side can cause handling issues as well as tire wear problems. Trailer weight distribution must be set so that the proper amount of weight is forward on the hitch or pin box in the case of fifth wheel trailers.

Overweight units that are involved in an accident may be weighed by the insurance company and claims denied if the unit is found to exceed critical measures.

■ RV Weight Terms

In 1996, the Recreational Vehicle Industry Association (RVIA) established a list a list of weight ratings that manufacturers had to post inside every RV they made. In 2000, they added a few more ratings to the list to help RV owners. In 2008, all those were superseded by new regulations adopted by the National Highway Traffic Safety Administration that mandated separate and specific RV weight labels. That means the list on your RV may very well be different from another RV produced in another year.

■ The critical RV Weight Terms are as follows:

Cargo Carrying Capacity (CCC) – The CCC is the GVWR minus the UVW, the SCWR, the weight of a full tank of propane, and the weight of all fresh water in the system including a full fresh water tank and a full water heater.

Curb Weight – The weight of a basic RV unit without fresh or waste water in the holding tanks but with automotive fluids such as fuel, oil, and radiator coolant.

NCC (Net Carrying Capacity) – Is the maximum weight of all passengers (if applicable), personal belongings, food, fresh water, supplies – derived by subtracting the UVW from the GVWR. In 2000, the RVIA started using Cargo Carrying Capacity (CCC) and added a sleeping capacity weight rating

GAWR (Gross Axle Weight Rating) – The manufacturer's rating for the maximum allowable weight that an axle assembly is designed to carry. GAWR applies to tow vehicle, trailer, and fifth-wheel and motorhome axles.

GCWR (Gross Combination Weight Rating) – Is the maximum allowable weight of the combination of tow vehicle and trailer/ fifth-wheel, or motorhome and dinghy. It includes the weight of the vehicle, trailer/fifth-wheel (or dinghy), cargo, passengers and a full load of fluids (fresh water, propane, fuel, etc.).

GVWR (Gross Vehicle Weight Rating) — How much weight a vehicle is designed to carry, set by the manufacturer. The GVWR is typically listed on a data plate near the driver's doorframe, and includes the net weight of the vehicle, plus the weight of passengers, fuel, cargo and any additional accessories. It assumes that the towed vehicle will have its own braking system. This why motorhome owners shouldn't tow a vehicle without a supplemental braking system.

GTWR (Gross Trailer Weight Rating) – Maximum allowable weight of a trailer, fully loaded with cargo and fluids.

Hitch Rating – Stamped into the hitch receiver or a placard attached to the rear of a motorhome. The number includes the maximum trailer or towed vehicle weight as well as the tongue weight on the hitch.

Hitch Weight – The amount of weight imposed on the hitch when the trailer/ fifth-wheel is coupled. Sometimes it is referred to as conventional trailer "tongue weight." Hitch weight for a travel trailer can be 10-15 percent of overall weight; fifth-wheel hitch weight is usually 18 to 20 percent of the overall weight.

NCC (Net Carrying Capacity) – Added in 1996, it is the maximum weight of all passengers (if applicable), personal belongings, food, fresh water, supplies – derived by subtracting the UVW from the GVWR.

Occupant and Cargo Carrying Capacity (OCCC) – The CCC was modified in 2008. CCC still applies to towable RVs but motorized RVs use the OCCC. It is calculated by taking the GVWR and subtracting the UVW and propane weight. It is the maximum allowable weight of all occupants including the driver plus the weight of all food, tools, fresh water tanks, full propane tanks, and all personal belongings.

Payload Capacity – The maximum allowable weight that can be placed in or on a vehicle, including cargo, passengers, fluids and fifth-wheel or conventional hitch loads.

Sleeping Capacity Weight Rating (SCWR) – Is calculated by multiplying the number of sleeping positions by 154 pounds.

Tongue Weight – The amount of weight imposed on the hitch when the trailer is coupled.

Tow Rating – The manufacturer's rating of the maximum weight limit that can safely be towed by a particular vehicle. Tow ratings are related to overall trailer weight, not trailer size, in most cases. However, some tow ratings impose limits as to frontal area of the trailer and overall length. The vehicle manufacturer according to several criteria, including engine size, transmission, axle ratio, brakes, chassis, cooling systems and other special equipment, determines tow ratings.

UVW – (Unloaded Vehicle Weight) – Introduced in 1996, this is the weight of the vehicle as delivered with full fuel, oil, and coolant, but without manufacturer's or dealer-installed options and before adding passengers, driver, propane, or fresh water.

Weights – Water (weight): 8.3 lbs. per gallon; LP gas (weight): 4.5 lbs. per gallon; Gasoline: weighs 6.3 pounds per gallon; Diesel fuel: weighs 6.6 pounds per gallon; Propane: weighs 4.25 pounds per gallon.

Wet Weight – Term used by RVers to describe the weight of a RV with all storage and holding tanks full. i.e., water, propane, etc.

■ Tires and RV Weights and Measures

Tires are undoubtedly the most important component of the RVs chassis. Besides supporting the vehicle's weight, they transfer acceleration and braking forces to the road as well as keep it going in the proper direction.

Tire manufacturers provide charts for each type of tire with what tire pressure is required to support a particular amount of weight. RV manufacturers must select a tire that will support the weight of the properly loaded RV. We all know tire failures can be catastrophic. A front motorhome tire failure will certainly cause the rig to veer suddenly in the direction of the bad tire. Later on we will discuss a method to safely guide a motorhome with a blown front tire to a stop. Tires can sometimes literally explode and take out fenders, holding tanks, and anything else close to the bad tire.

CHAPTER 7

EQUIPPING YOUR RV

■ What do You Need in Your RV?

This is a listing of the interior stuff Kathy considers essential for enjoying the RV lifestyle.

■ Stuff to Cook With

This is a very personal decision. I'm not a gourmet cook so I do not have a big mixer, or a food processor and it is no big deal to me. However, you will need pots and pans, plastic glasses and dishware, silverware, serving dishes, storage containers and utensils, and almost everything you would use at home to cook and eat simple meals. Some rigs have much more space in the kitchen area than others, so consider what you will need. If you don't own an RV or you are moving up to a bigger unit, consider this area. We don't eat out a lot, so cooking space is important. The pantry in the RV is small, however you can always find a store to buy groceries, and with a little planning, it's not hard to keep things from overflowing. A good rule of thumb is "a place for everything and everything in its place." When we first started out I had enough food for what seemed to be about three years of eating. I have learned to cut it down, and every six months I will go through the pantry and get rid of things I have not used in the last six months or that have expired. Organizing the pantry is quite simple. Most weeks we eat about the same meals; we have our favorites, so I always check to make sure I have plenty of the ingredients for those. Then there are times I want to make something special, so I take a list to the store and purchase just what I need for that meal. I always have some snacks on hand for when people come by and we are sitting outside talking. Cheese and crackers or cookies work well for that. We also keep a cooler outside the rig for drinks. This gives us more room in the refrigerator. It's really up to you what you have on hand. Some parks will have a box for the local food bank so nothing is lost. Many RVs will have a double door refrigerator, but these are not the same size as the home ones. They can hold about 4-5 bags of cold groceries and we all seem to have way too much anyway.

You will have both a convection oven and a two or three burner stove top and maybe even a propane oven. I have very rarely used the propane oven, other than for storage. I use just the convection oven for any baking I want to do. The only thing I miss is a broiler, as the convection oven doesn't have one. I would only use one three to four times a year, so it's no big problem for me.

■ Stuff to Read

If you enjoy reading, consider a Kindle or some other type electronic book reader. There is not much space for lots of books. However, almost every campground has a small library which is usually a "bring one, take one" swap. I have found some great books in these libraries. I take one, read it, and pass it on to the next campground, then pick up a new one. It's a great place to get rid of the extra books you may have. They will also have DVDs, CDs and VCR movies, and puzzles to borrow. You will never be bored with nothing to do on a rainy day. We know of one guy who loves to do puzzles, but there was no place to do them in the rig. He couldn't leave it on the table, so he placed a piece of Plexiglas over the puzzle on the table when it was time for dinner. The puzzle is safe and there is peace in the family. That works for him.

■ Stuff for an Office

Most rigs do not have an office or desk. Finding space to do the computer work can be difficult. We have a side entry on our motorhome so the passenger seat area is where our desk is. We bought a collapsible table and store it alongside the sofa when we are traveling, then pull it out and set it up in front of the passenger seat when we are stopped. We actually have two foldable tables. I use one to bead on, and our dining table is used for dinning. There are many places that will build a custom cabinet or desk for you.

■ Stuff in the Living Area

One of my big pet peeves is that the TVs in most motorhomes is up above the driver's seat. I about broke my neck watching TV because the sofa faced the side of the rig and the TV was to the left. To solve this problem, we had the TV moved from the front and put along the side with a cabinet underneath, then exchanged the sofa for two Lazyboy chairs. It is very comfortable now – feels just like a real living room. The place where the TV was previously is now storage where we keep our travel books. They did a beautiful job, and we are pleased with it. Think outside the box for what you need and be creative. This is your home, so just as you might remodel your home, you can remodel your home on wheels.

■ Stuff to Wear

Life on the road is very simple. Summer is shorts, tee shirts and sandals, winter clothes are jeans, sweatshirts, wind breaker jackets, and tennis shoes. We like to attend church, so I have a nice pair of slacks and several tops. Since we don't stay too long in one place, there is no need for an extensive wardrobe. We store the winter clothes under the bed in the summer and the summer clothes there in the winter. It's not too far away if the weather changes. I really dislike Laundromats, so we have a combo washer/dryer in the rig that I use all the time. I really like it, and so far, we have had no problems. But it does take up a lot of space. Many campgrounds will have a coin laundry so you will not have to go into town to do the laundry. Laundromats are not always located in the safest part of town. Most are coin operated, but a new trend is a card much like a credit card. You purchase the card at the camp store, then put money on the card and use this instead of quarters. There are several companies doing this so not every campground will have the same system. I think it would be a great idea if they did. I have the card in a sleeve and write on it which campground it is good for. Just remember to keep saving your quarters.

■ Stuff to Socialize With

There seems to be an unwritten rule for socializing. If the door to the rig is closed that means company is not welcome. If it is open or you see people moving about, than come knock on the door. With the rigs being so small, it is not often as neat and tidy as your host would like, and you don't want to embarrass your newfound friend. This mostly applies in good weather. Most socializing is done outdoors. Be sure to have 4 chairs so everyone has a seat. Or if you invite someone over, ask them to bring their chairs. We have a gadget called Campfire in a Can that is a small container that is a propane burner with artificial logs. It is just like having a small campfire; when you are done, just turn off the propane and the fire goes out. We have roasted marshmallows and cooked hot dogs on it. It works for us. Transporting wood from one state to another is now prohibited in the west as there is a western pine beetle that is eating up the pine trees. They are trying to contain it by not allowing firewood of any kind to be brought in from different states. Please be aware of what can happen if you bring wood from somewhere else. There is firewood for sale everywhere open fires are allowed. Help to be an asset to our wonderful forests.

We have found that our ideas about a lot of the stuff we thought we would need just weren't true. This lifestyle is quite simple and your camping friends are just happy to hang out with you. The type and style of clothing is not important. Being comfortable is what is important, and having a tee shirt from all the places you have been is a great conversation starter. I have a shirt from Bryce Canyon that has started many conversations. People either have been there or want to go, or they will tell you of a similar park they have been to and enjoyed. Of course, you have to add that to your bucket list.

What Other Stuff Will You Need?

This section contains all the stuff that John feels are essential for a well equipped RV.

■ Electrical Surge Protection

In our opinion, all RVs should be protected from power surges as well as over and under voltages. This is the very first accessory you should buy. A power surge or a lightning strike on power lines can destroy electrical and electronic items in your coach such as stereos, satellites, microwaves, televisions, and refrigerators. Surge protection is protection against voltage spikes on power lines. Direct lightning strikes are so catastrophic that no device can effectively protect against a close or direct lightning strike. Over or under voltage protection is effective for a gradual increase or decrease in voltage, exceeding the maximum or minimum voltage for which appliances are rated. Over voltage and under voltage protection removes primary power from the RV when the voltage drops below 102V or above 132V (safe mode).

Devices are available that can protect from these conditions as well as improperly wired electrical pedestals in RV parks. They can be directly wired into the RV or connected to the electrical pedestal and the RV plugged into the protective device. If you have a fifty-amp electrical system in your rig, be sure to purchase a fifty-amp power protector. A good place to look for these is at Amazon.com or the RV Upgrade Store www.rvupgradestore.com.

■ Water Filters, Hoses, and Sewer Equipment

Most RVers will quickly accumulate an assortment of sewer and water hoses along with some sort of fresh water filter.

■ Water Filtration and Treatment

Most late model motorhomes and fifth wheel trailers have "whole house" water filters plumbed in, usually located near the water/sewer service bay. The filter element of choice in these is a sediment filter. Water with noticeable haze or murkiness is carrying particulate matter that is referred to as sediment. Large particles settle out of water pretty fast, so what water is carrying are very small particles. Besides the noticeable effect on water clarity, sediment can also create problems by plugging up other filters you may be using, causing them to fail prematurely.

The whole house filter(s) must also be changed as they get filled with sediment and other contaminants. Check the first sediment filter every several weeks and look for a brown color throughout the filter media. That is the time to change it out. If it is very bad, check the next filter in line also. Carbon filters only last three months in our system.

If you find yourself in an area with high sodium (salt) content in the water, none of the above filters will remove the salt from the water.

Enter the reverse osmosis (RO) water filter system. It uses a semi-permeable plastic membrane to filter out most of the contaminants in water, including almost all biologic pathogens, minerals and salts, and some other chemical contaminants. The output side of the membrane produces pure water. The waste, dissolved solids, and contaminants which are called brine, are flushed down a drain. The costs for an RO system are much higher than regular filtration, but may be the only answer unless you buy bottled water.

■ Fresh Water Hoses, Pressure Regulators, Etc.

Plastic or rubber garden hoses are not suitable for fresh water use. The hoses you use for supplying fresh water to your rig should be purpose designed for supplying fresh potable water. They are constructed so they won't impart taste or odor to the water. Typically, these hoses come in either one half inch or five eighths inch diameter and in various lengths up to one hundred feet. The larger diameter hose will provide more flow and are the best choice. We carry two twenty-five foot hoses. Most campsites will only require one length, but some need more. I would not want to have most of a fifty-foot hose coiled up under my rig. Other shorter lengths of four to ten feet are useful for hooking up filters and for bypassing them if necessary. If you use a hose to flush your holding tanks, use one made in other colors than your fresh water hoses. The same goes for hoses used to wash your rig. We use a fifty-foot green plastic garden hose for that purpose. When you buy fittings such as "Y" connectors and shut-off valves, avoid the temptation to go cheap and use plastic ones. Spend a little more and buy brass fittings, and you won't be surprised some night when one of them lets go and you have a high pressure flood on your hands. This is the voice of experience talking.

There are special drinking water hoses made especially for cold weather use. They have a heating element permanently woven into the hose and use electricity from the power pedestal to keep the hose from freezing if the outside temperature drops below freezing during the night. They are expensive, costing as much as one hundred dollars for a twenty-five-foot length. We try to avoid areas where this might happen, but we aren't always successful. A less expensive and quite effective method is to purchase an electrical "heat tape" and connect it to the length of the hose. These usually have a thermostat that activates when the temperature drops past a set limit. Cover that up with inexpensive pipe insulation and you won't have problems with your hose freezing.

When you pack up to depart your campsite, blow all the water out of your hoses and roll them up with the ends screwed together. This will keep them sanitary and easy to store. If at all possible, do not store fresh water hoses in the same compartment as sewer hoses and fittings. This could possibly result in some nasty consequences. Poop and drinking water should never mix. Enough said about that.

A water pressure regulator reduces the park water pressure down to less than fifty pounds per square inch, forty being preferable. This is to prevent high water pressure from damaging plumbing lines and fittings buried deep down in the bowels of your rig, and keep it from flooding. A good water pressure regulator will reduce pressure but allow maximum flow, thus ensuring an adequate shower pressure. Most will have a gauge to measure the outlet pressure and can be adjusted to your desired pressure. This type of regulator should cost somewhere in the fifty to sixty-five-dollar range.

■ Sewer Hoses, Etc.

No matter what the rig, you must dump that pesky black tank from time to time. Sewer hoses come in a rainbow of colors and many lengths and thicknesses. Some press fit together, and some use bayonet type fittings. I prefer the positive locking bayonet type coupling as it will not pull apart. The material used for the hose should be as thick as you can find. Hose sidewall material ranges from 10 mils thick to over forty. The thicker material is much better. The thin stuff can develop pinhole leaks that can spoil your day. Usually, the sidewall material is stretched over a coiled metal wire so the hose can be compressed for storage. Unfortunately, when stepped on, these hoses will never be round again. A new material has no metal coil and can be compressed and stepped on and will return to the original shape. These hoses come in ten to fifteen foot lengths. We carry three ten footers and one fifteen footer. There have been several occasions where we have had to use all of it to reach the sewer connection.

An essential accessory is a threaded connection to the sewer with a bayonet fitting on the other end for the hose. Some municipalities require a rubber "doughnut" fitting between hose and sewer hole, so keep one on hand. Other places require the sewer hose to be supported several inches above the ground. We have a "slinky" device for this as well as a length of plastic gutter and PVC supports for longer runs. You should also have caps for both ends of each hose to keep things clean and dry in the compartment where your sewer gear is stored.

This seems like a good time to remind you that the black water holding tank in your rig has a three inch opening to the sewer valve. Thirty or forty gallons of black water sludge can gravity feed through that opening at an alarming rate. This is why you want to double check all your sewer connections before you open that valve. It's amazing how much of that tank will empty on the ground before you can reach the valve to close it. "I'm just saying".

Another method of dumping the black holding tank is the electric macerator. This is a twelve-volt device very much like a sink disposer. A motor turns a set of metal knives to chop and shred all solids coming down the line and then pump it out a garden hose sized hose to the dump. It can also pump uphill several feet as well as quite a long distance. A great advantage to an electric macerator is if you are parked next to a house. You can run the hose to a sewer clean-out and evacuate your tanks. These range in price from two to four hundred dollars.

■ Ultra Violet Radiation Protective Covers

Ultra Violet Radiation, or UV, will damage surfaces exposed to constant sunlight.

■ Windows

The windshield of a motorhome will expose all seats and dashboard areas to this. UV resistant covers can be made to fit any motorhome and are sold in sets that include the front side windows as well as the windshield. A side benefit is that they will keep the rig cooler. Large windows on fifth wheel trailers can also benefit from these covers. They can be made to fit inside the rig with suction cups, or outside with snap or twist fittings. There are also covers available for side mirrors and windshield wipers.

■ Tires

Tires are especially susceptible to premature aging due to UV radiation. White tire covers will protect them as well as keep them cooler than black covers. Some attach over each tire with stretch cords to keep them on. Others attach to the outside of the rig with snaps or other fasteners. I think the latter are far easier to attach and take off.

■ Outdoor Gear

This is the stuff you need to enjoy your campsite when the weather is good.

■ **Seating**

The first thing that comes to mind is outdoor seating, either as chairs or lounges. Just remember that the large lounges can be hard to store. We prefer the director style chairs as we find them to be more comfortable than the "bag" style chairs. They cost a little more, but some even have built-in trays for drinks and snacks. Whatever you buy, remember that you must find room for it somewhere in the rig or towed vehicle. We recommend sitting in a lot of different chairs to get the most comfortable "sit".

■ **Tables**

We have several folding tables to use when we go to flea markets and sell our bead products. We have two four footers and a small two by two-foot table we used to use for our radio show. Now, we use one of the four foot tables for the grill. Our experience with campground picnic tables has been mixed. Some are nice, six or more feet long and made of artificial materials. Most however are old wooden tables with plenty of splinters. We have a heavy duty vinyl cover for six-foot picnic tables and matching covers for the seats. We use it often. This is dependent on there being tables at all. Our experience is about half of the campgrounds we visit have them.

■ **Grills**

We believe a good outdoor grill is an essential piece of gear for the full time RVer. A key consideration is finding storage space for the grill. If you have plenty of room in your pickup truck for a large home style grill, bring it along. Most of us will have to live with smaller portable grills that will fit in basement storage compartments. We keep ours in a large plastic tub to keep grease and other debris away from the storage compartment. These grills can cost as little as ten dollars for a cheap charcoal model to over five hundred for a deluxe stainless steel beauty. By far, most of the grills we see in campgrounds are propane gas models. We use a Wal-Mart low end model that costs around thirty dollars. I'm on number four after almost eight years on the road. Usually, the bottom rusts out. We also use a twenty-pound gas bottle instead of the one pound canisters because we can refill the bottle much more economically than constantly purchasing the canisters. From what I have found in campgrounds and in internet surveys, the

Coleman "Road Trip" and the Webber "Baby Q" are the most popular gas grills in use by full timers.

■ Portable Campfire

I included this item because we have one, and I am starting to see more and more of them appear in campgrounds. The brand name is "Little Red Campfire" or Campfire in a Can". It is basically a propane gas burner with ceramic fire logs on top. You remove the red top and unwind the gas hose and regulator. Hook it up to a propane source and light it and you have an instant campfire. We always ask if we can use it in areas where there are "No Open Fires Allowed" signs due to drought conditions. We have not been refused, yet. These little guys put out enough heat to keep your feet warm on cold nights and they draw people in to talk around the campfire.

■ Propane "Extend-a-Stay"

The Extend-a-Stay can be used for two purposes. First, if you run out of LP gas in your motorhome propane tank; and second, to hook up the Extend-a-Stay to an outside LP/propane cylinder. This lets propane gas into your system from the outside cylinder allowing you to have continuous gas supply without having to move your RV and refill your permanent propane tank until you are ready to move. Additionally, you can use LP gas from your propane system to fuel high pressure appliances like grills and camp stoves straight from your RVs permanent LP gas system.

The standard kit includes brass tee fitting and 5' flexible pigtail for hooking up an outside propane cylinder to fuel your RV LP system. The deluxe kit also includes 12' of high pressure appliance hose to fuel your high pressure appliances directly from your RVs LP Gas system.

These kits are available at most RV stores. The standard kit costs around seventy dollars, the deluxe kit is around one hundred dollars. Installation is pretty straightforward if you are handy with tools. Any modification to your LP gas system should include a leak test and a pressure drop test. These tests are best done by a professional.

■ Ladder

A good ladder is essential for putting up sunscreens as well as washing your rig. The main concern should be the posted weight capacity of the ladder. Flimsy folding ladders contribute to dangerous falls. An RV ladder should be compact enough when folded to store easily. We store our ladder on a rack hanging from the built-in ladder at the rear of the coach. We bought a Werner brand ladder at a hardware store rated for three hundred and fifty pounds.

■ Safety Equipment

Every RVer needs to take a good look at safety equipment that could possibly save your life.

■ Flares and Towing Insurance

I'm sure you've seen semi trucks along the side of the road with three triangular reflectors spaced out behind it. They are there to alert people to move over a lane as the rig is disabled for some reason. These triangles are inexpensive and should be in your RV emergency kit along with several flashlights and road flares to signal a night break down. Obviously, the best piece of emergency equipment is a cell phone to call for help. Hand in hand with the cell phone is towing insurance. We believe the best contracts are available from the Good Sam Club www.goodsamclub.com as well as Coach-Net http://www.coach-net.com/. Once you are registered with a towing service, they will send a tow truck with the proper equipment to tow your particular rig. They can also provide emergency fuel or change a tire if you have the proper size spare. Most towable RVs either come with a spare tire, or have a place to store one. Some Class B and C motorhomes may have spare tires also. Class A motorhome tires are large and quite heavy when mounted on a wheel. My motorhome has a storage bay that is shaped to hold a spare tire, but the space is better used for tools in my case. If you routinely travel far from regular services, a spare tire may be a good idea. Some RV travel sources recommend you carry an unmounted spare when traveling to Alaska. There are services there to mount a tire, but it isn't likely that your specific size will be available.

■ Fire Extinguishers

Most RVs come with at least one fire extinguisher, usually of the powder type. This type of extinguisher has a pressure gauge with a red/green indicator. While the gauge may read green, the unit might not function correctly after sitting in one position for a long time; the powder settles and clumps in the bottom of the extinguisher. Pick this type unit up and turn it upside down several times every six months or so to loosen the powder. This is also a good time to check that the gauge is in the green area.

Kathy and I have been to a number of RV safety seminars, including some with live fires to put out. We can't emphasize enough the importance of this vital safety training. It is available at most large rallies. Check out http://macthefireguy. com/ for information on the location and times for this training. We were given advice to have a number of extinguishers on hand. You should have one for your car or truck, one for an outside compartment, one in the bedroom, and one near the kitchen area. These small extinguishers will not put out an RV fire that has been going for more than a couple of minutes. You have them to beat down the flames so you can get out of your rig. Even the largest RV can be reduced to a pile of smoldering ashes in five or six minutes. There are many videos on the internet showing this. For that reason, you must get out quickly. Your "stuff" isn't worth your life or your family's life. These four extra fire extinguishers can be purchased for as little as sixty or seventy dollars.

There are automatic temperature activated units for the both engine and the generator compartments. These use a gas such as Halon to displace the oxygen and extinguish the fire. There is also a Halon unit available for the refrigerator compartment to combat refrigerator fires. These units are expensive, but they provide peace of mind.

■ Fire Alarms

If your rig has a fire alarm, or smoke detector, test it for proper operation and change the battery at least annually. If not, go out and get one immediately. We have found that the alarm is usually placed outside the bedroom and near the gas range. Consequently, it will go off every time you fry bacon. We switched ours to a unit made by Kidde that has a push button switch that turns the alarm off for ten minutes, and then automatically returns the unit to normal operation. We highly recommend it.

■ Gas Alarms

Today's RVs have several propane gas appliances including the hot water heater, range top, and stove, refrigerator, and at least one gas furnace. Most RVs will have a propane gas alarm mounted near the floor by the kitchen. This is because propane is heavier than air and will sink to the floor. These alarms may be battery operated or permanently connected to twelve volts from the RV battery. In either case, test these units according to the manufacturer's instruction book.

If your rig does not have a carbon monoxide alarm, get one immediately and place it in the sleeping area near head height. Carbon monoxide or CO is odorless and colorless and will displace oxygen. Carbon monoxide gas is produced by combustion such as from a generator or even an engine running outside your rig. CO can kill you and your loved ones. Don't take a chance without having a functioning CO alarm. Check and replace the alarm battery annually with the smoke detector battery.

Both Carbon Monoxide and propane detectors have a useful service life of around 5 years. There are test kits available to check for proper operation. If you buy a used rig over 5 years old, you should replace these alarms immediately.

■ Weather Radio

We consider our weather radio an essential piece of emergency equipment. We turn it on and tune to the one of seven frequencies that is strongest, and we get National Weather Service (NOAA) forecasts and severe weather alerts for our area. Our radio also can use the Specific Area Message Encoding (SAME) system. A programmed NWR SAME receiver will turn on for the alert message, with the listener hearing the 1050 Hz warning alarm tone as an attention signal, followed by the broadcast message. At the end of the broadcast message, listeners will hear a brief digital end-of-message static burst followed by a resumption of the National Weather Service broadcast cycle. To program NWR SAME receivers with the proper county(s) and marine area(s) of choice, you need to know the 6-digit SAME code number(s) for that county(s). Once you have the number, follow the directions supplied the manufacturer of your NWR SAME receiver for programming. The number is available either online at the http://www.nws. noaa.gov/nwr/indexnw.htm , or by telephone at 1-888-NWR-SAME (1-888-697-7263) for a voice menu. Your campground management will have information on the name of the surrounding counties. We use a Midland Model WR 120, which has the SAME technology. It retails for about fifty dollars but can be found at many stores for around thirty. We don't always program our radio as it will give broad area information including severe weather alerts constantly. Our radio is on constantly, so we check its internal battery often.

We also use weather apps on our Android smart phone. These are "The Weather Channel" and my favorite, "Radar Now" which uses the built-in GPS and shows live weather radar in your area.

■ Tools

The selection of tools you carry should be determined by your expertise in fixing RV related systems. This can include tools for working with PVC piping to fix RV plumbing issues; electrical testing devices such as digital voltmeters for troubleshooting electrical problems, an assortment of general purpose tools such as screwdrivers, wrenches, and sockets for general repairs. There are many books available to help with repair of RV systems as well as the manuals that came with the RV for those items. One tool I find invaluable is a two-pound short handle sledge hammer for pounding stakes in the ground to anchor awnings and ground mats. Another must-have is a battery powered drill and extra battery. My favorite source for tools and even specialty tools is Harbor Freight Tools http:// www.harborfreight.com/ because they have stores across the country as well as internet ordering.

■ Maps and Navigational Aids

You will not be on the road long before you have a collection of stuff to help you find your way.

■ Paper Maps

In spite of all the electronic gadgets we have to help us find our way around our beautiful country, paper maps are still handy and can be easily marked up to find your way around. We use a large type road atlas by the American Map Company that we have replaced three times because the pages get dog-eared and torn. We also obtain state maps from the various welcome centers we visit. If you will stay in one state and tour it for an extended time, it is a good idea to buy a detailed state road atlas. We also carry a Motor Carriers Road Atlas available at truck stops. This will have low clearance bridges and hazardous cargo (propane) restrictions listed by state. Last but certainly not least, we have the Mountain Directory East and Mountain Directory West. They list most of the mountain grades of five percent or more that a large truck or motorhome might encounter and describes them. This is a lot of weight to carry and store, but it is peace of mind for us as we travel through new territory.

While not exactly a map, we carry a wonderful book called The Next Exit. This is also available as an application for Android and iPhones. The book is divided by state and then by Interstate highways. There is an entry for each exit with information on facilities available and even nearby campgrounds. What makes this guide a "must have" for RVers is that facilities that can accommodate large rigs are printed in red. This way you can look ahead to see where RV friendly stops are located.

■ Campground Guides

We carry the Good Sam Campground Directories. This gives us information on campgrounds, fairgrounds, state and national parks and other places to camp across the country. Often we refer to it several hours before we stop for the night and call one campground we have found for a reservation. The directory includes prior year's pricing information, number of sites, a description of amenities, phone number and website, and directions to the campground. There is also a campground rating system included to give you ratings on the facilities as well as recreation opportunities near the property. There are other campground guides, but this is the most comprehensive of all. These are fairly large paper bound books and the information is available on-line at http://www.woodalls.com/ and on a CD. We prefer the paper version as our laptop screen has lots of glare while we are on the road.

We belong to several campground clubs and each one has its own guidebook. We carry a guide for Passport America, RPI, Thousand Trails, Escapees, and several others. Those are mostly used for trip planning.

■ Electronic Mapping Programs

There are a number of programs that run on a personal computer that are helpful for trip planning as well as providing Global Positioning System (GPS) information in real time. We use Street Atlas from the DeLorme Company, http://www.delorme.com/, mostly for trip planning. Co Pilot Live, http://www.copilotlive.com/, from ALK Technologies is another system that also will run on a PC as well as Android and Apple cell phones and tablets. These programs require a learning curve to use all the features available, but I find the one I use invaluable to give me information on mileage to travel as well as fuel usage. There are after-market overlay files for use with these programs that will overlay symbols indicating special points of interest such as campground clubs, fuel stops, restaurant chains, and many others of use to RVers. These files are available on the Discovery Owner's Association website, http://www.discoveryowners.com/cginfo.htm and are available free of charge.

■ Global Positioning System (GPS)

GPS systems for vehicles have been around for years and are quite helpful for directing you in unfamiliar territory. Recently, new models have been introduced specifically for the RVer. They provide input of the height, width, length, and weight of your rig so as to not route you on roads with low bridges and weight restrictions. They also come pre-loaded with many points of interest such as campgrounds and parks as well as fuel sources. These units are being introduced constantly, and the best bet is to look them up in RV specific publications.

Cellular telephones and tablet computers are often GPS equipped, and there are many applications or apps available for the RVer. I believe the best is an app called "All Stays." This app is available for Android and Apple phones and tablets. We have it running on an Apple iPad and it will indicate campgrounds along the way. When you click on the symbol, all information about that campground will appear as well as reviews by previous campers.

RV SYSTEMS

Today's RVs are made up of many RV Systems. Whether the RV is a motorhome or a towable, there are many common systems that make the modern RV so desirable. There are 2 electrical power systems, 120 volt AV and 12 Volt DC. There are 3 water systems consisting of the Fresh, Gray, and Black tanks and associated plumbing, pump(s) and hardware. There may be a hydraulic system that operates the leveling jacks and often slide out rooms. Most RVs have an LP gas system that fuels appliances such as the hot water heater, gas range and oven, forced air furnaces, and absorption refrigerators that work on gas and 12-volt electricity. Diesel motorhomes will also have an air compressor system to supply compressed air to the braking system as well as to the air horn and to the air bags in the suspension system.

CHAPTER 8

RV FRESH WATER SYSTEMS

The RV fresh water system ensures the RV has clean water for drinking, washing, showering, and toilet flushing. Besides the fresh water tank, covered elsewhere, is the water pump, the hot water heater, the fresh water inlet valve, and all the plumbing associated with hot and cold water.

■ RV Water Pressure Regulators

Water pressure also varies from campground to campground. Some have in excess of one hundred pounds per square inch pressure. Modern rigs are designed for less than fifty. If you do not use a water pressure regulator, you could rupture an interior water hose. Believe me; you do not want to clean up after that, not to mention the expense of a very difficult repair.

Most folks don't know the difference between pressure and flow, but you should in order to understand the difference. "Flow" is a measure of volume of water delivered in a period of time, usually measured in gallons per minute or gpm. The poor shower is caused by low flow, as are most other RV water supply problems. "Pressure" is a measure of the force of the water, and it is measured when no water is flowing ("static" pressure). It is measured in pounds of pressure per square inch or psi.

RV plumbing systems in an RV Fresh Water System are generally tested to a pressure of 100 to125 pounds per square inch (psi), but to prevent warranty problems, RV manufacturers may recommend only 40-50 psi. Unfortunately, this may not provide the shower you're looking for. Most house plumbing operates at about 60 psi, and this can be adequate for RVs, too.

The cheaper (under $10) pressure regulators are really water flow restrictors, and you will notice the restriction when you have to dance around under the shower to get wet. The best way to go is with an adjustable water pressure regulator with a pressure gauge so you know what water pressure is entering your rig. There will be an adjusting screw to raise or lower the pressure. I set ours between 45 and 50 pounds per square inch (PSI.) Get one of these, available at RV parts stores or on-line. You'll be glad you did.

■ RV Fresh Water Hoses

The hose you use to connect your RV to the water supply may be the first cause of flow restriction in an RV Fresh Water System. Many RV water hoses are pretty cheap, and they are prone to kinking or collapsing. If your hose does that, you are suffering from a flow restriction. The solution here is to use a better hose that resists deformation. We prefer a 5/8-inch diameter hose instead of the common 1/2 inch. The reason is that 5/8 inch gives you increased flow. Whatever hose you choose, make sure it is designated for potable water use.

■ RV Fresh Water Pump

Just about every rig with holding tanks has a 12-volt DC electric water pump. It is the heart of the RV Fresh Water System. It pumps water from the fresh water tank to the faucets and shower head. Unfortunately, many manufacturers use inexpensive lower flow and pressure pumps. This produces wimpy showers and just more than a trickle from the faucets. Can this be remedied? I'm glad you asked!

Yes, you can replace that weak sister pump with a more robust higher pressure and higher flow pump available from several manufacturers. Aquatec, SHURflo and Flojet are the big players in the 12-volt water pump market. The trick is to get a pump that will provide the flow and pressure you need.

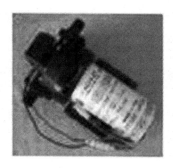
Aquajet Pump

Pump Strainer

Pump Controller

Many RVs come with SHURflo pumps. They are adequate but most folks complain that they are noisy and irritating, they don't pump enough water at a high enough pressure, and they cycle constantly during low flow conditions. For a motorhome with 2 sinks and a shower as well as an outside shower, you need plenty of flow and the pressure to get the water to more than one tap at a time.

We use the Aquajet RV model made by Aquatec which provides 5.3 gpm at 65 psi. Aquajet models are direct replacements for SHURflo pumps. The OEM pumps usually draw around 7 amps of power when running. Due to its higher performance, the SHURflo pump draws 10 amps. You must replace the pump controller with a 10-amp model when upgrading to a better pump.

A high flow pump requires a strainer on the inlet side. Small particles can destroy the pump head if they get in the water stream. The wire strainer prevents this.

CHAPTER 9

RV WATER FILTRATION

RV water systems comprise water flow from the inlet coming from the campground hose bib through the Fresh Water System and then through either the fresh, gray or black Water Holding Tanks. The 12-volt water pump moves the water when not connected to park water.

■ Water Filtering

Please understand that water quality varies from place to place, and you **must** filter the water you put in your rig. There are lots of contaminants that are found in water, and they can be in 2 groups. There are those that affect only our senses of sight, smell, and taste. The other group are those that affect your health. We should address both groups of contaminants when choosing a filtration system for their RV. RV Water Filters are installed on most late model motorhomes and fifth wheel trailers usually plumbed in near the water/sewer service bay. The filter element of choice in most of these is a sediment filter. Water with noticeable haze or murkiness is carrying particulate matter that is referred to as sediment. Large particles settle out of water pretty fast, so what water is carrying are very small particles. Besides the noticeable effect on water clarity, sediment can also create problems by plugging up other filters you may be using, causing them to fail prematurely. This is a good place to mention that the folks we consider experts in RV Water Filters are the people at the RV Water Filter Store. Check them out at: http://www.rvwaterfilterstore.com/

■ Sediment Filters

The first group of contaminants can usually be handled by sediment or "sed filters" that are measured in "microns" or one thousandth of a millimeter. A twenty-micron filter will remove particles twenty microns or larger in diameter, while a five micron filter will remove sediment five microns or bigger. Sediment filters strain out the sediment and hold it. At some point, the filter is plugged and must either be cleaned (if possible) or replaced.

A sediment filter should always be the first filter in an RV water filter system. It will protect your other downstream equipment from premature failure by removing the junk that could cause a problem.

■ Carbon Filters

The things that affect taste and odor of water will go right through a sediment filter, so you must use something else to remove them. Enter the carbon filter. The carbon can grab onto the bad stuff in water, leaving it clean-tasting and odor-free. It can only pull out a fixed amount of contaminants, so it will not last forever. You can't clean a carbon filter, so you must replace it when full or when water pressure and flow drop to an unacceptable level. Usually, carbon filters will last twice as long as sediment filters, but they're also more expensive. The second group of contaminants that affect our health can sometimes be removed by high quality Carbon block filters.

■ Our RV Water Filter System

In my own water filter system, I use a ten-micron sediment filter followed by a five micron sediment filter and follow that up with a carbon filter. The filter canisters are standard household units bought from a hardware store and plumbed together with brass fittings. This filter follows a water pressure regulator to maintain no more than fifty pounds per square inch of water pressure. Some parks have much higher pressure that can damage RV plumbing if not regulated. The regulated and filtered water is connected to the coach water inlet port. I have placed a "Y" valve just prior to the entrance to the filter so unfiltered water goes to the black tank flush inlet. Someplace in that water line to the black tank flush should be a backflow preventer device, also available at a hardware store. That will prevent the possibility of black water coming back down the line and contaminating your fresh water and filter system.

Rigs with automatic icemakers installed often have a filter in-line to the ice-maker. There may also be a separate spigot on the sink to dispense filtered water. That filter, available at Camping World, must be replaced periodically. We change ours every three months.

The whole house filter(s) must also be changed as they get filled with sediment and other contaminants. Check the first sediment filter every several weeks and look for a brown color throughout the filter media. That is the time to change it out. If it is very bad, check the next filter in line also. Carbon filters only last three months in our system.

We have found the RV Water Filter Store http://www.rvwaterfilterstore.com/index.htm to be both a great source of both information and a source of products for RV water issues.

This is our wet bay with three stage water filter.

Note the rubber glove supply ready for use.

■ Reverse Osmosis

If you find yourself in an area with high sodium (salt) content in the water, none of the above RV water filters will remove the salt from the water. Enter the reverse osmosis (RO) water filter system. It uses a semi-permeable plastic membrane to filter out most of the contaminants in water, including almost all biologic pathogens, minerals and salts, and some other chemical contaminants. The output side of the membrane produces pure water. The waste, dissolved solids, and contaminants which are called brine, are flushed down a drain. The costs for an RO system are much higher than regular filtration, but may be the only answer unless you buy bottled water. The RO filter removes most of the contaminants in water, including virtually all biopathogens, minerals and salts, and some other chemical contaminants.

■ Water Softeners

We carried a water softener for the first four years on the road. It was a black plastic thing that looked like a miniature fire hydrant. It came with hardness test strips, so I know it worked to reduce the calcium content in hard water. This calcium build-up can be a real problem for RV water heaters. The calcium crystals form and flow through the fresh water system and clog the aerators in sink faucets. They are easy to clean, but it's inconvenient to have to do this every other day or so. The same goes for RV washing machines. Unfortunately, our softener was heavy (sixty-five pounds) and only treated three hundred gallons before needing to be recharged with rock salt pellets. That container was another forty pounds or so and took up a lot of space. Consequently, we sold it. Newer units use table salt and treat up to two thousand gallons. We're looking into these.

CHAPTER 10

RV WATER PROCEDURES

We will cover three very important RV Water Procedures every RVer needs to know. We'll cover sanitizing and winterizing the fresh water system and flushing and cleaning the RV water heater.

■ Sanitizing the Fresh Water System

The quality of the water in the fresh water tank is vitally important to your health. Algae and other possibly harmful bacteria can grow quite well in your tank if you don't pay attention to a few precautions. If you are a part time RVer, you should sanitize the fresh water tank before every trip, and full timers should do this at least annually. It is a simple but lengthy process:

Start with a nearly full fresh water tank.

- Turn off the external water supply and turn on the water pump.
- Turn the water heater off, and let the water cool.
- Dilute 1/4 cup of household bleach for each 15 gallons of tank capacity into a gallon of water. Don't pour straight bleach into your tank.
- Add the chlorine/water solution to the water tank.
- One faucet at a time, let the chlorinated water run through them for one or two minutes. You should be able to smell the chlorine
- Top off the RV fresh water tank and let stand for at least three hours.
- Drain the system by flushing all the faucets and the shower for several minutes each. Don't forget the outside shower if your rig is equipped with one.
- Open the fresh water tank drain valve to speed up emptying the tank and open the hot water tank drain plug and drain until it is empty.
- Close all valves and faucets and drain plugs.
- Fill water tank with fresh water.
- Turn off cold water supply.

- Open a faucet in the RV to relive pressure.
- Pull out handle of the Pressure Relief Valve and allow water to flow from the valve until it stops.
- Release the handle on the valve. It should snap shut.
- Close the faucet and turn on cold water supply. As the hot water tank fills, the air pocket will be replenished.
- Flush each faucet for several minutes each repeating until the tank is again empty. Make sure you are using the water pump and not an external water supply.
- Fill the tank again. The water should now be safe to drink but if the chlorine odor is too strong you can repeat the fresh water flush.

Your RV fresh water system should now be safe for use.

■ Winterizing the RV Fresh Water System

If you aren't a full-timer yet, you will probably need to winterize your fresh water system. Winterizing can be a simple process, if you just follow the steps below. There are other ways to do this; I have given you the most common.

If your rig does not have one, an important accessory you can add to your RV is a water heater by-pass. It is a simple device; one or two valves that isolate the tank from the rest of the water system. A water heater tank is normally about 7 gallons. If you do not have one of these, you will have to fill the tank with seven more gallons of expensive RV antifreeze than you need. Installation is a pretty simple do it yourself project, or any RV dealer can install it for you. You will save the cost of the valve in just a few years with the value of the antifreeze you save.

RV antifreeze is safe to use in drinking water systems. Please do not use automotive antifreeze as it is poisonous and can cause serious illness and possibly death.

So let's get started. Here are the steps for winterization:
- Drain fresh water tank.
- Drain hot water heater.
- Dump and flush both black and gray water holding tanks, leave gray water valve open.
- Turn off fresh water supply
- Screw a compressed air adaptor into the fresh water inlet. The adapter is

available from Camping World or most RV dealers.

- Apply compressed air, keeping the pressure less than twenty pounds per square inch.
- Open each faucet, one valve at a time, allowing the compressed air to force the water out of the line. Don't forget the shower and toilet.
- Remove the drain plug from the hot water tank and allow the compressed air to blow out the remaining water. Reinstall drain plug.
- Disconnect the compressed air and the adapter.
- Close the water heater by-pass valve.
- Remove the water line that runs between the fresh water pump and the fresh water tank, where it joins the fresh water tank. There is an inexpensive adapter kit to make this easy and it is available from most RV parts dealers.
- Insert the end of the line into a gallon jug of RV antifreeze. (Again, do NOT use automotive antifreeze.)
- Start the fresh water pump. It will run for a few moments, sucking antifreeze from the jug. It will stop as pressure in the system builds up.
- Open each valve of each faucet, one at a time, until the red antifreeze appears; then shut the faucet. Don't forget the shower, toilet, and outside shower.
- Remove the line from the jug of antifreeze and reattach it to the inlet side of the water pump or close the valve if you have an adapter.
- Pour a cup or two of antifreeze into each drain including the shower.

You're done!

■ Flushing the RV Water Heater

As a result of our traveling to different places around the country in our RV, we encounter water with varying degrees of hardness or mineralization. It is important to flush the hot water heater tank in order to extend the life of the inner tank and to eliminate the buildup of mineral deposits. This should be done two or three times a year, especially at the start of the RVing season. Mineral deposits settle to the bottom of the tank, so simply draining the tank will not usually rinse out these deposits. The smaller particles move up the hot water line and clog the shower head and sink aerators. They must be cleaned individually.

- Turn off the switches for gas and if so equipped, electric hot water. Make sure the water inside has cooled.
- Turn off the water pump and the city water connection to de-pressurize the system.
- Drain the water heater by opening its drain valve (or removing the plug/anode). You can also lift the pressure and temperature relief valve handle to increase the flow. To aid in draining, open all hot water faucets throughout the RV.
- Now is the time to use a tank flush tool and thoroughly flush out the tank and remove mineral deposits trapped below the drain opening. The Tank Flush Tool is available at Camping World and most RV parts stores
- Close all hot water faucets opened earlier and turn on the city water or the water pump (the higher the pressure, the better).
- Open the pressure and temperature relief valve and allow water to gush from the drain opening as fresh water rushes in.
- Allow this flushing to continue for five to ten minutes. This will remove any stagnant water along with any residual mineral deposits that may remain.
- After flushing, turn off the water source, reinstall the drain plug/anode (or close the drain valve) and close the pressure and temperature relief valve by allowing the lever to snap shut.

Note: Inspect the anode rod if so equipped and replace if more than 50% is missing. Anode rods are used on Suburban water heaters.

- Turn on the water pressure again and open all the hot water faucets inside the coach until water flows freely from all hot faucets.
- Now, turn off the water and all but one of the hot faucets, then open the pressure and temperature relief valve again to release any water and to establish a cushion of air on top of the water in the water heater. When water stops dripping from the pressure and temperature relief valve, close it and the last hot faucet inside the RV. The heater is now ready for use and you can turn on the gas or electric switch to heat the water in the tank.

CHAPTER 11

RV HOLDING TANKS

RV Holding Tanks are installed in almost all RVs today to contain fresh water and gray and black waste. These and extra batteries make modern RVs "self-contained". There are usually three main storage tanks in a camper or motorhome. They are the Fresh Water, Gray Water, and the Black Water tanks. These holding tanks are great conveniences, but you must be knowledgeable, as well as understand the basic preventive maintenance that must be done to keep them working as designed.

■ Fresh Water RV Holding Tank

The largest of the three types of RV holding tanks is the fresh water tank. These are mostly made of a plastic material. They can be either black or white. The black color will inhibit the growth of algae. We find that the larger the rig, the bigger the holding tank. Small rigs might have as little as ten to twenty-gallon capacity. We have a ninety-gallon tank, and I have seen some rigs with as much as a hundred and fifty gallon storage.

Water weighs a little more than eight pounds per gallon. This means we are hauling more than seven hundred and twenty pounds of excess weight if we travel with a full tank. Fear not, we don't do it. We put about a quarter of a tank in when we travel so we can flush the toilet with a little left for hand washing. There will be a valve somewhere close to the tank for draining the tank. I try to drain the fresh tank as often as possible to maintain fresh and clean water. Most campgrounds will let you do this on your campsite.

■ Gray Water RV Holding Tank

The gray tank is designed to collect and store the water that goes down the sink and shower drains and from a clothes washer if you have one. This water has soap and detergent in it but no sewage so it is called Gray Water. The tank is designed with a capacity that varies with the size of the rig. You should have enough capacity to hold up to a week's worth of gray water from two people. This probably does not include use of a washing machine. The gray water tank is the biggest constraint to boon docking, or living off the grid without external utilities. It is usually almost equal or slightly larger than the black or sewer tank.

Campgrounds do not allow the dumping of gray water holding tanks onto the ground at a site. It must be dumped at the same Dump Stations as the Black Water tank. Dumping of Gray water when boondocking is a controversial subject. Some folks advocate dumping in arid areas to add water to the ground. I have no opinions on this.

To this end, the standard for gray water and black water tank dumping connections is the same for all campers and RVs.

When you look in the service compartment of an RV, or under a camper, you will recognize the same 3-inch connectors; and on many RVs, the black water and gray water lines go to a T-type connection with one common 3-inch connector. This is for ease of connecting and dumping of waste.

Some fifth wheel trailers have a separate galley holding tank for the kitchen sink drain. There will be a third handle to empty this "other" gray water tank.

■ Black Water RV Holding Tank

The Black water tank holds the water that goes down the toilet. Some rigs with two toilets may have two black tanks. I can't imagine why, but there are some instances of a manufacturer building a rig with only one holding tank that contains the gray water and the black water. I'm sure this saves some money, but I don't think the designer ever traveled and camped in an RV. Both the black and gray tanks will be vented to a fitting on the roof of the RV, just as a home plumbing system does. It is possible to get odors from that inside depending on whether the roof vents are open and the direction of the wind.

It is easier to clean out a sewer hose with soapy gray water than any other way. That's why it is recommended that you dump the black water first, then the gray. Doing this will allow the gray water to flush out the waste that is left in the hoses from the dumping of the black water tank, and helps clean the hose system, leaving only (or at least mostly) Gray Water waste in the hoses.

In the chapter where I covered buying sewer hose, I recommended you have plenty to reach distant sewer fittings. This did not mean hooking all of them up and letting them flop around on the ground in a heap of coils that look like a resting boa constrictor. Use only as much as you need to make a straight run and elevate it off the ground with one of the many available types of plastic gadgets that look like slinkies made for that purpose.

When you check into a campground, you will be given material about the rules; often there will be a statement telling you to use a threaded sewer connector. Other instructions may tell you to use a rubber sewer gasket or doughnut to seal up the space between your sewer hose and the campground sewer connection. Please read these instructions and heed them as local ordinances direct these actions.

■ RV Toilet Paper

Here is the scoop on toilet paper for use in an RV. Unless you like to throw money down the toilet, don't buy the expensive "RV" brand. Many other common brands work quite satisfactorily. What you need to know is that it will break down in the tank. To test toilet paper, place a few sheets in a covered cup of water. Gently shake it for a minute. Remove the top and the paper sheets should be shredded into pieces. If not, it probably will not break down in your tank either.

■ RV Black Tank Chemicals

There are probably hundreds of chemical products to put in the black tank. Most are to cut down on odors. Others add chemicals to help break down and liquefy the waste. Whatever you use, try to stay away from any product using formaldehyde. This is definitely an environmentally unfriendly chemical and will kill the beneficial bacteria in septic systems. Try to find an enzyme based product. We use a tablet type, but it also comes as a powder, liquid, and even a premixed, dissolvable pack. Unfortunately, these enzymes will not work in very hot or very cold temperatures. They also need more time in the tank than most of us have. We dump before the enzymes have had time to do their job. We solved the hot weather issue with a product called "Odorcon" which contains stabilized chlorine dioxide. This stuff works great. Check them out at http://www.3rodorcon.com/ . They also have a great product for your fresh water tank.

■ The Geo Method

The Geo Method addresses the fact that RV owners should be concerned with maintaining its wastewater tanks. Problems with wastewater tanks can and should be avoided. Wastewater tank repair is expensive. Due to health concerns, many service facilities will not work on wastewater tanks and lines until the tanks have been completely emptied and sanitized. This may be quite difficult when the tank(s) is in need of repair. So, common sense dictates that the tanks should be kept relatively clean at all times. Additionally, improper use of the wastewater tanks can lead to a buildup of solid wastes, which in itself may cause the system to fail.

The following material on the Geo Method is reproduced with permission of the author, Charles Bruni

I've discovered very simple, effective, and inexpensive methods of maintaining my wastewater tanks in a relatively clean condition at all times. It is the Geo Method. I developed these methods myself through my understanding of chemistry, physics, and biology with a smidgen of common sense thrown in for good measure. I also read my RV owner's manual. Although we are not full time RVers we use our fifth wheel camper at least one weekend a month. We never use public bathing and toilet facilities. In other words, our wastewater tanks are fairly heavily used. Since I've met a number of RVers who don't seem to know how to maintain their wastewater tanks I thought many RVers would find my tips useful. If you have not been maintaining your tanks I believe you will be pleasantly surprised the first time you employ these tips. I do these things and they work.

RVs are equipped with waste water HOLDING tanks; NOT septic tanks. Those holding tanks are nothing more than chamber pots. Chamber pots should be cleaned and sanitized after their contents are disposed of. The Geo Method is based on this fact.

■ Dump a Full Tank

When you are camping and your RV is connected to a sewer/septic intake, leave the drain valves closed until the tank is full and ready to dump. Dumping a full tank provides a sufficient quantity of water to flush solids from the tank. Leaving the drain valves open allows the water to drain off without flushing out solid waste. That solid waste will collect in the tank(s) and cause problems over time. If your tanks are not full when you are ready to dump them, fill them with fresh water first, and then dump them.

■ Dump Tanks In Order From Dirtiest To Cleanest

In other words, dump the black (commode) water tank first, then dump the galley tank, then dump the bathroom tank. This way you will be flushing out the dirtiest water with progressively cleaner water.

■ Use Water Softener And Detergent,

This is the heart of the Geo Method. This stuff is amazing and it works. Buy a couple of boxes of powdered water softener at the grocery store. You'll find it located with or near the laundry detergent products. I prefer Calgon Water Softener because it dissolves quickly in water. Cheaper water softeners work just as well but dissolve more slowly. Dissolve two (2) cups of the water softener in a gallon of hot water. Then, pour the solution down the drain into the empty tank. Use two cups of softener for each wastewater tank in your RV. The tank's drain valve should be closed otherwise the softened water will just drain out. Then use the tank(s) normally until it is full and drain it normally. Add a cup of laundry detergent to the black (commode) water tank at the same time you add water softener. This will help clean the tank. The gray water tanks should already contain soap through normal use. Water softener makes the solid waste let go from the sides of the tanks. If you've ever taken a shower in softened water, you know that after rinsing the soap from your body your skin will feel slick. That's because all the soap rinses away with soft water. Softened water also prevents soap scum from sticking in the tub. Get the connection? With softened water gunk washes away instead of sticking. The same thing applies to your RVs wastewater tanks.

I use a clear plastic elbow connector to attach my sewer drain line to the wastewater outlet on my RV. It allows me to see how well things are progressing during a wastewater dump. Before I began using water softener regularly the black water tank›s water was brown, the galley tank›s water was brownish, and the bathroom tank›s water was white. The first time I added water softener to the tanks the water coming from the black water tank was actually black (not brown) and the kitchen tank›s water was also black (not brownish). The bathroom tank›s water remained white. That told me that the water softener had actually done what I had intended for it to do and made solid waste, which had been stuck to the interior of the tanks, let go and drain away. I added water softener (and laundry detergent to the black tank) to all the wastewater tanks for the next few dumps to be certain all the solid waste possible had been cleaned away. The wastewater only appeared black on the initial treatment. I now add water softener and detergent to each tank once after every few dumps to maintain the system.

Too little water softener may not be of sufficient concentration to work effectively. Too much water softener will NOT hurt the tanks. So, if the amount you used didn›t quite do the job, then use more the next time. Don›t forget the laundry detergent.

■ Use A Water Filter On Your Fresh Water Intake Line

Most fresh water contains sediment. Sediment will accumulate in your wastewater tanks and your fresh water lines. It also tends to discolor your sinks, tub/shower, and commode. I use the disposable type and have found that they eventually fill up and begin restricting the fresh water flow resulting in low pressure. That's how I know it's time to get a new filter. It works, it's cheap, it avoids problems, do it. When I fill my fresh water tank I attach the filter to the end of the hose and fill the tank with filtered water.

■ Some Other Thoughts About The Geo Method

WATER, WATER, WATER – and more water! The Geo Method assumes you are hooked up to a plentiful clean water supply, and that you have access to a sewer. The water softener will make the gunk let go. That's only half the battle. After the gunk lets go it must then be flushed through the relatively small drain opening in the bottom of the tank. That takes water. Lots of water. I use a Flush King (Google it) to make rinsing more effective and faster.

CAUTION should be used when mixing chemicals. All I did when I came up with The Geo Method was use normal laundry products (water softener, laundry detergent, and chlorine bleach) and put them in the holding tanks which already contain water. I was NOT experimenting with chemicals. I simply applied laundry chemicals in normal combination to the waste water tanks. There are chemical products under your kitchen sink, in your laundry room, and in your garage that can injure or kill you when mixed. If you can do your laundry without harming yourself, you can successfully employ The Geo Method. Don't go playing around with novel chemical combinations concocted from household products.

What was novel about The Geo Method was not in the combination of chemicals (all household laundry products intended to be used in combination) but in their application in cleaning RV waste water tanks. Common experience, if you›ve done laundry, tells you The Geo Method is safe. Doing laundry doesn›t damage your washing machine, rot out your plumbing, or destroy waste water treatment systems. The Geo Method won›t either. However, substituting other cleaning agents may not be safe.

There›s nothing special or fragile about the materials used in RV plumbing. RV plumbing materials are made from the same stuff that household plumbing is made from. The problem arises in figuring out how to clean and sanitize the inaccessible interior of a holding tank. Water softener prevents gunk from adhering to the inside of the tanks, detergent removes the dirt, and chlorine bleach kills germs/odors. Soaking gives the chemicals time to work. Agitating the mix by driving down the road helps the process. Think of it this way; you can put some really nasty stuff in your washing machine, yet the inside of the washing machine doesn't get dirty. It stays clean – right? Same goes for your automatic dish washer. The same thing applies to RV holding tanks.

Those people who claim The Geo Method is somehow harmful just plain don›t know what they›re talking about. Their objections defy common sense and common experience. Anyone who thinks The Geo Method is harmful has a simple solution available to their simple minded concerns – don't use it. At one time, daily bathing was thought by some to be harmful to one's health, and many people argued against it advising others to remain dirty. Those who object to The Geo Method fall into the same category of enlightened thought.

Will The Geo Method work even if most of the time I›m NOT hooked up to water and sewer? YES! Just use common sense. If you dry camp ninety percent of the time just keep water softener and detergent in your tanks (especially the black tank) while you're dry camping. This will keep gunk from sticking to the tanks. When you are hooked up to sewer and water take the opportunity to fill the tanks with fresh water and flush the tanks. Keep flushing them until the water runs clear. I know it works because I've done it.

Caution: Never put regular toilet tissue in your RV's black tank. Only use toilet tissue which is approved for RV and/or septic tank use. Regular toilet tissue may eventually dissolve, but not before causing a clog in your black tank.

Occasionally traveling with partially filled wastewater tanks containing softened water and detergent promotes cleaning by agitating the water. The same goes for chlorine bleach.

I believe this process works faster and more efficiently during warm weather. However, I know it works well even during cool/cold weather.

The process works best the longer the water softener and detergent remains in the tanks. So, I don't add water softener during periods of heavy wastewater generation. I wait until I know we won't be generating wastewater quickly so that the softened water remains in the tanks for several days before dumping.

If you have an older RV you may have to use water softener and detergent several times initially to completely clean the tanks of residue.

Water softener is NOT fabric softener, nor is it the rock salt used to recharge mechanical water softening systems.

Water softener is hard to find for a variety of reasons. Mostly it's because folks don't use it much. Most Wal-Marts I've been to stock liquid Calgon. Even though I know exactly what I'm looking for I still have a hard time spotting it on the shelf. Please don't write to me asking where to buy it. Seek and ye shall find.

Liquid water softener, liquid laundry detergent, and liquid dishwashing detergent all work too. The key points are water softener and detergent. I prefer powder because it's cheaper by volume and weighs less by volume. I have plenty of cheap water on hand to hydrate it and pitch it down the commode and drains.

I add a small amount of chlorine bleach to the fresh water tank twice a year to disinfect and sanitize it and fresh water lines. A weak chlorine bleach solution will not hurt you. However, it certainly makes the water taste bad. When we have chlorine in the fresh water system we use bottled water for drinking and cooking until the chlorine is gone – or, you can drain the system and refill it. YES, we drink the filtered water that we have in the fresh water tank. NO, it has never tasted funny or caused any problems.

Folks write to me all the time saying their tank holds X gallons, so how much detergent and water softener should I use? I don›t know. How could I? It will depend on the age of the RV, how much the tanks have been used, how well they›ve been rinsed in the past, how often they›ve been allowed to dry with crud in them, etc. I›ll say this; brand new rigs shouldn›t need The Geo Method for several dumps (6-12, or more – maybe less). An OLD rig will likely require a lot of detergent and water softener over several applications allowing the solution to soak for a week or more. Then, you›ll have to do a lot of rinsing to wash the crud out of the tank's drain. Without getting too graphic, I've helped a fellow who had never closed his black tank's drain valve. The experience of cleaning his tanks took forever and was literally nauseating – to both of us. I'll never, ever, do that again.

No, I do NOT do the ice cube thing. The Geo Method works without ice cubes. (Why not try walnuts instead? At least they won›t melt within five minutes. No, I›m not serious.)

I don›t believe these chemicals harm commercial septic tanks. If you think otherwise, then simply use The Geo Method only when dumping into a sewer system. Or, don't use it at all. It's your rig.

I›ve seen forum posts lately indicating that some RV parks are asking customers what kind of chemicals are in their waste water tanks, and in their cupboards. I find this hard to believe. It›s none of their business. I feel no obligation to answer questions that the questioner has no business asking. Especially when I›ll be penalized for a wrong answer. So, the correct answer that I would give is, «I don›t use any chemicals at all.» That should end the inquisition. If it goes beyond that it›s time to take my business elsewhere. They most often need my business way more than I need their park.

Don't be afraid to use your tanks. Just use common sense about their care and maintenance.

These tips are inexpensive to do. Some of them don't cost anything. You have nothing to lose in trying them and I encourage you to do so. I actually feel a certain amount of pride in the condition and cleanliness of both my waste and fresh water systems. Naturally, these tips make dumping a much more pleasant and sanitary procedure.

If you have odors in any of your water systems, these procedures should eliminate them. Odors indicate a sanitary problem and degrade the enjoyment you derive from your RV.

When my RV is parked and not in use I place stoppers in the sink and tub drains. This forces the wastewater tanks to vent through the vent pipes to the outside instead of through the drains into the RV. Water evaporates. Once the drain traps dry out during periods of non-use, nothing is there to prevent gasses (odor) from venting into the camper. Use stoppers when your RV is stored.

All statements in this article are those of Charles Bruni.

■ Flushing the RV Toilet

When you step on that pedal, hold it down for a while. Most RV toilets have another pedal position that will allow you to add water without flushing. If the flush contains toilet paper, fill the bowl with water and then flush. More water in the black tank will make it easier for the enzymes to work if you use that type of black tank treatment.

■ Dumping and Rinsing the Black and Gray RV Holding Tanks

OK, you have set up your sewer hose, tightened everything up and have two full tanks. Let the fun begin. Not so fast. It is a wise person who plans ahead. When the black water comes cascading down that three-inch hose, there is a lot of weight behind it. When it is turned loose, it could lift that sewer hose right out of the connection if it isn't tightly threaded or weighted down with several pounds of weight on top of that end of the hose.

We have a solution to the hose lifting out of the hole. We spared no expense on this device. I found the worst and most stretched out pair of sweat socks I could find, filled each with gravel, tied them together, and draped it over the business end of the sewer hose. It's hard to believe how much of that stuff will spread out on the ground and cover your shoes before you can close the valve. Whatever you want to call it, this is nasty stuff. You may have heard this called the black water dance. Now you know why. The thing that an RVer learns very quickly is that this is not a septic tank, but just a temporary holding device for some extremely nasty stuff!

This tank was designed to hold the excrement, urine and toilet paper of a typical couple for about a week. Please do not put anything else down there. If you accidentally drop something you want to keep down there, rethink it. The complications and downright nastiness of a clogged black tank are not worth it.

Hopefully you purchased a short clear section of plastic sewer pipe attached just below the dump valve. This will allow you to see when the dump is complete and see the condition of the flush water. Did I mention that you should wait until the tank is nearly full before you dump? Here we go. First you will want to pull the black tank valve handle all the way out. You will be rewarded by a rush of brown stuff followed by a gurgle. Hopefully, your rig is equipped with a built-in black tank rinse system. This is one or two nozzles plumbed into the side of the black tank to rinse out the interior. Hook a short water hose up to the rinse hose connection and start the water running. You will see all kinds of stuff flowing out of the tank you just dumped. Keep this up for a minute or so and then close the black tank valve while the water is running. This will start to fill the black tank with water. At this critical point, do not let yourself become distracted. This is because the black tank has a vent to let sewer gasses escape out of a fitting on your roof. If you forget to turn off the water, the tank will fill and there will be strange noises coming from the toilet. Do not step on the flush valve unless you want to be rewarded with an explosive shower. In short order, the water will start to rise through the vent pipe and provide you with a really good reason to clean your roof. Wait no more than about eight minutes for a forty-five-gallon black tank and pull the black tank valve. The extra water will do a good job of removing stuck toilet paper from the sides of the tank. At some point, the clear section should show the water running clear.

At that point, the tank is clean and rinsed. Let several gallons of water run into the tank to coat the bottom with several inches of water. Close the black tank valve and open the gray tank valve. The gray water will run out as a solid stream and then finish with a rush of bubbles. A nearly full gray tank will do a good job of cleaning out the sewer hose. Now is the time to put the chemicals in the black tank.

■ RV Holding Tank Sensors

Until quite recently, the sensors inside the holding tanks were metal rods threaded through the side of the tank at intervals to indicate the liquid level in the tank. This works quite well in fresh and gray water tanks. Unfortunately, toilet paper remnants and other stuff will get hung up on these and the tank monitor will usually read much higher than what it really is. The only sure cure I know of is to have the tank professionally steam cleaned. The folks who do this have a video camera attached to the hose and they can find and remove all the remaining stuff in the tank. This costs around four hundred dollars for both the black and gray yanks and is the only way I know of to get those pesky sensors clean. Guess what? It won't be long and they will be clogged again. Newer sensors are taped to the outside surface of the RV holding tank and are quite accurate. Retrofit kits are available that use existing wiring.

■ Holding Tank Hookup at a Campsite

When you pull in to a campsite, one of the first things you will do is hook up your sewage connector to the one at your site. Even though you hook up, DO NOT open any valves until the tanks are full. If you dump a partially filled black tank, there won't be enough volume to remove most of the waste. There was a time when we left our gray valve open all the time, but now we keep it closed until it is full. Typically, we dump gray twice as often as black. We will do it more often when using the washing machine. Please do not leave the black tank valve open all the time. The waste will harden due to a lack of water in the tank, and you will soon find out what we mean by pyramiding. You will eventually clog up the black tank and will have a very expensive tank pressure cleaning job to look forward to. Leave the valve closed, and open only when full and ready to be dumped.

■ Holding Tank Hookup On the Road

Some folks will leave a site and drive to the next campground in the same day. They will dump the black water tank and fill it with water for the trip. This will allow the water to shake around during the bumps and turns of the trip, and can then be dumped again when you arrive at the next site. This agitation during the trip can really help clean both RV holding tanks. We have heard that putting ice cubes down the toilet will help this agitation. Unfortunately, the ice will melt quickly. Another idea is to put about ten pounds of rock salt of the type used in ice cream freezers into the black tank. This should last longer than the ice.

CHAPTER 12

RV 12-VOLT DC ELECTRICAL SYSTEM

Like oil in an engine, 12-volt power is the life-blood of an RV. This is true even more in a motorized RV considering all the sensors and black boxes used in modern engines, both gas and diesel.

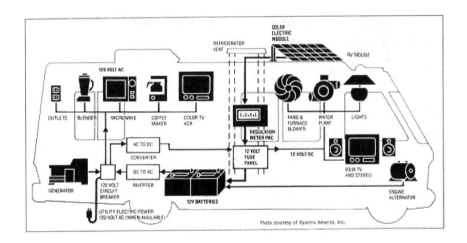

This diagram includes both AC and DC systems

■ Batteries

The source of 12-volt power is the battery, or multiple battery bank. Automotive and RV batteries are made up of multiple cells that when connected internally produce either 6 or 12 volts.

The starting or chassis battery on a motorized unit is designed to produce a lot of current(Amps) to turn the starter motor and start the engine. This starting current is measured in Cold Cranking Amps(CCA). The 12-volt chassis battery(s) are usually recharged by the vehicle alternator when the engine is running. This battery supplies 12 volts to not only the starter motor, but to all the electronics such as engine control units. Chassis air conditioning and heating blower motors and controls as well as the radio and dash controls are also supplied from the chassis battery. Both electric levelers and hydraulic leveling system pumps get their power from the chassis battery.

The "House" or coach battery is usually a bank of what is known as "Deep Cycle" batteries. They are usually measured in the time it takes to discharge a particular current (amps) over a certain time. This is Amp Hours. According to Wikipedia "A **deep-cycle battery** is a lead-acid battery designed to be regularly deeply discharged using most of its capacity. In contrast, starter batteries (e.g. most automotive batteries) are designed to deliver short, high-current bursts for cranking the engine, thus frequently discharging only a small part of their capacity. While a deep-cycle battery can be used as a starting battery, the lower "cranking current" imply that an oversized battery may be required.

A deep-cycle battery is designed to discharge between 45% and 75% of its capacity, depending on the manufacturer and the construction of the battery. Although these batteries can be cycled down to 20% charge, the best lifespan vs. cost method is to keep the average cycle at about 45% discharge. There is a direct correlation between the depth of discharge of the battery, and the number of charge and discharge cycles it can perform."

These deep-cycle lead-acid batteries generally fall into two distinct categories; flooded and valve-regulated lead-acid, also known as Absorbed Glass Mat (AGM). The flooded type are the most common as well as being the least expensive. Flooded cell batteries with regular maintenance can be expected to last 4 to 6 years in RV use. AGM batteries are sealed and require no regular maintenance, but are much heavier and almost twice as expensive as flooded cell types. They should last much longer than flooded cell batteries.

The maintenance required for flooded cell batteries is to keep the electrolyte mixture at a level above the lead plates in the cells. This is done by adding just enough distilled water to cover the plates or reach the mark inside the battery. The tops of the batteries should be kept clean and free of grease and oils to avoid short circuiting them. The battery contacts should be inspected regularly and cleaned of any corrosion. Any time you are working around batteries, you should wear eye protection and ensure there is good ventilation.

Lithium Iron Phosphate (aka LiFePO4 or LFP) Batteries are the newest technology in battery banks. Early lithium batteries were prone to fires and even explosions. The newest versions are non-explosive. You need to make sure that it is impossible to overcharge or overly drain the lithium batteries, which can permanently damage them.

Caution: You need to make sure in particular that it is impossible to overcharge or overly drain the lithium batteries, which can easily permanently damage them.

To do this, many lithium systems incorporate some sort of EMS (Energy Management System) that can cut off current to/from the batteries when necessary. I believe the very best information about Lithium battery banks for RV use is from the folks at Technomadia. Here is a great article on this subject: http://www.technomadia.com/2011/11/lithium-update-3-lithium-battery-cost/

■ House 12-volt system

All the things that are basic to enjoying your RV are provided by the house 12-volt system. The battery provides power for interior lights; demand water pump; the furnace, kitchen, and bathroom fans; the thermostat that controls heating and air conditioning; Slide-out motors, control boards for propane appliances such as the refrigerator and water heater; hard-wired LP and Carbon Monoxide detectors, and the inverter if so equipped.

Using a propane heater on overnight can discharge the house battery quickly if you are dry camping. This is because the blower motor draws a lot of current. The halogen or incandescent lamps in most RVs can draw a lot of current if many are left on. This is the reason LED lamps are becoming so popular as they draw about 1/5th as much current as the regular lamps. Some demand water pumps require almost 10 amps of current when they are running. Prolonged water pump usage can cause excess battery drain. An inverter if you are so equipped will draw current in proportion to the AC load placed on it. Heavy use of AC powered appliances can cause excessive battery drain.

■ Fuses

Each separate 12-volt circuit in an RV has a protective fuse somewhere in the line. These are to protect the device being powered and the wiring from over current due to short circuits. Unfortunately, these fuses can be almost anywhere. Our diesel motorhome has three 12-volt fuse panels under the dash, another below the 120 volt breaker panel, and others spread around. Some are individual fuses in a line and not in a panel. Try to get a wiring diagram from your RV manufacturer to help you find these fuses.

NOTE: Never ever put a larger fuse in place of the one that is blown. Electrical circuit fires are a major cause of total loss RV fires.

■ Phantom Loads

Most RVers don't know about phantom loads. These are loads placed on the 12-volt system from appliances that are on 24 hours a day. These can be illuminated switches, clocks, gas detectors, stereo memory, motion activated lights and the circuit boards in refrigerators and thermostats. These loads can draw down your battery in a few days without regular battery charging.

■ Battery Charging Converters

When your rig is plugged in to park power, many rigs have a converter that changes 120 volts AC to 12 volts for use by all the 12 volt circuits inside. Sometimes the converter also has a battery charging function to keep the house batteries charged. Many of these are of low quality and can overcharge a battery and boil the electrolyte causing the battery to fail prematurely. There are several aftermarket chargers that have three stage safe battery charging circuits inside.

■ Inverter/Chargers

These systems contain a 3 stage battery charger, a 120 to 12-volt converter, and an inverter to convert 12 volt battery power to 120 volt household power. The charging circuit in a 3 stage charger is as follows:

Bulk Charge – This is the first stage of 3-stage battery charging. Current is sent to batteries at the maximum safe rate they will accept until the voltage rises to near (80-90%) of full charge level. Voltages will vary from 10.5 volts to 15 volts.

Absorption Charge – In the 2nd stage the voltage remains constant and current gradually tapers off as internal resistance increases during charging. In this stage the charger puts out maximum voltage around 14.2 to 15.5 volts

Float Charge – The 3rd stage is after batteries reach full charge, and charging voltage is reduced to a lower level (typically 12.8 to 13.2) to reduce gassing and prolong battery life. This is the maintenance or trickle charge.

This 3 stage type of battery charging will allow for the longest battery life.

■ Generator

The rig's generator (if equipped) will provide 120 volts of AC household current to power up the battery charging circuit. Many boondockers use their generators morning and evening to keep batteries charged. Bear in mind you are using up fuel at a rate of about 1 gallon per hour of generator use on average depending on the AC load on the generator.

■ Solar Panels

Many folks use solar panels to charge their batteries to allow them to camp off the grid for as long as their holding tanks will allow. There is a separate chapter on solar, but each system has a Charge Controller. It is a regulator that goes between the solar panels and the batteries. It is designed to keep the batteries charged at peak without overcharging. Meters indicating Amps from the panels and battery volts can be added as an accessory and are highly recommended. We have a good sources of solar systems and knowledge in AM Solar http://www.amsolar.com/.

■ Wind Power

We are seeing more and more RV mounted wind generators. Obviously you need adequate consistent wind to produce the rated output of these units. Here is good information on them: http://turbineel.net/rv-wind-turbines/

When all else fails, you can start your rig and the alternator will charge the batteries, but this is a noisy and fuel consumptive way to do it.

CHAPTER 13

RV 120-VOLT AC ELECTRICAL SYSTEM

The 120-volt system is identical to household electricity. Similar wall sockets and circuit breakers are used in RVs. This power comes from a number of sources that include the campground pedestal, your inverter (if so equipped), and your on-board generator (if so equipped.)

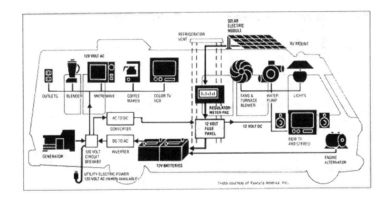

This diagram includes both AC and DC systems

■ RV Park Power

The more modern campground pedestals will usually have three types of plugs; one 20-amp receptacle that looks like a household outlet, a 30-amp receptacle for RVs that require 30-amp power, and a 50-amp receptacle for larger rigs that require 50-amp power. A very small trailer or pop-up that doesn't have an air conditioner can use the 20-amp plug. Larger travel trailers and some small 5th wheel trailers and some motorhomes are wired for 30-amp power. These rigs usually have only 1 air conditioner. Some have 2 air conditioners, but must use only one at a time. The rigs wired for 50-amp power usually have at least 2 air conditioners and need this level of power for the AC powered onboard systems.

There are adaptors available in case the park only has 20 amp or 30-amp power. You can certainly run any RV on 20 amps, but you will only be able to use one or at the maximum 2 appliances. It is not recommended to try to run an air conditioner on 20-amp power. There are adaptors to run a 50-amp rig on 30-amp power with reduced capacity. Only one air conditioner at a time with that configuration. There are also adaptors to run a 30-amp rig on a 50-amp receptacle, but you will still only have 30 amps available to the rig on only one leg of the 50-amp circuit.

An AC circuit in an RV requires 3 prongs in the receptacle. One is the ground, one is the hot 120-volt wire, and the other is the 120 volt return wire. 30 amp circuits have heavier wire and thicker terminals in the plug and receptacle to handle the increased current. The 50-amp circuit has a 4 pronged plug. Again one is the ground terminal, there are 2 120 volt hot terminals, and there is a common 120 volt return terminal. The 50-amp circuit has even heavier and thicker wire to handle the increased current. Each leg of a 50-amp circuit is a 50 amp 120-volt circuit, so actually you have a total of 100 amps supplied to the RV.

Here are some of the appliances that use 120-volts
- Air conditioner
- Microwave oven
- Refrigerator (if a residential unit)
- Satellite Receiver
- Television
- Household appliances
- Converter

We covered converters in the 12-volt DC chapter, but again, the converter converts 120 volts AC to12 volts DC. When your RV is powered up by campground power, both 12 volts DC and 120 volts AC are provided by the campground receptacle.

Where we had many fuses protecting the 12-volt DC circuits, the 120-volt AC circuits have resettable circuit breakers very similar to the ones found in a home breaker box. Manufacturers locate the breaker panel in all kinds of places and it's a good idea to locate it in case a circuit becomes overloaded and trips a breaker.

In our rig, there are even 2 circuit breakers located on the inverter that powers the microwave and the bathroom and kitchen Ground Fault Interrupter(GFI) circuit GFI outlets are usually located near sources of water and will trip when it sees a near short. The circuit breakers can usually be found behind a metal panel, close to where the power cord enters the RV. Make it a point to familiarize yourself with the circuits and label them.

■ Common Campground Electrical Problems

Many older campground electrical receptacles are cracked, and discolored from too much heat. Plugging in to one of these causes a poor connection which will cause heat build-up to the point that it can melt your power connector. If your connector has warped and corroded blades, the same situation exists. A little steel wool and some elbow grease will prevent this condition.

Sometimes a campground outlet will be miswired. We use an inexpensive electrical circuit analyzer available at hardware stores and camping supply stores for less than $10. Plug this analyzer into the 20-amp receptacle and look at the lights on the analyzer and compare the pattern to the chart on the front of the analyzer. You will quickly know if the circuit is properly wired. Use a 30 amp to 20-amp adapter and plug the analyzer in to the 30-amp receptacle and repeat. You will need a volt-meter to check the 50-amp receptacle. Notify the campground office immediately if you find a problem and do not plug your rig in until the problem is fixed or find another site and do the checks all over again.

If the analyzer shows reversed hot and ground wires, you have a "Hot skin" condition and electrical shock is likely if you touch the rig while standing on the ground. Change sites immediately. There is an inexpensive tool every RVer should have handy to check for this "Hot Skin" condition. It is a non-contact AC voltage detector and is available at most hardware stores for around $20. Take the detector outside and while standing on the ground, touch any metallic part of the RV with the tip of the detector. If it flashes or emits a sound, you have "Hot Skin" and must carefully remove the rig's power plug and find another site.

Quite often, especially with 30-amp power, the campground receptacle will have a "Nervous" breaker that will trip for no apparent reason. Breakers do age and get weak with age and high current running through it. The campground maintenance personnel can very easily replace that "nervous" breaker and restore reliable power to your rig. Sometimes the trick is to convince the campground folks that that is the case.

Any power line can be subject to surges (over voltage above 130 volts) and sags (under voltages below 100 volts.) These conditions can damage the electronics in many appliances, televisions, and other sensitive RV electronics. Enter the Surge Protector, otherwise called the Energy Management System These protective devices plug into the park power and the rig power plug is inserted into the surge protector. Internal circuits in the surge protector will remove power to the rig when incoming voltage exceeds the high or low set points built into the protector. After a time delay, power will be sampled for good voltage and power will be reapplied to the rig. Many of the better units have testing circuitry that will sample the power at the pedestal and analyze it for proper wiring connections before power will be applied to the rig. Indicator lights or even remote control panels will keep you informed of what is going on. We recommend that ever rig be protected with an appropriately sized surge protector. It will keep you from loosing thousands of dollars' worth of electronics in your rig.

■ **Inverters**

Another source of 120-volt AC power is the inverter that converts 12 volts DC from your batteries to 120-volt AC. These inverters can be stand alone devices, or they can contain the inverter, converter, and a 3 stage battery charger all in one box. Older inverters produce what is known as "Modified Sine Wave" output. Household current looks like a continuous ocean wave with peaks and valleys of the same size with smooth rounded tops and bottoms. The modified sine-wave inverter produces power that looks like the tops and bottoms are chopped off and become flat. This type of power is fine for most appliances, but modern electronic devices can fail over time by being powered by this type of power. Available now are pure sine-wave inverters that produce smooth household type power. If you have a residential refrigerator, you probably have a pure sine-wave inverter. The older units can be replaced, sometimes by drop-in replacements to save newer sensitive electronics.

■ Generators

The third source of 120-volt AC power is the generator. These are measured by how many thousands of watts (kilowatts) are produced. Our diesel motorhome has a 7.5 kilowatt generator. This allows us to use appliances that total 7,500 watts. We can run both air conditioners and the microwave at the same time.

Some generators run with LP gas as the fuel. Once the tank is empty, no more generator. The bulk of RV generators run off of either gasoline or diesel fuel provided by the rig's fuel tank. Most of these are set up with the fuel line going into the tank about a third of the way up, so you will have fuel to start your rig and go and get more fuel.

Many rigs with generators will have an "Automatic Transfer Switch" that routes park power off and generator power on when the generator is running. When the generator is stopped, the rig will revert to park power by virtue of relays opening and closing in the automatic transfer switch. In those rigs not equipped with an automatic transfer switch, the main power plug must be removed from the park pedestal and inserted in the generator receptacle inside the rig electrical bay so that generator power can flow inside the rig. For park power, the plug must be removed from the generator receptacle and reinserted into the park pedestal.

CHAPTER 14

RV LP GAS SYSTEM

Let's start with a definition of "LP." It stands for Liquefied Petroleum. When our tank(s) are filled, what goes in is a liquid under pressure. It is stored in the tank as a liquid and then we vaporize the liquid so it will ignite and burn to produce heat. The gas we commonly use is Propane and it will change from liquid to gas at room temperature if not stored under pressure. Propane is a colorless, odorless gas that is heavier than air. That's why LP gas detectors are mounted near the floor. An odorant is added to propane so we can smell it when there is a leak.

We use 2 types of tanks on RVs to store LP gas. Trailers and truck campers use Department of Transportation (DOT) cylinders mounted on the trailer tongue or in the case of truck campers and 5th wheel trailers, in exterior compartments. These are usually of the 20 and 30-pound variety. The DOT cylinders must be recertified every 12 years. The recertification date is stamped on the cylinder. Newer DOT cylinders are equipped with quick closing coupling (QCC) valves. They have 3 safety features. If the tank valve on the top is opened without having a fitting and hose attached, gas will not flow. There is a fuse that will shut off gas flow if it becomes too hot as in a fire. If the connected hose (also called a pigtail) breaks, the flow will be restricted. These cylinders have a left-handed-thread connection also known as a POL connector. The second type of tank is used on motorhomes and is called an American Society of Mechanical Engineers (ASME) tank. These are bolted to the frame of the RV and have a separate port for filling. ASME tanks do not need recertification.

Twin trailer Propane tanks

The propane in the tank is at a pressure of approximately 150 psi. Our gas appliances require much lower pressure, so a regulator is used to reduce that pressure. RV gas regulators are a two stage device that reduces that 150 psi to 0.4 psi. The first stage reduces pressure to about 10 to 15 psi. The second stage reduces to the 0. psi level. When pressures are this low, they are measured with a very specialized device called a manometer. The measurement is in inches of water column and 0.4 psi equals 11 inches of water column.

Two Stage Propane Regulator

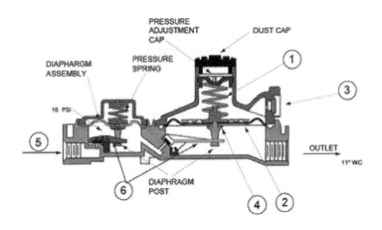

PRESSURE
ADJUSTMENT
CAP

DUST CAP

DIAPHARGM
ASSEMBLY

PRESSURE
SPRING

15 PSI

OUTLET

11" WC

DIAPHRAGM
POST

Inside detail of two stage regulator

These regulators are non-repairable and must be replaced if defective. The cost is quite reasonable for such a precision device.

Travel trailers, fifth wheel, and pick-up campers use an automatic regulator. Both tanks are left on at the same time, the regulator uses the "service" tank as indicated by a mark on a knob or lever. When the service tank is empty, the regulator automatically switches to the other tank and an indicator pops up indicating it is empty. Unfortunately, these devices sometimes get hung up by dirt and debris and fail to switch. Changing the pigtail gas lines will restore the gas flow.

All RVs that use LP gas should be equipped with leak detectors. Propane is heavier than air and will seek the lowest level. Electronic leak detectors have the sensors near the floor. When they detect gas, an alarm is sounded. Some RVs have a tank mounted solenoid shutoff valve that will shut off the gas when the alarm is activated.

From the regulator, the vaporized gas is routed to the gas appliances with flexible rubber gas lines. These must be checked as they age for cracks and tightness of the connectors. A mixture of water and dish soap can be painted on connectors and lines. If bubbles form, there is a leak and it must be repaired immediately. For this, you may very well find yourself spending some time under your rig. Oh, the joys of RV ownership!

CHAPTER 15

RV HYDRAULIC SYSTEM

There are hydraulic systems in all motorized RVs. Gas rigs have hydraulic actuated brakes. There are also hydraulic systems to open and close slide rooms as well as to actuate leveling jacks on all types of RVs.

■ Hydraulic Leveling Systems

If your leveling jacks are hydraulic (some are pure 12-volt DC electric), there will be a pump that moves hydraulic fluid from a reservoir through a series of high pressure lines to the piston of each jack. The pump will usually be powered by 12 volts DC from the chassis, or starting battery on a motorhome or the general battery bank on towable RVs. For that reason, many jack system manufacturers require that the engine be running when using the hydraulic system to prevent depleting the battery. There will be a manifold that directs the fluid to each jack when a solenoid is actuated for that particular jack. The fluid is put under pressure by the pump and moves the piston. Stiff springs return the jack when pressure is relieved from the line.

This is a Power Gear brand pump, manifold, and reservoir

Here are some cautions when using these type of leveling jacks.

- Hydraulic jacks are much stronger than manual screw jacks. Using them together, you can easily raise the entire motorhome off the ground. This is very helpful when the time comes to change a tire — because crawling under a motorhome can be difficult with a flat tire. When leveling, raising the tires off the ground can put extreme tension on the front suspension that can result in damage to those components. Use wood or plastic blocks for that.

- When using the hydraulic levelers, always lift either one complete side or one complete end of the RV. This will help you avoid twisting the unit which may cause damage to the structure. This twisting can also cause a motorhome windshield to pop out of its mounting gasket.

- It is a good idea to use jack pads under the leveling jacks. This will spread out the weight that can cause the jack to become buried in soft ground. If the outside temperature is high when you drop your jacks on an asphalt surface, you will most likely create a depression in the surface.

- Most of the newer leveling systems have a controller that can level automatically or manually. There will be a procedure to calibrate the system for proper operation in automatic mode. If you don't have it in the data you received with the RV, contact the leveling system manufacturer for those instructions. You should perform the calibration as soon as you get the rig and annually thereafter.

■ Hydraulic Slide out systems

Like hydraulic leveling systems, hydraulic slide out rooms have a motor driven pump, often the same one as the leveling system, that operates from 12 volts DC from the chassis battery on a motorhome or the general battery bank on a towable rig. The pressurized fluid actuates a hydraulic ram which pushes out or pulls in the slide out. The direction is controlled by a combination of valves.

Check the voltage of your battery and charge if needed before any troubleshooting. Most slide out systems provide a way to manually operate the slide out if problems arise. For hydraulic systems this usually requires relieving pressure in the hydraulic ram and physically pushing the slide out or in. You may need some help from your friends

Besides lack of 12-volt power to the hydraulic pump, hydraulic slides can fail due to low hydraulic fluid level, fluid leaks and defective valves. There is also a float switch in the hydraulic reservoir that will close if the fluid falls below a preset level. This will actuate an alarm on the slide room or jack control panel. If this happens, deactivate the jacks or being in the slide room. Then check the level and add more fluid if low.

CHAPTER 16

RV COMPRESSED AIR SYSTEM

Virtually all diesel motorhomes over 30 feet long have an onboard, engine driven air compressor. Air pressure is used to power the service brakes, emergency brakes, air bags, air horns, and occasionally used to fill a low tire. Many times there will be a manifold where an air hose can be connected so you can inflate boats, bike tires, and even power air tools.

The compressor pressurizes 2 or more permanent air tanks. When the pressure in both tanks gets near 125 psi, the compressor stops pressurizing the tanks. The air goes through an air dryer with one or two filters to remove moisture generated by the compressor. This dryer receives a signal to expel the accumulated moisture when the compressor stops, and you will hear a hissing sound. When the air is used for stopping and other functions such as leveling, honking the air horn, and filling the suspension air bags, the pressure drops and the compressor cycle starts again after pressure drops below about 90 psi. Those air tanks are isolated from one another by check valves to retain pressure in the tanks when one leaks. Many RV applications have a separate air tank for left and right brakes. On our rig, there is a third tank for the air bags, air chuck, and air horn

Air is used for both the service brakes and the emergency braking systems. The brake pedal opens a valve that allows air to flow to the brakes depending on its position. When the pedal valve is pressed slightly, a few psi of pressure is applied to the drum or disk brakes on both sides of each axle. As the pedal is pressed further, more pressure is applied to the brakes. When the pedal is fully depressed, then all the air available in the tanks is applied to the brakes (120 psi). Most new RVs have ABS (Anti-Lock Braking Systems) that prevent full pressure being applied to each brake to prevent wheel lock up during emergency stops. If no ABS system is present, then full pedal movement provides enough pressure to lock up all the wheels. That's why you see the double black marks on the highway where large vehicles have had to stop quickly. As the pedal is released, the air pressure is released making the characteristic whooshing sound. The compressor then turns on to make up the air pressure used by this braking process. That is why you should not "pump" the brakes to slow down while descending a steep mountain grade, because the compressor typically can't keep up with the air usage. You should keep a steady slight pressure on the air brakes to keep the vehicle at a safe speed. Even better is to be in the proper lower gear, going slower, and using an exhaust brake so the service brakes can be saved for real emergency braking actions.

The Emergency Brake is a separate braking system. When there is no pressure in the system, large springs apply enough pressure to the brakes to lock them solid. On engine start, these special air/spring mechanisms are pressurized to make the springs release the mechanical pressure on the brakes. The emergency brake requires at least 60 psi of pressure to release the springs. In case of a large leak, or if the compressor fails, or the regulator fails while you are driving, the air in the tanks will reach 60 psi and the spring brakes will lock the wheels. An audible "low pressure" warning happens at 80 psi so drivers have a chance to get the rig to the side of the road.

Testing the effectiveness of the emergency brake is recommended each time you start driving. To do this, put the emergency brake on, which is usually the up position, then try to make the vehicle go forward with about 1200 rpm engine speed in low gear. The vehicle should not move. Make sure that going forward a few feet will not cause damage or injury and be ready to apply the service brakes if the emergency brake does not work.

■ Air Suspension

There are several designs of air suspension systems using one air bag per axle side, two air bags per side, one air bag and a leaf spring per side and so on. All these systems use a way to control the air pressure in each air bag to maintain a level and stable ride for the vehicle. The valves that control each air bag modulate the air by measuring ride height between the axle and the vehicle frame. Air usage for this control varies depending on the road the vehicle is traveling on. On roads that curve sharply and dip repeatedly, more air is used than when traveling on a level Interstate Highway. The air compressor will then cycle more often, perhaps every few minutes. When on level highway, the compressor should cycle very infrequently unless there is a leak in the system somewhere.

■ Dashboard Air Conditioning

Some motorhomes use air pressure to create vacuum to operate the dashboard air conditioning system. These vacuum generators use a small amount of air and make an occasional soft hissing sound. If there is a leak in the vacuum system, then more than normal amount of air usage will cause more frequent cycling of the air compressor.

■ Air Horn

Air used for the Air Horns uses only a small amount of air pressure.

■ Air Brake Adjustment

Air Brakes are normally automatically adjusted. They use "automatic slack adjusters" to keep the brakes properly adjusted. If you have an older rig without automatic adjusters, you either need to learn how to get under the coach and adjust the slack adjusters, or pay a shop to do it. It's necessary to drain the moisture that might have collected in the air tanks by opening a small spring operated valve in the bottom of each tank. Usually there will be steel wires somewhere up front near the generator. Pull on them one at a time briefly. You may here a small hiss as the moisture is released. Do this weekly unless you never find any water in the tanks, and then go to monthly. If the air dryer is working correctly, there should be very little if any moisture in the tanks. There are filters in the dryer that need to be changed periodically. Check your chassis owner's manual for the details on changing them.

■ Air Brake System Testing

At least once per week when you are operating your vehicle, you should perform this basic Air Brake Recycling Test.

Air Leakage – With the air tanks pressurized to 120 psi and the engine off, walk around the vehicle listening for any sound of air leakage. Then have your partner press the brake pedal down and hold it down while you walk around the vehicle again listing for the sound of air leakage. If you hear a hiss sound, then there is a leak and it should be fixed.

The air brake systems should be tested before each day's driving. This is a very important safety test and is repeated in the Driving Tips chapter. The process is as follows:

- With a fully-charged air system (typically 120 psi), turn off the engine, chock the wheels, release (push in) the parking brake button (all vehicles), and trailer air supply button (for combination vehicles), and time the air pressure drop. After the initial pressure drop, the loss rate should be no more than 2 psi in one minute for single vehicles and no more than 3 psi in one minute for combination vehicles.

- Turn the key to the on position. Rapidly apply and release the service brake pedal to reduce air tank pressure. The low air pressure warning signal must come on before the pressure drops to less than 60 psi in the air tank. If the warning alarm/signal doesn't work, you could be losing air pressure without knowing it. This could cause the spring brakes to activate suddenly. Only limited braking can be done before the spring brakes come on.

- With parking brake, (all vehicles) and trailer air supply button (for combination vehicles) released (pushed in), apply firm pressure to the service brake pedal. Watch the air supply gauge and listen for leaks. After the initial pressure drop, the loss rate for single vehicles should be no more than 3 psi in one minute, and no more than 4 psi in one minute for combination vehicles. If the air loss rate exceeds these figures, have the air system repaired before operating.

- Continue to rapidly apply and release the service brake pedal to further reduce air tank pressure. The trailer air supply button (if it is a combination vehicle) and parking brake button should pop out when the air pressure falls to the manufacturer's specification (usually between 20 to 40 psi). This causes the spring brakes to come on.

- When the engine is operating at 1800 RPM, the pressure should build from 85 to 100 psi within 45 seconds in dual air systems. (If the vehicle has larger than minimum air tanks, the buildup time can be longer and still be safe. Check the manufacturer's specifications.) If air pressure does not build up fast enough, your pressure may drop too low during driving, requiring an emergency stop. Don't drive until you get the problem fixed.

- Wait for normal air pressure, release the parking brake and trailer air supply button (for combination vehicles), move the vehicle forward slowly (about 5 mph), and apply the brakes firmly using the brake pedal. Note any vehicle "pulling" to one side, unusual feel, or delayed stopping action. This test may show you problems which you otherwise wouldn't know about until you needed the brakes on the road.

CHAPTER 17

RV ABSORPTION REFRIGERATORS

RV refrigerators are one of the things that makes RVs self sufficient, along with waste holding tanks and Propane heat and hot water. The absorption refrigerator has been around a long time, and 40-year-old units are still operating like new. The inner workings of this special refrigerator are quite complex. Metal tubing is bent and stretched into diverse angles to accommodate several chemicals that, when heat is applied, cause the fins inside to become quite cold, thus cooling the inside of the unit. When the heat is applied using propane, the refrigerator will cool normally without 110 volts. This makes living off the grid much more pleasant.

■ How an RV Refrigerator Works

If you are interested in exactly how an absorption refrigerator works, here is a great article by Gary Bunzer, the RV Doctor, that goes into much more detail than I can.

▶ http://www.rvdoctor.com/2001/02/rv-absorption-refrigeration-cooling.html

■ RV Refrigerator Tips

- Before you turn on an RV refrigerator, ensure the rig is level within a few degrees both side to side and front to back. RV refrigerators depend on gravity to work properly, and can be severely damaged if operated off level.
- Always pre-cool the refrigerator overnight before putting food in it. You want to make sure you're not trying to cool the food and the warm refrigerator at the same time.
- You might want to cool and freeze food at home first and load it into the RV refrigerator after it is cool.
- Pack food loosely so air can circulate freely. You can add a small battery operated fan to help air circulation.

- Uncovered liquids and food can cause condensation and frost buildup on the interior fins. There are inexpensive aftermarket fans that clip to the fins to keep them from freezing up.
- Try to keep the refrigerator door closed as much as possible. It has been said that each minute the door is open; it takes an hour to regain the cold temperature. Never cover shelves with foil or large pans, as this will keep cold air from circulating.
- Check the door gaskets often. Close the doors on a dollar bill and pull the bill out slowly and you should feel a slight resistance.
- To test interior temperature, set a glass of water with a thermometer in it on the top shelf inside the refrigerator for the most accurate reading. Temperatures in the mid 30's are ideal.
- If you smell ammonia, turn off the refrigerator immediately, open the doors, and ventilate by opening windows and roof vents. Unfortunately, the ammonia smell means the cooling unit is irreparably damaged and must be replaced.

■ About RV Refrigerator Problems

The two major manufacturers of RV refrigerators are Norcold and Dometic, both major players in RV appliances. Unfortunately, these units have gotten a bad name due to defects that can cause cooling units to fail catastrophically, as well as cause fires.

This is the cracked boiler section of the cooling unit in our Norcold Refrigerator.

Note the greenish residue. This happened 6 weeks after the recall kit was installed.

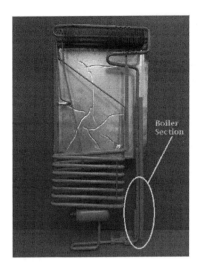

RV refrigerator Cooling Unit hi-lighting the Problematic Boiler Section

■ RV Refrigerator Recalls

The Norcold company, now a division of Thetford, has had a constantly expanding RV refrigerator recall on certain models of RV refrigerators that started in 2002. The recall has been expanded from the original cooling unit manufacturing dates of 1996-1999, each time including units manufactured at progressively later dates. RV fires caused by the affected refrigerators have occurred in units 5 to 7 years old. There have been several thousand RV refrigerator fires as a result of this problem. Some have resulted in deaths and many caused complete destruction of the RV.

■ What caused the RV Refrigerator Recall

The actual defect is a fatigue failure that can be either cracked welds or cracked tubing in the boiler section of the cooling unit which contains the refrigerant and is subject to the most heat. These cracks could allow the liquid solution to slowly leak from the cooling unit. If a leak happens and the refrigerator is still on after circulation has stopped, the heat source could generate high enough temperatures that the steel material of the cooling unit could soften and rupture. If refrigerant gas is still in place when that happens, hydrogen gas may be expelled and could be ignited by the high temperature, possibly causing a fire.

RV refrigerators generate heat to cause a chemical reaction in the cooling unit to make the inside of the refrigerator cold. This Heat is generated by propane gas or by electric heaters. What that means is you can experience a failure when operating on either gas or electricity.

■ Is My Refrigerator in the Recall?

Currently, models included in the recall are 4-door model numbers 1200, 1201, 1210, and 1210 manufactured between 1997 and 2010. There are many single and double door units included in the Norcold recall as well. for the same reason.

▶ Norcold Recall information Notice http://www.norcoldrecall.com/

▶ Dometic Recall information http://67.238.126.140/recall.php

Once you determine that your unit is part of the RV refrigerator recall, make an appointment with an RV repair facility that can do the work. The cost of the parts and labor are borne by the manufacturer. The recall kit includes installation of a metal sleeve toward the base of the refrigerator chimney/flue. On the sleeve is a thermal switch, which is designed to cut all power to the refrigerator in the event of excessive heat being generated. When power is cut, the refrigerator will not run on gas OR electricity. Unfortunately, this kit does not fix the underlying defect of thin wall tubing and deficient welds. Once the heat is high enough to cut off power, the entire expensive cooling unit is usually defective and must be replaced.

■ Norcold Class Action Lawsuit

There is a class action that is the Norcold lawsuit. The following information is copied directly from the website of the law firm filing the class action suit against Norcold for the RV refrigerator defects.

■ Details of the Norcold Lawsuit

On December 27, 2013, 22 consumers filed a motion for class certification status in their lawsuit alleging that the manufacturers of Norcold-brand gas absorption refrigerators, used in Recreational Vehicles (RVs), knowingly sold defective refrigerators that posed a serious fire risk, but hid that information from the public and federal regulators. The class action lawsuit, filed in the Central District of California, is seeking relief on behalf of all persons who purchased or owned RVs in California, Florida, Texas, New York, Pennsylvania, Maryland,

Tennessee, Oregon, North Carolina, Washington, Illinois and Arizona, equipped with three models of Norcold-brand gas absorption refrigerators. The lawsuit names Norcold, Inc., and its parent companies, Thetford Corporation, and Dyson-Kissner-Moran Corporation (DKM), as Defendants. The three Defendants now have until the end of January, to file a response to the motion. A hearing is scheduled in March 2014 before Judge Staton to decide if the case will proceed as a class action. The class action lawsuit seeks to force Defendants to warn the Class and repair the defective cooling units before further leaks occur, exposing consumers to unreasonable safety risks.

The lawsuit alleges that since 1999, thousands of Norcold's gas absorption refrigerators have had their boiler tubes corrode and leak flammable gas in the vicinity of the unit's heaters, presenting a dangerous fire risk. The refrigerators contain flammable gases – including hydrogen gas – under high pressure. Fires are caused when defects in the refrigerator's cooling units cause the boiler tubes to corrode, leak and release the flammable gases close to a heat source, which can then ignite.

The lawsuit alleges that since 1999, thousands of Defendants' N6, N8 and 1200 series gas absorption refrigerators have had their boiler tubes corrode and leak. Yet, Defendants still refuse to fix the actual defect that causes the leaks. The lawsuit alleges that rather than eliminate the design defects, Defendants have instead concealed the true nature of ongoing dangers through a series of low-cost, limited recalls proposing to retrofit the cooling units with devices they present as adequate repairs in recall notices. But the critical problem with all of these retrofit devices, the lawsuit alleges, is that: (1) none of them actually fix the defect that causes the boiler tubes to leak; (2) the retrofit devices are simply temperature sensors designed to minimize resulting damage in circumstances where a leak has already occurred, and (3) they often fail to work as evidenced by the large number of leaks and fires that have continued to occur in retrofitted units. As a result, each class member continues to possess a defective cooling unit which exposes them to unreasonable safety risks:

Hence, the recalls and retrofit devices amount to little more than placing a band-aid on a cancer victim – a so-called "remedy" that does not come close to fixing the underlying problem, which remains. Class members acting diligently in obtaining the recalls, therefore, are lulled into a false sense of security, never being *informed of the truth. Plaintiffs seek, through this class action, to hold Defendants accountable and to secure necessary relief for the Class under applicable consumer protection and warranty laws.*

Link to the Norcold lawsuit

▶ http://www.zimmreed.com/norcold-rv-refrigerator-fire/63879/

CHAPTER 18

RV MAINTENANCE

Let's face it, you have made a major investment in your rig, and you will want it to give you many years of fun. Routine preventive maintenance will help to ensure that. Since Kathy and I full-time, we are doing maintenance constantly. Some of you may have to store your rig for a season and I'll touch a little on that. The first maintenance thing I did when we bought the rig was to purchase a Maintenance Logbook. It was a general purpose book for all types of rigs, but all the pertinent stuff for our diesel pusher motorhome was there. I lined out the stuff that didn't fit.

I compared all the maintenance entries with the information in all the service manuals that came with the rig. If you do not have these, you can obtain them from the manufacturers of all the various appliances and other items that are in your rig. I got quite a few from websites with downloadable documents. The rig manual can be obtained from the rig manufacturer. Also make sure you have engine and transmission maintenance data from those manufacturers. If your manufacturer is no longer in business, try the Forum section on http://www.rv.net or http://www.irv2.com.

Next, I set up my maintenance log in accordance with the information I found in the manuals. Then I had to decide what preventive maintenance steps I could accomplish myself, and what needed to be done by professionals. Anything having to do with engine, transmission, and brakes was left to either Freightliner, the chassis maker, or Cummins Engine, the engine maker. Fortunately, there are service centers across the country that can handle maintenance on almost every make of RV.

We change engine oil every five thousand miles or yearly, whatever comes first. Included with that service is a thorough chassis lubrication and replacement of oil and fuel filters. Make sure whoever does your work will follow exactly the manufacturer's guidelines. You don't want them to skip any steps. Explain what you want and get them to put it in writing on the service ticket. We usually have the generator's oil and filter changed at that time as well.

On diesel rigs with air brakes, there are replaceable air dryer filters that must be replaced periodically. Allison automatic transmissions are on most diesel rigs, and they need filters and transmission fluid changed periodically. Although I could probably do the generator maintenance myself, it's just too easy to let the professionals do it along with the engine maintenance.

Beside oil changes, fuel filter changes, tire air checks, fridge service checks, furnace checks, AC checks, battery checks, water heater checks, and many more must be done.

Any of these items listed above can cause you a lot of heartache while traveling if they stop working properly, so you really need to see that they are in good shape before your trip.

If you store your rig for a season, and then plan to use it for a long trip, schedule all the preventive maintenance at least a few weeks before you want to depart. Problems can appear and parts will have to be ordered. I believe you should give the drive train and brake system first priority, along with tire checking and battery charging. Those are the things that get you there. Next, complete the maintenance steps for your appliances and other systems. Plan ahead and you will depart on time with peace of mind that your rig has all maintenance done.

These are the other things that will need periodic preventive maintenance. Get it done before a big trip so you won't have to scramble for a repair shop in an unfamiliar town.

There are some RV system items that might be better left to a qualified mechanic. These are mostly propane fired appliances. Now you are looking at the possibility of a fire. Some of the maintenance steps can be done by a handy RV owner, but doing other required steps to determine LP gas pressure and leaks require expensive, specialized equipment. Those steps should not be skipped. These appliances include the following:

■ Refrigerator

The owner's manual has a simple list of items that the owner can do, but there are others that should be done by a certified technician.

■ Furnace(s)

You don't want it to stop working in the middle of a freak cold snap because all the proper steps of the maintenance were not done. Leave this maintenance to the pros.

■ Water Heater

I have spent more than a few hours working on our water heater. I have cleaned the tank of calcium crystal growth from heating hard water. I have replaced the electric heating element twice. I've replaced the inlet and outlet hoses because the original ones had cheap plastic connectors that broke and caused floods in the bedroom. What fun that was in the middle of the night. I leave anything having to do with the gas system to the pros.

■ Air Conditioner(s)

The primary user maintenance for RV air conditioners is to keep the filter clean. These can be removed and washed with warm water. This should be done every two weeks during the AC season. If you are comfortable working up on your roof, remove the shroud or large fiberglass cover and check the pan for moisture. If there is standing water, clear the drain holes. Check between the cooling fins and the fan for leaves and other debris. This should be removed with compressed air. Clean the evaporator coils with a soft brush. Inspect, clean, and straighten any bent condenser fins on the unit. Use a knife or any other thin and sturdy metal edge. The cooling system is sealed. Leave that to the pros!

■ Batteries

Battery cables should be intact, and the connectors kept tight at all times. Always use insulated tools to avoid shorting battery terminals. Clean the terminals and cable end connectors with a water and baking soda solution. Use a stiff brush and clean until shiny and the green is gone. Make sure the entire top of the battery is clean and free of dirt and corrosion. Always use distilled water to replenish batteries. Check batteries at least monthly, more often in the hot summer. You may find that it is difficult to open the battery covers because of all the heavy wiring on top of the batteries. We use a battery watering system called "Pro-Fil" we found at Camping World. It consists of new cell top covers that form a water manifold that will water all your house batteries at one time. A small bulb siphon pump brings the distilled water from its container and into the manifold. When the bulb is too hard to squeeze, all cells are at the proper level. We have all four of our six volt house batteries hooked up with this system. This is also available for twelve volt batteries. Too easy!

■ Wiper Blades

Operate the wipers often. If there are constant streaks, replace them with new units of the same length. Also exercise the windshield washers. Replace the hoses if needed. The openings can be cleared with a needle.

■ Window & Slide Seals & Gaskets

Check the window and slide-out gaskets and seals. They should be lubricated with a silicone based spray twice a year to assure that they remain pliable and do not dry out and crack.

■ Slide-out mechanisms

Check your owner's manual for maintenance steps for your slides. Ours has a rack and matching gear at each end. Both should be lubricated according to the manufacturer's specifications. While you're at it, check the manual slide in and out system for proper operation. You will need it at the worst possible time, like at night and or in the rain. I'm just sayin'.

■ Leveling Jacks

Like the slide system, the jacks must be lubricated in accordance with the maker's specifications. Ours are hydraulic, and have grease fittings on each jack. The shiny part of the cylinder should be sprayed with a silicone based spray as well. I also check the hydraulic fluid level in the tank every two months. Some other systems are electric and have different requirements.

■ Roof

Let's face it, the roof is what keeps you dry when it rains. Older rigs may have a metal, or aluminum roof. Later model rigs will have a roof covering made of either fiberglass or rubber, also known as EPDM (you don't want to know what this is short for). Primary maintenance for all is to keep them clean and inspect the seals and gaskets of the roof mounted stuff like air conditioners, vents, antennas, and sewer vents. We clean our roof four times a year and more often if we have been parked under trees dripping sap and other nasty stuff. Pay special attention to the area where the front and rear fiberglass caps are joined. If you find cracking or deterioration in the seals, clean the area and add sealant material on and around the area.

EPDM roofs require some special care. Never clean them with a petroleum or citrus based cleaner as it will harm the EPDM material. There are many cleaners on the market specifically designed for rubber roofs. The chalking or streaking you see is a normal part of the aging process for this material. Look carefully for cuts or tears in the rubber membrane that will cause leaking. Repair with special EPDM repair material available in RV supply stores like Camping World.

■ Emergency Exit

Every RV has an emergency exit besides the main door. Exercise this at least monthly, and lubricate it as needed to ensure it will open smoothly when you really need it. If it is a window like ours, cut and notch a piece of wood to hold it open. Otherwise, it will slam on your hand or fingers to add to the stress of going out of your window during an emergency.

■ Tires

Inspect your tires, the sidewalls in particular. Unfortunately, you should look at the inside surfaces too. This is not fun on rear dual tires, but an inspection mirror and a flashlight will help. Check for cracks and cuts. A cut on the open road can lead to a blowout. Cracks in the sidewall are a sign of dry rot. If you find signs of dry rot, plan on replacing all the rig's tires. Also look for blisters in the sidewalls and missing tread pieces.

Next, you must check air pressure in all the tires, both rig and towed vehicle, or truck and trailer. Get a good quality air gauge that can handle the pressure required in your tires. It is best to check pressure in the cool of the morning. Never let air out of a hot tire. The proper level of air in your tires is all there is between you and the road surface. This is a good place to suggest a tire pressure monitoring system. It works all the time and can also monitor tire temperature.

It will warn when any tire falls below a preset pressure or temperature so you can stop before you have a blow-out. There are many different systems on the market. I suggest you consider a system with replaceable sensor batteries. This is so you won't have to buy new ones when the batteries die.

There are many other things that must be checked to keep your rig ready to go, and every rig is different. What I have listed above is a minimal list, and you must look for those other things. There are many resources available to help you with maintenance and repair of RV systems and appliances. I have the Trailer Life RV Repair and Maintenance Manual by Bob Livingston. It is available at Camping World and other RV supply stores. There are also numerous video's available on the internet to help with rig maintenance.

SECTION III

ALL ABOUT TOWING

CHAPTER 19

RV TOWING TERMS

Many of the definitions below are not standardized throughout the towing products industry. For the definition of those terms we have tried to choose the definition most generally in use.

■ Glossary of RV Towing Terms

Ball mount — the part of the hitch system that supports the hitch ball and connects it to the tow bar or trailer coupler. Adjustable ball mounts allow a hitch ball to be raised or lowered in order to level the towing system.

Base plate — see "mounting bracket."

Binding — when the tow bar is difficult to detach because of excessive pressure, the tow bar is said to be "bound."

Car-mounted — a tow bar designed to be mounted and stored on the towed vehicle.

Class 1 rated hitch — hitch receiver with a capacity of up to 2,000 pounds and 200 pounds' tongue weight.

Class 2 rated hitches — hitch receiver with a capacity of up to 3,500 pounds and 300 to 350 pounds' tongue weight.

Class 3 rated hitches — hitch receiver with a capacity of up to 6,000 pounds and 600 pounds' tongue weight. It is sometimes used to refer to a hitch with a 2-inch receiver, regardless of the weight rating.

Class 4 rated hitches — hitch receiver with a capacity of up to 10,000 pounds and 1,000 pounds' tongue weight. (Many times any hitch with a capacity greater than 6,000 pounds is referred to as a class 4.)

Class 5 rated hitches — hitch receiver with a capacity greater than 10,000 pounds and 1,000 to 1,200 pounds' tongue weight.

Converter — a "3-to-2 converter" converts the electrical signals in a tow vehicle with separate (3-wire) brake and turn signals to tow vehicles with combined

(2-wire) brake and turn signals. Conversely, a "2-to-3 converter" converts the electrical signals from combined to separate.

Coupler — the component that connects the tongue of a trailer or tow bar to the hitch ball.

Curb weight — the total weight of a vehicle and all necessary fluids (water, coolant and oil) and a full tank of gas, when not loaded with either passengers or cargo.

Diode — Diodes allow the towed vehicle's brake and turn signal lights to mimic the motorhome's (which is required by law) without damaging the towed vehicle's electrical system. They allow current to flow in only one direction, thereby eliminating electrical feedback, which could damage the towed vehicle's wiring, fuses or other electrical components.

Dry weight (or "DW," a.k.a. "Unloaded Vehicle Weight") — this is the weight of the motorhome (or towed vehicle) without adding fuel, water, propane, supplies and passengers.

Fishwire — a technique used to install many automotive aftermarket accessories. For example, if the available space is too small to position an attachment bolt by hand, a length of wire is threaded onto the bolt and the bolt is maneuvered ("fishwire") into position using the wire, which is then removed.

Gross Axle Weight Rating (or "GAWR") — is the maximum allowable weight that a single axle (front or rear) can support. GAWR applies to tow vehicle, trailer, and fifth-wheel and motorhome axles. The GAWR is typically listed on a data plate near the front of the vehicle.

Gross Combined Vehicle Weight (or "GCVW") — the actual weight of a towing and towed vehicle, including all passengers and payload.

Gross Combined Weight Rating (or "GCWR") — the maximum allowable weight of the combination of the motorhome and towed vehicle (or the tow vehicle and trailer or fifth wheel). It includes the weight of the vehicles, the cargo, passengers and a full load of fluids (fresh water, propane and fuel).

Gross Vehicle Weight Rating (or "GVWR") — how much weight a vehicle is designed to carry, set by the manufacturer. The GVWR is typically listed on a data plate near the driver's doorframe, and includes the net weight of the vehicle, plus the weight of passengers, fuel, cargo and any additional accessories.

Hitch (or "receiver hitch") — a device which attaches directly to a tow vehicle, providing the connection to the ball mount and trailer. Note: tow bars are sometimes incorrectly referred to as hitches.

Hitch adaptor — fits onto the receiver tube of a hitch and converts it from one size to another (from 1¼" to 2", or from 2" to 1¼"). A hitch adapter may reduce the weight capacity to the rating of the adapter.

Hitch ball — the ball-shaped attachment on the ball mount onto which a coupler is attached. The coupler mounts and locks on top of the hitch ball and encompasses the hitch ball.

Motorhome-mounted — a tow bar designed to be mounted and stored on the motorhome.

Mounting bracket (a.k.a. "bracket" or "base plate") — connects the towed vehicle to the tow bar. All mounting brackets are bolted on to the sub frame of the towed vehicle.

Proportional braking — a supplemental braking system which brakes at the same time and intensity as the motorhome is said to be "proportional."

Quick-disconnects — the connection point between the tow bar and the tow bar mounting brackets. These components allow the tow bar to be quickly connected and disconnected. There is one quick-disconnect ("QD") for the driver's side and one for the passenger side. Quick-disconnects also allow for the mounting of accessories.

Quick links — used to attach the safety cables. They look like one link in a chain, and have a nut which can be threaded up or down to open or close the link.

Safety cables/safety chains — required by law, safety cables connect the towed vehicle to the towing vehicle. They are a secondary safety device to hold the vehicles together if the towing system separates for any reason. (Safety chains are commonly used with trailers or fifth wheels)

Stinger — the part of the tow bar that inserts into the motorhome's receiver hitch. A hitch pin and clip secure the tow bar to the motorhome.

Supplemental braking — an independent braking system that brakes the towed vehicle in tandem with the motorhome or towing vehicle.

Tongue weight — the downward force exerted on the hitch receiver by the towed vehicle, which is typically listed by the manufacturer. Tongue weight should be between 10 and 15 percent of the towed weight.

CHAPTER 20

TOWING A VEHICLE

Most motorized RV owners end up towing a vehicle. This goes for almost all motorized RVs with the possible exception of the Class B van conversions. This vehicle becomes the "Toad", a beloved term for a towed vehicle. A lot of planning must go into towing a vehicle. Will you want to tow it with all 4 wheels on the ground? Are you more comfortable towing a trailer with the car in it? How about a 2 wheeled tow dolly? Whatever method you choose, it is all about having a source of transportation available for touring and shopping while our motorhome is set up at a campsite.

You must be concerned with the motorhome's capability to tow the weight of the vehicle and trailer if so equipped. Each rig has a gross combined weight rating (GCWR), which includes the weight of both rig and towed vehicle. Under no circumstances should this ever be exceeded. The installed hitch on the motorhome also has a weight rating as to how much weight can be pulled.

No matter the towing method, you need a way of slowing and stopping the towed vehicle. A motorhome is designed with brakes capable of stopping with a full load up to its gross vehicle weight rating (GVWR). The weight of a vehicle in tow, possibly with the added weight of a dolly or trailer, will add distance to the vehicle stop when the service brakes are applied. Stopping a 10 to 15-ton vehicle is hard enough without adding another several tons pushing from behind. For this reason, many states have laws requiring auxiliary braking systems installed in the towed vehicle, or the dolly or trailer.

I can't emphasize enough the importance of having such a system on your tow. At the end of the day, all this means we have to be concerned with towing the weight as well as stopping it.

■ Tow Dolly

A two wheeled towing dolly is an excellent way to tow a front wheel drive vehicle with the front wheels secured to the dolly and the rear wheels on the ground turning. A new Towing Dolly will cost between $1200 and $2500 dollars. Some may have integrated braking systems that are either electrically actuated, or inertia actuated also called surge braking. You will not be able to back up your rig when the loaded dolly is attached. If you do, dolly tire damage is a real probability. Without the car attached, the dolly can be backed like any 2 wheeled trailer. You will need to find a place in your campsite for the empty dolly.

■ Trailer

Towing an unmodified vehicle with rear wheel drive may require either an open or closed trailer with at least 2 axles. This type trailer usually comes with electric brakes installed. Such trailers can cost $2,500 and up. Enclosed trailers capable of hauling a vehicle will cost considerably more. A vehicle on or in a trailer may be backed up normally. A major safety consideration with a trailer will be the maximum tongue weight rating of the motorhome's hitch as well as the maximum towing weight rating. Besides the added weight, another downside of any trailer is where to park it. Most RV parks do not have room to park it on site.

■ Towing a Vehicle 4 Wheels Down

Towing "4 down" is a very popular way of towing a vehicle behind a motorhome. Unfortunately, very few vehicles can be towed 4 down without some sort of modification. The best list I have found is from Motorhome Magazine http://www.motorhome.com/download-dinghy-guides/ . They have listings going back to the year 2000. The very best and most reliable source of information on whether a vehicle can be towed 4 down is from the manufacturer. Even the ones that can be towed may have certain restrictions as to speed or time as well as fuses that must be pulled. A great after market product is a wired switch placed in the fuse wiring. Here is a link to a source for these. http://www.rv-partsplus.com/RVing-fuseswitch Most Standard shift transmission vehicles can be towed 4 down, but again, the manufacturer is the final authority. Otherwise you risk voiding the vehicle warranty.

As of this writing, many Jeep models, Chevrolet Malibu's, many Ford models, and Honda CRVs through model year 2014 are flat towable with some restrictions. There are others as well as the now out of production Saturn line of vehicles. Fortunately, there are aftermarket modifications that can render many more vehicles towable. Chief among these is the drive line disconnect for rear wheel drive, and the automatic transmission fluid pump for front wheel drive models. Made by Remco http://www.remcoindustries.com/Towing/ ,this equipment can be installed by many RV repair facilities.

Base Plate – Towing a vehicle 4 wheels down will require a special connection between vehicle and motorhome. First is the base plate that is bolted to the frame and specific to the particular vehicle. Because they are mostly a bolt-on accessory, they can be installed by anyone familiar with basic tools. Some cutting of the plastic fascia may have to be performed to fit the base plate. The base plate contains the connection points for the tow bar as well as for the safety chains.

Base plate Assembly

Tow Bar – The Tow bar completes the mechanical connection from towed vehicle and motorhome. Most will fit into the 2-inch hitch receiver on the motorhome and remain on the motorhome when disconnected.

There are some models that mate up to a hitch ball and remain on the towed vehicle when not in use. There are many models of tow bars, some with integrated surge brake actuators. Make sure you choose a tow bar rated to tow the weight of your vehicle with a 20 percent safety margin. It is also wise to get a base plate made by the manufacturer of the tow bar so they will be compatible. The two major tow bar manufacturers are Blue OX and Roadmaster.

▶ http://www.blueox.com/
▶ http://roadmasterinc.com/index.php

Auxiliary Lighting – When you are towing a vehicle, auxiliary lighting of some sort is required so the tail lights of the towed vehicle will signal turns and stops, as well as be lit at night. Both tow bar manufacturers make lighting systems with all the wire, lamp sockets, umbilical cable and socket to connect to the motorhome. There are also magnetic lights that stick to the rear fenders and are either connected by a cable to the motorhome lights, or wireless models.

Auxiliary Braking System – As with using a trailer, towing a vehicle will likely require some sort of auxiliary braking system. There are many different types on the market. Many have a unit sitting on the floor under the steering wheel and connected to the brake pedal. They can be actuated by the brake light signal or by accelerometers in the system. Another very popular system is made by SMI http://www.smibrake.com/index.html that fits under the hood of the towed vehicle. These are available for motorhomes with both air brakes and hydraulic brakes.

Every auxiliary brake system I have found has either an available or included emergence breakaway switch. It is absolutely imperative that you install this vital safeguard. If the tow bar or other part fails, the switch will be actuated and the towed vehicle's brakes will be actuated. You don't want your toad to pass you!

Auxiliary braking systems require 12 volts from the towed vehicle. The vehicle's ignition switch must be in the "Aux" position so that the steering is unlocked. Anything activated in the Aux position will be a drain on the battery. Many folks find a dead battery after a day of towing. We recommend a charging line between the battery of the motorhome and the towed vehicle battery. I have found a great solution from LSL Products called the Toad Charge. http://www.lslproducts. net/ToadChargePage.html It provides a fused charge controller under the toad's hood connected to the motorhome battery. It is safe and trouble free. I have been using one for 10 years.

As you can see, there is a lot to getting a vehicle ready for flat towing, but you only do it once. We flat towed a 2003 Hyundai Santa Fe for 10 years. It had a transmission lube pump to make it towable and we had no trouble with towing it over 60,000 miles. Now we have a 2014 Honda CRV towed 4 down.

CHAPTER 21

MATCHING TRUCK TO TRAILER

Matching truck to trailer involves many physical factors that must be considered. In an ideal world, someone who wants to have a truck and towable RV will find just the right RV, and then buy a truck that is capable of safely towing it. Unfortunately, the world isn't perfect, and many folks have a truck and try to find a trailer to pull or vice versa. In this page we will lay out all the considerations to help you make a choice that will be both safe and effective. Some of this is fairly complex. I wish I could make it easier, but these are things you should understand.

Unfortunately, many folks rely on information they get from a salesman at an RV dealer or truck dealer. Salesmen are in business to make money by selling you a vehicle or RV. They are educated on how to sell. They are not educated about RV safety or all that goes into making a smart decision. They just don't know much that can help you make an informed decision. Please base your buy decisions on your knowledge, not that of a salesman.

According to the RV Safety and Education Foundation(RVSEF) at http://rvsafety.com/, who weighs thousands of rigs every year, 57% of all RVs on the road exceed one or more weight safety ratings. Additionally, the following exceed at least one rating:

- 60% of all tow vehicles
- 51% of all travel trailers
- 55% of all 5th wheel trailers
- 50% of all trailers exceed the GVWR

What we want to accomplish is to familiarize you with the terms you need to know, as well as other issues so you can make an informed decision on matching truck to trailer, as well as what will work safely and what will not.

■ Specifications for Matching Truck to Trailer

■ Universal Terms

There are several universal terms we will use throughout this discussion that you should know thoroughly. They are:

GVWR (Gross Vehicle Weight Rating) — how much weight a vehicle is designed to carry, set by the manufacturer. The GVWR is typically listed on a data plate near the driver's doorframe, and includes the net weight of the vehicle, plus the weight of driver, passengers, fuel, cargo and any additional accessories. (Driver and passengers are figured at 150 pounds each)

GCWR (Gross Combination Weight Rating) – is the maximum allowable weight of the combination of tow vehicle and trailer/ fifth-wheel, or motorhome and dinghy. It includes the weight of the vehicle, trailer/fifth-wheel (or dinghy), cargo, driver, passengers and a full load of fluids (fresh water, propane, fuel, etc.).

GTWR (Gross Trailer Weight Rating) – Maximum allowable weight of a trailer, fully loaded with cargo and fluids.

GAWR (Gross Axle Weight Rating) – The manufacturer's rating for the maximum allowable weight that an axle assembly is designed to carry. GAWR applies to tow vehicle, trailer, and fifth-wheel and motorhome axles.

MLTW (Maximum Loaded Trailer Weight) The maximum weight that a tow vehicle is rated to tow. Hitch Ratings: The hitch on a tow vehicle will have two distinct and important ratings. The TOW rating, which defines the maximum weight of a trailer in tow. The VERTICAL or TONGUE rating, which defines the maximum vertical hitch load that the trailer can impart to the tow vehicle.

There are also some other ratings that concern dry weight, which is how the trailer comes off the factory production line. We know no body will arrive at a campground with a dry, unloaded rig, so we discount those ratings.

■ The Truck

Our next step in matching truck to trailer is to look at the specifications from the truck manufacturers. This can be quite confusing as some do not use the same terms. Most folks will want to know it their truck will tow a particular trailer and that's where the Maximum Loaded Trailer Weight rating comes in.

First you must know the loaded weight of your truck. The only way to find that out is to put your truck with the load you would use on a scale with full fuel and all passengers. You might want to drive the truck on the scale, get the total weight, and then drive the front axle off the scale to get the rear axle weight.

Then you subtract the total truck weight from the Gross Combined Vehicle Weight (GCVW). The answer is the total the trailer can weigh to be towed safely.

■ The Trailer

Now the trailer part of matching trucks to trailers. If you already have a trailer, hook it up and drive it on the scale with the truck off the scale. Next drive forward till the front trailer axle is off the scale. Repeat if there is a third axle. If the total truck and trailer weights exceed the GCVW, you need to decide what to remove to get to a safe total weight.

Every trailer has a tag or plate that shows either the tongue weight if a Travel Trailer or the pin weight if a fifth wheel trailer. It is a dry weight. Earlier I listed a specification of GAWR or gross axle weight rating. You have the weight of the rear axle with trailer from the scale. If you exceed the GAWR, you must remove weight from the front of the trailer. As long as you are not over the combined vehicle weight rating, you can move things around towards the back. Now it starts to get complicated. Remember I had you get the weight of each trailer axle? You want them to be as close as possible to equal to avoid uneven tire wear.

■ The Weakest Link

The weight ratings for trucks and trailers are there because the manufacturer uses components that can handle the specified weight. Trailer axles have weight ratings. If you have 2 7000 pound axles on your trailer, that is 14000 pounds. You don't want to load it to 16000. That makes the axle a weak link. Trucks rear springs have a weight rating. If exceeded, handling will be affected and the springs can deteriorate. Both truck and trailer brakes are weight rated. When you are overweight, the brakes heat up and will fade. Your stopping distance will increase dangerously. Tires also have weight ratings. If you are loaded beyond the maximum tire weight rating, you are looking at a blowout. Selection and proper installation of a hitch that is rated properly is an essential part of matching truck to trailer. The hitch must have a tow rating at least equal to the GVWR of the trailer. The vertical rating of the hitch must be at least equal to the vertical load imparted by the trailer to the tow vehicle.

I mentioned weighing your rig at a weigh station or truck stop. The very best way to do this is to have all tire positions weighed. The aforementioned RVSEF does this as well as the Escapees RV club SmartWeigh program. http://www. escapees.com/SmartWeigh/Default.aspx

1 Scales at each wheel position

■ **Changing Weight Ratings**

Many owners make modifications to their rigs to improve the load capacities or performance with components certified by the manufacturer. They are trying to force matching the truck to the trailer. Air lift systems, helper springs, higher capacity wheels and tires are some things owners add to their rigs to improve the vehicle towing or load capacity, or performance. Unfortunately, a set of stronger springs will not affect the capacity of the rear axle.

Those owners automatically assume legal responsibility for all modifications made to their rigs, and they will assume the risk. An insurance company may well deny a claim if they determine that unofficial changes have been made.

■ **There's a Video for That**

The RV Safety and Education Foundation(RVSEF) has developed a video called Matching Trucks to Trailers. Here is a link:

▶ http://rvsafety.com/rv-education/matching-trucks-to-trailers

■ There's an App for That

Much of the research for this matching truck to trailer was with material from the folks at http://www.fifthwheelst.com . Their website is a treasure trove of safety information for those towing trailers. They have developed the "5th Wheel ST" fifth wheel and Gooseneck Towing Weight Calculator and Safety Report as an App for android and IOS devices. You simply enter information from data plates and scale readings and the readout will tell you 7 points indicating the safety margin or overload conditions. This could well be the best $1.99 you will ever spend. Check it out at http://fifthwheelst.info/

Welcome to the industry-leading towing calculator that can safely answer age old questions like these:

- "How much can I tow?"
- "How much can my truck tow?"
- "How much can my SUV tow?"
- "What is my truck's 5th wheel towing capacity?"
- "What is my SUV's towing capacity?"
- "What is my fifth wheel towing capacity?"
- "Can my truck tow a 5th wheel as well as my conventional trailer?"

Another tool from the folks at fifthwheelST is the upgraded web-based RV Tow Check 2.0 app is available for free and it's accessible on Smartphones and tablets at http://RVtowCheck.com.

The minimum requirement for RV Tow Check 2.0 requires three inputs by the buyer or dealer. They are: gross combination weight rating (GCWR), gross vehicle weight rating (GVWR) and the gross vehicle weight (GVW). The user has the option to select a fifth wheel hitch if it's not already installed in the truck. They may include any additional unscaled weight for cargo and additional **passenger weight**. The app does not assume everyone weighs 150 pounds, like the manufacturers do.

CHAPTER 22

TOWING A TRAVEL TRAILER

We will deal with information for towing a travel trailer that you will need to know in order to be safe and protect your life and property. Adding the weight and bulk of a trailer to your tow vehicle turns it into an altogether different animal to drive and maneuver. The various sections of this chapter should enable you to drive it with confidence. There is a lot of material here. I know it can be intimidating, but it is all important so you will be able to safely and efficiently tow your Travel Trailer.

■ Trailer Hitch and Receiver

We'll start with the hitch receiver, the square tube under the bumper. These come in classes from I to V depending on how much weight you will be pulling. It's a good idea to give yourself some safety room here and go heavier than your current trailer. The receiver should also be welded to the frame of the tow vehicle with long weld beads, not just spot welded. Inside the receiver will be a steel bar with the hitch ball on one end. Make sure that your hitch ball is the same height as the trailer hitch. The trailer should ride evenly without a down or upward pitch. The maximum tongue weight should be 10 percent of the hitch rating. The hitch ball is rated for the total weight.

Class IV Hitch

Safety chains should be crossed to form a saddle to hold the trailer up in case of failure of the hitch ball or other components. Don't let them drag on the ground, as they can be ground down and lose strength.

Now we'll look at the trailer's coupler. This connects the load (the trailer) to the hitch on the tow vehicle and must be able to handle the weight of your loaded trailer. The trailer hitch will work in many situations, but there are some excellent additions that will help distribute weight and prevent trailer sway. That is the "tail wagging the dog" action that sometimes happens.

A weight distributing hitch uses spring bars to help the installed hitch. They apply leverage to either side of the hitch, which transfers the load pushing down on the rear of the tow vehicle to the axles of the trailer. This provides a smooth, level ride and allows you to tow the maximum weight allowed.

A weight distributing system uses the actual loaded tongue weight to determine which system to use. If the bars are rated too high, you will have a rigid ride and possibly bounce in your trailer. If they are not rated high enough, they won't be able to distribute the weight and will not help at all.

Weight distributing hitch

Sway-control devices are recommended for most weight-distribution systems. Trailer sway has several causes. Crosswinds, the load being too far back, and wrong spring bar tension in the weight-distribution system are the main ones. If your trailer starts to sway, most likely the trailer and tow vehicle haven't been set up properly. The first thing is to not panic. Trailer sway usually starts gradually. As soon if it starts, slow down and let the vehicle slow without using the tow vehicle brakes. You can manually actuate the trailer brake controller. Once you're down to a safe speed, carefully apply the brakes and stop. You can readjust the load or figure out why this is happening.

Sway Control Kit

No discussion of trailer hitches would be complete without mentioning the Hensley Arrow hitch. At around $3000, it is the Cadillac of hitches, but with good reason. To quote from company literature: "The Hensley Arrow uses a converging linkage system, which only allows the trailer to turn by forces applied by the tow vehicle and never by forces applied to the side of the trailer, such as wind or uneven roads. It works as a uni-directional tool.

Forces applied to the trailer must move the tow-vehicle and trailer together, making the vehicle and trailer perform like one solid unit. The tow vehicle, however, still maintains the ability to turn and control the trailer. It's simple geometry, but it's amazing what it does to completely **eliminate trailer sway**."

Hensley Arrow Hitch

■ Hitching Up the Trailer

You will need to raise the tongue of the trailer a little higher than the hitch ball on the truck. Use the installed manual or electric jack to do this. Now back the truck up to the trailer SLOWLY so that the hitch ball is centered to receive the trailer coupler. When the receiver is directly above the hitch ball, put the truck in park with the hand brake on. Lower the trailer onto the hitch ball until it's completely seated. Then flip the locking mechanism.

After the hitch is lowered onto the ball of the truck and latched on, the following sequence should occur.

1. Using the tongue jack (electric hopefully) raise the tongue of the trailer back up, actually taking some of the weight of your tow vehicle. I'm not suggesting you pick the rear wheels off the ground, just add a few inches of height.

2. Insert the WD spring bars (which each weigh as much as a couple of bowling balls) into the special head of the hitch stuck in the receiver of the tow vehicle.

3.   Using a trial and error method the first time, determine which link of the chain is the best choice to give the proper amount of torque in order to level out the tow vehicle and trailer tongue. Paint that link purple.

4.   Hook this link of the chain over the hooks on each side of the trailer tongue.

5.   Find the piece of pipe supplied with the hitch. (Usually it can be found at the last campground you visited because it was left sitting on the bumper.) Now with all your might, using the pipe as a lever, lift up on the bracket until the hook and chain pop over center. Insert locking pin. (This is where lifting the tongue jack helps you out. Otherwise, you'd be lifting all that weight with your own strength).

This is a dangerous time. If your hand slips, that pipe will come flying back down at the speed of sound right before it breaks your arm in two or moves your jaw over about a foot and a half. Be careful!

Unhitching should follow the exact same procedure in reverse.... lift the tongue jack, use the pipe to flip down the chain hook. This part is even more dangerous because it's hard to judge how much potential energy is stored up on the system. You can unexpectedly send that pipe into near earth orbit, break your jaw, or embed the pipe a foot deep into the back of your truck if you're not careful.

This description is for the most commonly used setup. There are other slightly modified systems using various linkages, etc. that are slightly less life threatening.

Next, plug the trailer's wires into the towing vehicle's electrical outlet. The last thing is to attach the safety chains in a crisscross pattern, allowing enough slack for turns, but short enough to not drag. This is a great time to check that the truck and trailer lights are working properly as well as to test the trailer brakes.

NOTE: Many Thanks to Living the RV Dream podcast listener Jason Paulsel for the description of hooking up the equalizer bars. This is one reason I do not have a Travel Trailer.

■ **Trailer Brakes, Tires, and Wheels**

OK, you're hooked up and ready for towing a travel trailer. Not so fast young Jedi. You must first ensure the trailer brakes are operational and able to stop the trailer in a straight line. Most Travel Trailers are equipped with electric brakes. They may be controlled with a surge device mounted on the trailer or remotely by a brake controller in your tow vehicle. Personally, I would opt for the truck mounted brake controller. Some less expensive trailers only have brakes on one axle. This could certainly be problematic in a panic stop. There are kits available to convert your brakes to electric or surge activated disk brakes on all wheels. This would certainly be my preference when towing a travel trailer. Whatever setup you have, test it to ensure the trailer brakes actuate at the same time the tow vehicle's brakes do.

While we're talking about safety upgrades, now is the time to look at the tires. The air in your tires is all that holds up the load when towing a travel trailer. Special Trailer(ST) rated tires prior to 2010 that were of Chinese origin have had many problems and frankly are junk. Buy the best tires you can afford from a reputable company you trust. Get the highest load range that is available as well. Trailers have higher wheel loading than passenger cars or trucks. The axles do not steer, and the wheels are subjected to high twisting side loads in tight, slow turns. This causes the wheel to flex which tends to loosen wheel lug nuts over time. Check lug nut torque before each trip. A suitable torque wrench costs about $80 and is a worthwhile investment considering the value of your trailer.

NOTE: The most common causes of tire failure are overloading and under-inflation. Both result in excess flexing of the sidewall which causes heat buildup and eventual failure. Continuing to run with a flat can cause it to catch fire as well as destroy parts of your trailer.

Wheel lug nut torque is usually much higher than that specified for passenger car wheels. Check your particular trailer's recommended specifications. Most are in the 90-95 ft.-lb. range. On a new trailer, check the torque on all wheels after the first 25-50 miles of towing. Also recheck any wheel that has been removed and replaced after towing 25 to 50 miles. Do not drive a loaded trailer with a missing lug nut or damaged lug bolt.

Your axle wheel bearings will need occasional attention. Feel with your hand at the hub to check for one that may be running hotter than the rest.

Note: If the bearing is adjusted too tight or is running without grease it can get VERY hot!

You must pay immediate attention to a hot bearing. They will either need more grease or adjustment, but replacement may be necessary. This is an excellent application for an infrared thermometer that will indicate the temperature at whatever it is pointed.

■ Trailer Lights

Before towing a travel trailer, all the lights on the trailer must be connected through an umbilical cable to the tow vehicle's light circuits. Trucks with towing option installed will have the connections already made and a receptacle for that cable someplace on the bumper. In addition to turn signal and brake lights, the trailer's running lights must also come on when the tow vehicle's lights are on.

■ Loading a Travel Trailer

Towing a travel trailer safely involves a careful loading process. The heavier items that you load into the trailer should be placed as close to the middle as possible, but first they must be tied down so they won't shift while the trailer is moving. Start with the top heavy items. Lay them down and secure them. Arrange these items so they are protected in their location. Tying them down is not good enough. They need to be tied off at several angles or they could shift in a speed change. Your smaller items can act as filler material as long as they are securely fastened down.

Now is the time to start checking the tongue weight as you load. Sherline industries makes a great scale just for this and it is small and packable. They have models that will weigh up to 2000 pounds. Check them out on Amazon.com or direct from the manufacturer http://www.sherline.com/lm.htm . The smaller items can be loaded to help balance the load. Try to load the weight evenly from side to side as well. One side overweight can cause a serious problem when cornering, up to possibly turning over the trailer.

Note: Top heavy loads can cause trailer "dive" under hard braking, possibly reducing steering and braking control.

Do not put heavy things on add-on devices from the rear bumper or placed across the tongue frame. A bicycle is OK, but not much else.

■ **Weighing the Tow Vehicle and Trailer**

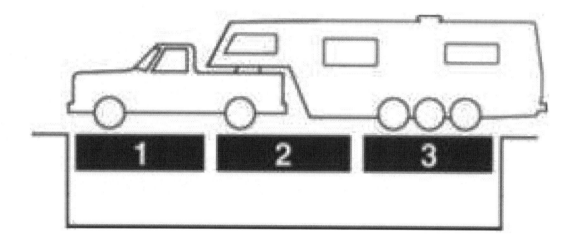

CAT Scale diagram

Now that you can tow and stop your trailer, it's time to weigh it. Because so many RVs are overweight and therefore unsafe, before towing a travel trailer, you should weigh it and your tow vehicle as soon as possible. You and your family's life may very well depend on it as well as people on the road around you.

As with any towing situation, the very first thing you must do is determine if your towing vehicle has the capacity for towing a travel trailer fully loaded. That means full water tank, water heater, and propane tank. It also means all the gear you will carry on a typical trip. First thing to know is the tow vehicle's towing capacity as well as rear Gross axle weight rating(GAWR). The very best way to determine if you are within rated limits is to weigh the rig all ready to go. First, enter the scale with only the front axle. Then the entire vehicle without the trailer. Circle around and hook up the trailer and weigh the tow vehicle with trailer attached. Next move forward until only the trailer is on the scale, and then move forward until only the rear axle is on the scale. You now have all the weights you need to determine your Gross Vehicle Weight, Your Tongue weight, and the total trailer weight as well as individual axle weights. All this information will tell you if either the tow vehicle or the trailer is overweight as well as the rear axle weight of the tow vehicle. With this you can also determine the proper air pressure to put in your tires according to the tire manufacturers tire loading charts for your particular model of tire.

What do you do if you are overweight? Oh, so many possibilities! If your tow vehicle is very much overweight, you may need to consider a larger and more capable one. If the trailer is OK but heavier on one axle than the other, you will have to shift tat weight around. Bear in mind that 10 to 12 percent of the trailer's weight should be on the tongue at all times. No more and no less.

Here is a YouTube video showing what can happen when you do not use weight distribution or sway control. http://www.youtube.com/watch?v=kwOqARlw1EI&feature=youtu.be

I hope this information on Towing a Travel Trailer will help you enjoy yours for a long time. We include this to alert you to certain safety concerns with towing a Travel Trailer.

CHAPTER 23

TOWING A
FIFTH WHEEL TRAILER

Fifth wheel towing starts with a quote from Wikipedia "Some recreational vehicles use a fifth wheel configuration, requiring the coupling to be installed in the bed of a pickup truck as a towing vehicle. The coupling consists of a kingpin, a 2-or-3 1⁄2-inch (50.8 or 88.9 mm) diameter steel pin on the front of the fifth wheel trailer, and a horseshoe-shaped coupling device called a *fifth wheel* on the rear of the towing vehicle. The surface of the semi-trailer (with the kingpin at the center) rotates against the surface of the fixed fifth wheel, which does not rotate. To reduce friction, grease is applied to the surface of the fifth wheel. The advantage of this coupling is improved towing stability."

This improved towing stability is one of the main reasons fifth wheel trailers are so popular. Ease of maneuverability is another reason to choose a fifth wheel trailer over a travel trailer.

■ Fifth Wheel Hitches and Accessories

Fifth wheel towing setups used in RVs have been around for a long time. Modern fifth-wheels since the 1990's can tilt to the sides and are easier to hook up because the coupler in the bed is "funneled" to capture the king pin on the trailer, which helps guide it into place.

Because fifth-wheel hitches are anywhere from 14 to 18 inches above the bed, they can be susceptible to chucking, where the coupler jaws grab the king pin. This is mainly a problem with less expensive setups. If you spend more on a better fifth-wheel hitch that adjusts to keep a tight grip on the king pin, chucking is all but eliminated.

The fifth wheel towing hitch must also be able to handle the loaded weight of your trailer. In this case, buy a more capable hitch in case you upgrade in the future.

Standard Fifth Wheel Hitch

An important issue when you select a fifth wheel hitch is cab-to-axle ratio, or the distance from the back of the cab to the center point of the coupler, usually located above or slightly forward of the rear axle. Requirements for a full-size bed are a no less than 48 inches behind the cab. For a short-bed pickup to pull a fifth-wheel, the measurement can be as little as 38 inches if you also use a pin-box extension (12-18 inches) and slide rails for the coupler.

Sliding Hitch　　　　**Pin Extension**　　　　**Bed Saver Attachment**

That pin-box extension is attached to the trailer. Its function is to extend the pivot point, or king pin, farther forward. The load of the trailer still rests above the axle but the trailer's front cap is farther to the rear to prevent interference with the truck's cab when turning. In addition to the pin box extension, a sliding style hitch can be used which moves front to back to help with low speed maneuvering, like backing into a space in a campground. You unlock the coupler from the slide rails, set the trailer brakes, and pull forward. Once you lock the coupler in place, you will have clearance for backing and tight maneuvering. Before you leave, you will have to unlock the coupler and slide it forward and then lock it in place for regular driving. This will save you from having to get body work done on your trailer and truck. Isn't fifth wheel towing fun?

Another fifth wheel towing accessory I see a lot is an air pin box. The air bag(s) help with the jolts the trailer takes from rough roads. There are also air hitches available,

Air Pin Box

Air Hitch

You will probably have to remove the factory tail gate for fifth wheel towing, or buy a special tailgate with clearance for the trailer's king pin.

■ Hooking up a Fifth wheel trailer

Back up far enough to ensure the king pin is in all the way and touching the front part of the coupler. Now pull the hand lever to lock the kingpin. Next, lift the trailer jacks as high as they will go. This is a good place to mention that you MUST ensure a solid mechanical lock between kingpin a d hitch receiver. Otherwise, when you drive forward, the kingpin will slide out and the trailer will drop on the bed of your pickup. You will probably see this "dent of shame" on other pickups in the campground that haven't been repaired yet. There is an accessory called a pin catcher that bolts on to the rear of the hitch that will catch and hold the pin so that the trailer doesn't drop. Perhaps a wise investment. You might need an extension harness that carries the voltage for the marker and signal lights. Some fifth wheels require a harness with fuses and relays all their own, but usually the extension is a length of cable and two seven-blade connectors. Next, check your lights, turn signals and brakes. This brake check is where you will make sure the kingpin is secure in the hitch.

■ **Fifth Wheel Towing Tips**

I could have researched and written a small section of fifth wheel towing tips, but our friend Ray Burris at www.loveyourrv.com wrote a really great blog post on this subject. Check it out here:

► http://www.loveyourrv.com/fifth-wheel-travel-trailer-towing-tips/

CHAPTER 24

RV BREAKDOWN TOWING

We will cover RV Breakdown Towing in several sections. First up will be vehicle insurance. No matter whether you have a motorized rig or a towable, you should have some form of towing insurance. This may be a part of your automobile policy if you are not a full-time RVer. You must contact your insurance company and add coverage for both the RV and the tow vehicle. Then we'll cover what to do first if you do break down. Then we'll cover actually being towed.

■ RV Insurance

If you have a motorhome and are towing a car(Toad), you must have a policy that covers both car and Motorhome. If you are in an accident, most likely both will be damaged. If you have policies with 2 insurance companies, you are looking at 2 deductibles and 2 claims. You are also liable if your car breaks loose from the motorhome and goes off on its own. Claims will be filed by drivers of other vehicles yours has hit, as well as property owners that have sustained damage caused by your errant car. These claims will most likely be against the liability portion of your RV insurance. Your motorhome insurance does not automatically extend to the car you are towing. This is why you should carry liability coverage on both your motorhome and towed vehicle.

There are other features you should look into as well. Does the policy pay for hotel stays while the RV is under repair? Policies change from company to company as well as in different states.

I know it's a lot to deal with, but you need to settle all this with your insurance agent before you take off on a trip. Not all insurance policies have this coverage. You may be forced to change insurance companies.

■ Full-time RV Insurance

People who live in their RVs more than 150 days per year are apparently considered full-timers by many insurance companies. Full-time RVers will need to obtain a full-timers comprehensive personal liability policy. This policy will change the coverage to be similar to your home insurance. Anyone injured inside your can make a claim against you, and this type of coverage is designed to cover such claims. Many full-timers don't realize they need this coverage until their insurance claims are denied because their RV is their primary residence. Another benefit of this coverage is higher limits of insurance on the contents of your rig. You are living full-time and the rig is your home. All that "stuff" you have should be covered. Of course the policy premium depends on the size of the deductible you set up. We try to have a $500 emergency fund just to cover deductibles.

■ RV Breakdown Towing Insurance

You should really consider some type of RV breakdown towing insurance. There are several companies that specialize in this. Among them, the best are Coach-Net (offered by several RV clubs), Good Sam (a part of the Affinity Group), and the American Automobile Association (AAA). Some automobile insurance companies purport to offer this type of coverage, but there isn't much data to support it.

▶ http://www.coach-net.com/default.aspx
▶ http://www.goodsamroadside.com/

This specialized type of insurance will cover having your rig towed in case of mechanical breakdown or becoming stuck in mud or soft ground. They will usually not cover towing in case of an accident. Your regular RV insurance takes care of that. You should compare the offerings of these companies to make sure they offer what you will need. You will want to ensure that if your truck breaks down and has to be towed, that the tow truck will then return and tow your trailer to a safe place. You must also make sure the towing company that the insurance company contacts for you has the proper equipment to safely tow your vehicle. Some policies limit the number of tows or the number of miles covered. This is very important as a 50-mile tow of a large motorhome can cost upwards of $800 or more.

None of these insurance companies actually own or operate tow trucks. They have agreements in place with tow companies all over the country. After they determine where you are, they usually contact the nearest towing company that has the equipment to handle your issue whether it's a tire change, battery jump, or actual tow.

Our friends Charles and Chris Yust are independent RV insurance agents who are also full-time RVers and understand our issues. Check them out at:

▶ http://www.candcrvinsurance.com

■ When You Have a Breakdown

If you have a breakdown, the first thing is to get your rig off the road and in a safe place. I know this is very hard as you are nervous and wondering what will this cost, and how long will my vacation be delayed; but just take a deep breath and try to relax for a few minutes. That will help to clear your head for what comes next.

Get pen and paper and write down everything that happened. What noises did you hear? Did you smell anything out of the ordinary? How about warning lights and gauges? Write it all down because it can be quite important when discussing this with a service writer later on. Can you start the vehicle now? Any noises that shouldn't be there? Shut it down immediately if there are strange noises or warning lights.

The next thing to do is call for help. If you have RV breakdown towing insurance, call the emergency number the company has given to you. Be calm and answer the questions clearly. They will want to know exactly where you are. Highway number and milepost would be great. If you have GPS, give them the coordinates. They will hang up while they arrange a mobile service call for you. Then they will call you back with the name and sometimes the phone number of the tow company and how long it will be before they are to arrive. The better insurance companies will continue to contact you until either you are on the road again or are being towed to a repair facility. If the police or highway patrol stops by, so much the better. They know all the local towing companies and can perhaps expedite them to your location. Without towing insurance, calling 911 is your best bet.

]If, after the tow truck operator arrives and you are unhappy with them, call your insurance company. It is up to you to sign off on a tow. If you have a motorhome, especially a large one, there are certain things that the tow truck operator must do. First they must raise the front wheels off the ground. This is where the first problems can happen. If the tow truck does not have a way to lift the tires off the ground and tries to lift the frame, the front cap can be damaged and even torn off. Assuming he has the proper equipment, next the drive shaft must be disconnected and tied up so it doesn't drop to the roadway while towing. With a diesel pusher, the whole drive shaft will be removed. It is about 2 feet long. If your rig has air brakes, the tow operator must air up the air tanks before towing. If you have a rain guard or sweep behind the rear wheels, it must be tied up high enough so it doesn't drag when the front is lifted. The tow driver will also have to hook up turn and brake lights. Nowadays, these are wirelessly controlled from the tow truck. You will not be able to ride in your rig when it is being towed. If you do not have a dingy vehicle, occasionally you can ride in the tow truck. Check with the RV breakdown towing insurance company first about that. All this being said, one of our breakdowns occurred near Yosemite National Park. The tow driver arrived with a very large flat bed tow truck and proceeded to put our rig up on the flatbed. It all worked fine, but is was distressing to see our rig leaning in the hairpin turns and switchbacks on the way down and to a repair shop.

Ok, you're underway, probably following your rig or waiting with your trailer for it to be picked up. You are on the way to a repair facility. The tow truck driver will not release your rig until the RV breakdown towing insurance company has paid the towing company. This can be an exasperating experience as you are put between the towing company and the insurance company. It has happened to us.

SECTION IV

FULL-TIME RVING

CHAPTER 25

"ARE YOU OUT OF YOUR MIND?"

Kathy and I dreamed about RVing for years before we even knew much about it or did anything about it. We would be driving on the interstate and see a big coach or fifth-wheel trailer and we would think and say together, "That will be us some day". We were convinced even then that touring the country in a big rig was the best way to travel. We didn't even imagine you could do it as a full-time lifestyle.

Can you imagine how we felt after we joyously sold our house and most of the stuff in it, moved into our new-to-us RV for a great adventure and lifestyle change and heard, "Are you out of your mind?" Unfortunately, this seemed to be the attitude of a lot of the people we know and love when we made the announcement. Many folks have a really high resistance to change. So many people are quite content and happy to live in the same house in the same town with the same people around them for their entire lives. That is perfectly fine for them and we don't want to change them. When someone in their circle decides to break away from that comfort zone, however, they find it hard to understand. You will be asked, "How in the world can you live 24/7 in that tin can?" "You'll go stir crazy and kill each other!" "How will you pay your bills?" and "How will you get your mail?" I can think of many other similar comments, but you get the point. Take heart my friend, because they will never feel the freedom of the open road. They won't see this country like you will. They won't do new things and meet new friends like you will every time you fire up your rig and hit the road for someplace new.

One common issue is that one spouse or partner is ready to jump into this lifestyle, sell everything, buy a rig and hit the open road, while the other has serious doubts. Often one or the other has serious issues with leaving their home and most belongings behind. If you live close to family and children and grandchildren, it can be hard to cut those ties. In some severe cases, the conflicts of a full-time lifestyle will not work for those folks. We aren't qualified to solve these conflicts and wouldn't want to come between people anyway. It's unfortunate, but this lifestyle isn't for everyone. Possibly you might want to try "Long Timing" or extended trips away from your sticks and bricks house before you jump off the ledge into full-timing.

One of the questions that was asked was "Won't you get on each other's nerves and argue and fight?" The answer is a qualified "sometimes". Hopefully, you and your partner have given a lot of thought to the 24/7 in a hallway thing. No matter the type of RV, from small travel trailer to a 45-foot luxury motorhome, all of them are narrow hallways. The best you can expect is about four hundred and fifty square feet, and that is exceptional. It won't take long and that space will shrink in on you unless you get your head(s) around it. We all need personal space and RVing is no exception. You can go outside, or to one end of your unit, but make sure you both realize the need for some "alone" time.

I don't want to start off with doom and gloom, but this is a reality. This lifestyle is not for everyone, but with early realization of the possible downsides and a good plan, it can be the most rewarding thing you have ever done. Kathy and I were married for thirty-eight years before we set out full-timing. We knew which buttons not to push so as to avoid conflict. We now live closely together in less than 400 square feet and there are certainly situations where we don't agree with one another. We have found the best cure is some alone time to do our own thing without one another. Kathy needs a certain amount of "Kathy" time to herself to read, or shop, or even think without me and I realize that. Consequently, we avoid most serious fights and arguments.

The nearest thing most people get to what we have is when they go on a vacation. They'll get on a plane or in the car and travel somewhere and check into a motel. Who knows who slept in that bed last and what did they leave behind? On the other hand, we can go far beyond airports and motels and restaurants. We sleep in our own bed and cook our food if we want to. We can even stay off the grid if we desire.

It took us almost a year to realize that we were embarking on a new and exciting *Lifestyle,* not an extended vacation. Initially, we fell into the unending vacation trap when we started out full- time. We felt we had to go, go, go, and see everything and do everything all in the first several months. In our case, this

"Express Touring" lasted for the first year. We also spent as much in that year as in the next three! We finally realized we had plenty of time to see things and we could return to see and do things we missed the first time.

A good case in point is our love of the Black Hills of South Dakota. We have spent four summers there and I don't believe we've seen it all yet. It's that way all over the country. So far, we have cherry picked the high points in our travels, but there would be so much more to see if we had stayed longer. We started the Living the RV Dream radio show four years into full-timing, and it was then that we realized we were truly living a very wonderful and special lifestyle. But, that is the beauty of it. You have the freedom to do what you want to do and when you want to do it. It's your choice. You can plan a trip down to the hour with all stops booked and attractions planned in advance; or you can have your plans set in Jell-O like we do. We'll discuss plans and goals in detail later on.

Something that came as a surprise were the many new friends we have made while traveling and during our volunteering and workamping assignments. We meet people with similar experience and lifetime friendships result. This would never happen in our insulated life in a sticks and brick house where we moved in a small circle of family and friends. Because we share this unique lifestyle, we bond much more quickly than before. Thanks to e-mail and social media, we continue to keep in touch. We may not see someone for a year or more, but when we meet again in some other place on the map, that friendship is still strong and it becomes a joyous homecoming.

Of course the naysayers had many other questions like "How will you ever learn to drive that great big thing?" and a host of other questions, some of which we didn't yet have answers to. Well, most will be revealed and much, much more as you read this book. I want to emphasize that Kathy and I are NOT experts in this RV lifestyle, but after being on the road since 2005, we are experienced and we have had much trial and error to get to good answers. Those are in the Lessons Learned chapter at the end of the book.

CHAPTER 26

DO YOUR HOMEWORK

The very first thing to do when contemplating the full-time RV lifestyle is a fair amount of what we call "homework" to arrive at good decisions. Homework starts with deciding what kind of lifestyle you will live. Do you love NASCAR, rodeos, visiting family, being a snowbird, seeing the country and its natural beauty? Perhaps you enjoy traveling around and doing volunteer work at churches or maybe Habitat for Humanity. That might determine what type of rig will be best for your lifestyle. You will have to figure out how you will handle your mail and bills. Do you know how you will finance this dream? You must do at least a preliminary budget to decide what you can afford. Will you have adequate healthcare insurance? How will you communicate with people? Have you thought about what you will do with your "stuff"? All this and more goes into the "Homework" part of getting ready to be a full-time RVers.

We started our homework at the local library. We read every book on RVing. Some were good and informative and some were not. Some talked about current RVing information and some were old and outdated. Various internet sites led us to more information and helped us to ask better questions. We looked at the manufacturer's web sites and we went to the Florida RV Super show and met up with two couples who were Escapees. They talked to us for more than an hour and a half about full-time RVing. We didn't even know what that was but it sounded exciting. Of course, we asked what the down side was and they paused and pondered the question and then like a choir they said "we should have done it ten years sooner".

OK, we were hooked, but there was still a lot more to investigate. We also looked around at all the different RVs and got their brochures to take home and study, and we took lots of pictures. John checked the underneath space and I pretended that I was living in the RV and made dinner and tried to make the bed. We must have walked twenty miles and looked into a hundred RVs. We then went to the local RV dealers within a hundred miles of our home. Many salesmen were informative and some were not. It helped us to decide on a motorhome for the lifestyle we were planning on living, instead of a 5th wheel or a travel trailer. John talked to service managers to find out which brands needed more service than others. We visited local campgrounds and talked with campers about their RVs and about their lifestyle. Some were full-timers and were really enjoying it, some were long timers who were gone from their homes for four to ten months at a time, and some were camping almost every weekend. They all enjoyed the camping lifestyle they had chosen. We learned what they liked about campgrounds and what they looked for when choosing the campground. They told us some horror stories about camping but they still loved it and were very informative about it.

Go to all the RV shows you can get to. Investigate the types and specific models within each category. By now you should have a pretty good idea what type of RV you want. Focus your RV show visits to that type. Look through all the manufacturer's brochures and compare specifications.

Talk to the Service Managers at a few dealerships about specific brands and what type of issues they may have. We did just that and eliminated several brands that were at the top of our list. You don't want to make a large investment and see it sitting in a service bay more than in your driveway.

We started to subscribe to Motorhome magazine and the Escapees magazine and read them from cover to cover. Gleaning all the information we could, we knew we needed to make the best decision possible. Buying a motorhome is expensive and I wanted to make the best decision for us. We finally decided on a motorhome and we picked out three different models that we liked when we were ready to buy. This process took almost two years and I am glad we did it. We have had our motorhome for ten years and we still like it a lot.

Homework is going to RV shows, dealerships, and RV club rallies as well as talking with a number of full-timers to get various insights. Visiting a dealership can be good if you make it quite clear to the inevitable salesman assigned to you that you are in the investigating stage and are absolutely not ready to make a purchase. Always take a small notebook and a camera with you when looking at RVs. By the time you have climbed into twenty or thirty rigs, they all tend to run together. Write down the model and what features you like and which ones you don't. Make a note of the MSRP (Manufacturer's Suggested Retail Price), but don't let that sway you. RV buying is a negotiation and MSRP is relatively useless as anything but a starting point, especially with used rigs. When Kathy and I look at rigs, I start with a walk around and look into all basement doors. This way I get a feel for how much storage is available, how easy it is to access engine filters, batteries, fuse panels, and other service items. This is also when I make a note of the age of the tires using the DOT code on the tire. If the rig is used and you are interested in it, go up on the roof and check out the conditions up there. Are there cracks in the caulking, tears in membrane material, black mildew? Are there loose items that will rattle and make noise at 55 miles per hour? These are issues that must be addressed prior to purchase. Kathy goes inside and will pretend to do routine household chores like cooking a meal, changing a bed, and other things we do on a regular basis. Is there enough counter space? One of her hot buttons is whether there is enough pantry space for food and supplies close to the cooking area. Is there adequate room around the bed to move easily? Is the dinette comfortable for eating? If the rig is motorized, I check out the cockpit for easy access to all driver controls, comfort of the driver's seat for long hours on the road, and other amenities. All this goes into the notebook. After a while, you will get a feel for what things are important and you might make up a check-list for evaluating an RV for possible purchase. I would resist the temptation to take a test drive at this point in the homework. You don't want the salesman to salivate and count his commission in advance, do you? Save that for when you have settled on a few models that you are interested in making a purchase decision on.

We do these same things when we look at rigs at RV shows and large rallies with RV displays. One thing to remember, today's "Show Special" will be just as special, and just as good a deal next week or even next month. At most shows and rallies, you will receive a plastic bag at the entrance with some brochures and show info. Stuff this bag with brochures on all the rigs you think might be a possibility for future purchase. This gives you valuable information for comparison of different rigs. You might even consider a backpack for carrying these and your notebook and camera. If a price is listed on a rig, write that on the brochure.

I wish we would have had a small voice recorder when we talked to full-timers and other experienced RVers. We spent over an hour with two full-timer couples at the Escapees RV Club booth at the Tampa, Florida Super Show talking about the full-time lifestyle. That conversation was a confirmation that full-time RVing was what we wanted to do. It was a year before we bought our rig. We still had a lot of homework to do even though we knew this was to be our future.

CHAPTER 27

WHAT ABOUT YOUR STUFF?

You have decided to go full-timing and now it's time to sell the house. Whether you choose a realtor or do it yourself, get ready. This is not a quick process. You will want the best price for your house, so consult someone who will help you decide what needs painting and/or repair, what price you can consider, and what's the bottom line you will accept for the house.

One of the first things to understand is that almost everything you own is "stuff". It can be replaced. What cannot be replaced, such as family pictures and artwork, can either be put in storage or on loan to your family. We started by calling our children and telling them to bring a U-Haul and take anything they wanted. After they did and we had taken out the few things that we considered non-replaceable, we scheduled 2 yard sales. This does take some time; you can usually get a yard sale kit from the local newspaper that will help you with the process. The most important thing to remember is that you are trying to get rid of everything, and price it accordingly. After the sale we contacted the Salvation Army to come and pick up anything that was left. This can be kind of hard to do, but there is only so much space in the RV for things that will be important. Choose wisely.

If there are some things that you cannot get rid of, find a storage unit and rent it for a year. After that year go through all of this again and make a decision. We have friends that had 3 storage units and they returned every year trying to cut down what they had stored. Finally, after about 5 years they were able to get rid of everything that they didn't need. Paying for storage units can be expensive, so really think about what you want to store. We made the decision to go the whole way and just sold everything we could.

You may also want to consider donating to your local church or charity. They will greatly appreciate whatever you can give and you will be able to take a tax deduction.

Do you have two cars? One must go. Since we bought a motorhome, we knew we would be towing and we choose the newer car. We took our second car back to the dealership and they gave us a great price for it and that took care of that. We also had to modify the car with a transmission pump to make it towable with all four wheels down. This decision was made because the car was already paid off and to buy a new towable car would cost a lot more money than the modification. Only you can decide what you want to do. Again choose wisely. The more money you have available to tour with will make your full-timing life more enjoyable.

CHAPTER 28

PICK A DOMICILE STATE

When Kathy and I started on the full-time adventure, we were unaware of the advantage of selecting a state for domicile purposes. We were in Florida and paid no state taxes and we thought that was enough. Not so! We paid seven percent sales tax on the motorhome purchase. That was a sizeable chunk of money we could have used for better purpose. We realized there were other possibilities when we were researching mail forwarding services. We went to the website of Alternative Resources, now called Dakota Post http://dakotapost. net/ and all the advantages of South Dakota residence were listed. At that point we purchased "Choosing Your RV Home Base" from Roundabout Publications at Camping World. This book is a must have if you are just starting out full-timing.

In it we found state by state listings of: financial liability by state; federal taxes for full-timers; state retirement exemptions; tax advantages of each state; vehicle licensing registration specifics; and voting rules and requirements. We were able to compare states and wrote down the things that were important to us. At the end of this process, we chose South Dakota for no state income taxes, low vehicle insurance and registration, and very friendly probate laws.

Unfortunately, we can no longer recommend South Dakota as a domicile state. Their insurance rates have more than doubled over the last 5 years. There is no portable (out of state) health insurance available, and you must return to SD to renew your driver's license. In our opinion, Florida and Texas are the best bets for domicile states for full-timers.

The RV lifestyle gives us the unique opportunity to choose any state to call "home". For anyone considering the full-time RV lifestyle, a state to establish a home base can be quite important and there are several factors that must be considered. Among the most important issues for full-timers are taxes, insurance, and RV fees. Which states have the best income tax advantages? Which states offer the best rates on RV registration, including annual vehicle taxes? If you pick the wrong state to establish an official residence, it could result in your spending thousands of dollars a year that could be saved by establishing a home base elsewhere. And just how does a full-timer establish an official residency? Is it enough to simply rent a post office box? I don't think so.

As soon as you arrive in your domicile state, you should establish a mailing address using a mail forwarding service. Then you surrender your current driver's license and get 5them from your new state. Next, you should go to an insurance office or on-line site and get insurance for your car and motor home. Your next stop should be at the courthouse for vehicle registration for new license plates for both vehicles. Next you should register to vote in your new state. Because we travel so much, we do not vote in local elections and use absentee ballots for federal elections. It is best to evaluate the complete picture as it fits your particular lifestyle when selecting an RV home base state.

It is not a good idea to use one state for mail forwarding, another for a driver's license, another as a legal address for tax filing, etc. States might think you are attempting to avoid paying their taxes or fees, and they do seem to have many ways of finding you.

CHAPTER 29

HOW DO I GET MY MAIL?

This is almost always the first question we get when we talk about full timing with people. To be honest, I would be happy to never get any mail. It becomes clutter, and we already have enough of that. But, until electronic means make it obsolete, we must still deal with mail. A lot of folks we know have their adult children take care of sending their mail to them. This is fine, but they are busy and sometimes the mail is a low priority for them. It's a hassle to package it, go to the post office, send it, and pay the postage.

When we started on the road from Florida, we used a Mailboxes, Etc., now called the UPS Store. www.theupsstore.com for forwarding our First Class mail. This worked out fairly well, but there were problems with "junk" mail and the service was comparatively expensive. Since that time, we are convinced that dedicated mail forwarding services are the best solution to getting your mail on the road. A recent Google check of "mail forwarding" yielded more than 80 actual mail forwarding services. We were in the process of changing our state of domicile to South Dakota, so we decided to use a service in that state. We ended up with a company called Alternative Resources, now called Dakota Post, one of the more popular mail forwarders from South Dakota. Most of these mail services work in a similar fashion. There is a monthly or annual fee for the service, and then a deposit of fifty to a hundred dollars for postage charged to a credit card, replenished when the postage account falls to a pre-determined low point. Like most of the larger services, they were quite flexible with what class of mail we wanted forwarded and what method, such as First Class, or Priority Mail, or even Federal Express or United Parcel Service. They were also flexible with how many shipments we would receive. We could have it shipped weekly, bi-weekly, monthly, or a one-time shipment when we were traveling.

One important thing to remember is that unless you are a seasonal resident, most campgrounds will not receive mail for you; they just don't have the staff, nor do they want to get into difficulties with the United States Postal Service. We use the General Delivery service at local Post Offices in the area where we are camped. Be careful in this as certain Post Offices will not handle General Delivery mail. Get the zip code of the campground where you will be staying and call that Post Office. Verify that they will accept General Delivery and also the zip code and address of that Post Office. This may seem like a hassle, but so is chasing a missed delivery with time sensitive material in it.

Of all the mail services we have looked into, the Escapees RV Club mail service is a world class operation. Located in Livingston, TX, it has its own zip code. You must be a member of the Escapees RV Club to use their mail service, however. Go to http://www.escapees.com/ . Recently, Escapees set up a Florida mail service and one in South Dakota is forthcoming.

Next up is Dakota Post, located in Sioux Falls, South Dakota. This is our choice as it is in our new home state. Go to http://www.dakotapost.net/mail-forwarding. Other South Dakota mail forwarders are www.mydakotaaddress.com in Madison, South Dakota and America's Mailbox in Box Elder, South Dakota at www.americas-mailbox.com . There are others available in South Dakota; you just have to search the web for South Dakota mail forwarding.

If you want to have your official domicile in Florida, a mail service located in Crestview, Florida is http://www.myrvmail.com/. Again, there are other mail forwarding services in Florida, just look them up on the web.

There are mail services based in many other states, I have only highlighted the major ones in the states most frequently used by full time RVers. Spend some time searching the internet to find the ideal service to fit your needs. You should also check out RV forums such as the one on http://www.rv.net/ for plusses and minuses before settling on this important part of the full time lifestyle.

CHAPTER 30

WHAT ABOUT HEALTH CARE

In the ten plus years Kathy and I have been on the road, she has had three surgeries and I have had one. I was also hospitalized for four days in Florida with a still unknown virus. If we had not possessed good health insurance, our life on the road would have been over. I am retired from the U.S. Navy and have the good fortune to have excellent health insurance for both of us. Now we are both on Medicare and the military insurance pays all costs Medicare doesn't. This is probably the best situation to be in. Many of you will have health insurance from a previous employer or from your state in some cases. That's great!

We have talked to fellow full-timers who have medical insurance from a previous employment that is only in effect if they are in the original state of that employment. Apparently there are supplemental policies for out of state travel, but the cost is high.

With the advent of the Affordable Care Act, or Obamacare, there are more options, especially if you have pre-existing conditions. That being said, not all states are alike when it comes to healthcare. In South Dakota as of press time, there are no plans that allow care out of the state. On the other hand, many Florida plans allow care out of state. Do your homework.

Affordability is in the eye of the beholder, but there are many companies that will provide varying levels of health insurance for a monthly or semi-annual fee. The obvious point here is even a short hospitalization can produce tens of thousands of dollars in costs and an office or urgent care visit with the attending tests can run into several thousands. If you set out on the full-time lifestyle without health insurance, you are betting everything you have that neither of you will become seriously ill. It's a crapshoot my friends. I cannot in good conscience recommend this lifestyle to you without your having adequate health insurance coverage.

Here is an insurance broker that works with RVers to find the best and most affordable coverage. https://www.rverinsurance.com/

This is a good time to mention medications. We have a mail order prescription service called Express Scripts. We give them a delivery address as we travel and get most of our meds that way. Some of our refillable prescriptions are through CVS and Good Sam Club pharmacies. Just show the packaging or the prescription number to the local store and you can get your meds that way. We use CVS primarily because they are found almost anywhere in the country. We asked our doctors to set us up with 1 year prescriptions in ninety day packages. This way we can plan in advance when we may be running low. No matter who you choose, make sure they have outlets where you will be travelling.

Here are some blogs and links to help you figure out what is best for you:

▶ http://rv-roadtrips.thefuntimesguide.com/2010/12/rv_medical.php
▶ http://www.technomadia.com/2013/11/chapter-12-healthcare-and-staying-healthy-on-the-road-2/
▶ http://wheelingit.us/2014/02/28/the-aca-aka-obamacare-its-impacts-on-full-time-rv-health-insurance/

CHAPTER 31

PLANNING AND SETTING UP GOALS

We got some good advice about planning when we started out full-timing. You're starting out on a journey such as you have never done before. The best way to approach this journey is with sound planning. You don't want to come off the road and regret that you haven't done the things you wanted to do.

■ Goals

The first and most important part of the planning process is to set goals for both yourself and your partner. Will you stay in RV resorts and tour the country, or will you move with the seasons (snow birding), or will you see every major league ballpark? Would you like to tour Civil War battlefields? You must have goals, or you will meander aimlessly; or perhaps that is your goal. You can have multiple goals; just remember how long you might be at this. It would be gratifying to accomplish your main goals and then talk about the stuff you did with friends and family. You might even convince someone else to try the full-time lifestyle.

■ Short Term Goals

Short term goals are the things you want to accomplish within the next year. This way, you can be specific and even lay out a tentative route. This is actually the most difficult type of planning because you will start executing the short term plan immediately. Better get it right before the meandering starts. This type of planning works hand in hand with the budgeting process. You need to know you can afford to do the things you have planned for the year ahead of you.

An example of a short term plan might be to visit all the state and national parks in several states. Another could be to attend a number of rallies across the country. Whatever you plan, try to keep it realistic. A business term I used to use is "don't boil the ocean". In other words, don't plan so much you couldn't possibly do it all in a year. Kathy and I only had one destination we had to do the first year, and that was to see Mount Rushmore. We did that and so much more.

If you are over fifty years old like we are, you must plan on visiting your doctor once a year to get physical exams and renew prescriptions. We have forgotten this and consequently we have doctors in three states.

■ Trip Planning

Trip planning, short term goals, and budgeting all work together. Once you set the goals, you are in a position to start planning the trip. Kathy and I do the goal setting together, and then I do the rough trip planning. I get out the maps, the campground guides, and the planning software, and lay out a route that takes us either directly to our destinations or near enough to visit by car. We make sure we will have the funds to do what is in the plan, or we revise the plan.

■ Midterm Goals

A good midterm plan might reach out five years or so. There are over four hundred National Parks in the continental U.S. You could realistically expect to thoroughly tour about a hundred and fifty or so in five years assuming you won't do much else. You could, however, visit forty-nine states and spend a month or so in each. If you snowbird from warm weather to warm weather, the midterm planning is easy. If you want to tour the country, seasons play a large part in the planning process.

Kathy and I continue to visit as many National Parks as we can when our route takes us near one. Of course we also do National Monuments, and there are a ton of those. Our main focus is to find new and interesting places to explore and then report on for our radio show.

■ Long Term Goals

Long term goals encompass your total full-time RVing experience. This could go out ten or twenty years or more. This is where you can do a little "blue sky" planning, commonly known as dreaming. Once you have it down on paper, figure out how you can make it happen. You might want to get another rig sometime in the future. Put it in the plan; you can always revise it later on. You might want to make allowance for the fact that we all age more quickly in those years. I hate trying to do stuff I love but just can't do it anymore.

■ Exit Plan

We are planning at least another ten years on the road as long as our health allows; but we are setting up a plan for being off the road. In Chapter 34, we discuss exit planning in more detail.

CHAPTER 32

BUDGETING FOR FULL-TIME RVers

No matter how you live the RV lifestyle, you will need money on a regular basis to continue to enjoy it. This isn't much fun to deal with, but it must be done to ensure you are able to continue this lifestyle. You have to decide how much you are willing to spend in order to maintain whatever level of RV lifestyle you desire. We have talked to folks that said they had to spend over five thousand dollars a month to be happy. Wow! We have discussed this issue with others that boondock in one place for long periods that can do it on as little as several hundred dollars a month. We fall someplace in between.

There are numerous variables that have to be considered to come to a reliable figure for you. To start off, you need to determine all your fixed monthly costs such as insurance, rig and car payments, phone, internet, television, and other communications expenses, and any others you may have. See the budget section for more ideas. Now we'll add in the variable expenses. You must decide on your basic lifestyle. Will you eat out in restaurants, or will you make most of your meals, or something in between? Will you boondock, or live off the grid, or will you stay in campgrounds and resorts? Will you travel a certain range of miles every month, or will you stay put for a season? Will you work while out on the road, and if so how much money do you expect to make or save? These and many other questions must be answered in order to come to a realistic dollar figure.

Once you have arrived at a monthly income requirement, subtract that from the total of your actual available income. Anything that is a positive number is great and can be put into savings. If you have a negative total, then you must reconsider your lifestyle desires. You may have to work to supplement income, or travel less to reduce fuel expense, or make other accommodations. In our case, workamping has brought us lifelong friends and some wonderful experiences. Check out our working on the road section for more information.

Budgeting and the need for it is probably one of the hardest things to explain.

Everyone has different desires, plans, incomes and expenses, but here are some basic expenses to consider when you prepare a budget for full-time RVing. How much does it cost to live the RV lifestyle? It can be as much as $150K or less than $11K a year. It all depends on how you want to live. With a larger income, you can live a more elaborate lifestyle by staying in more expensive campgrounds and resorts, eating out at restaurants, and driving a lot of miles. Smaller incomes may require more frugal living such as discount campgrounds, cooking meals on board and staying longer to enjoying the free activities offered at campgrounds and in nearby cities. Average full-timers we have talked with will spend about $25K to $35K a year. We take advantage of campground memberships, shopping at Wal-Mart Supercenters, military commissaries, thrift shops, and yard sales. There are many ways to cut expenses so you can enjoy the things that mean the most to you. Just decide where you want to spend your money.

■ Fixed Costs

Fixed costs are those that recur on a regular basis either annually, quarterly, or monthly. These are the must-pay items that you can't change easily.

■ The RV

If you do not pay cash for your RV this may be your biggest recurring expense. Whether you choose a class A, B, or C motorhome, 5th wheel, travel trailer or pop-up, you will have payments to make. We chose a Class A diesel motorhome and to tow a small car. The best advice we have heard is to buy you third vehicle first. Full-timing is hard on a rig, so try and buy the very best you can comfortably afford.

■ Towed or Towing Vehicle

If you have a motorhome you will probably need a towed vehicle. It is easy to park the rig and hop in the car and off you go for another adventure. Be sure and find out if the car is flat towable, which means 4 wheels down. You can modify your tow like we did because our car was paid for and it was less expensive to modify the car than buy a new one. If you have a 5th wheel or travel trailer you will need a tow vehicle. Make sure you check the towing specifications for your tow vehicle and match it to the weights of your trailer.

■ Vehicle Insurance

By registering in a less populated state, your insurance costs can be lower. We were in Florida when we first bought our rig, but decided on South Dakota as our state of domicile. Not many people live in South Dakota and our auto and motorhome insurance cost went down by a third. Unfortunately, this is not the case 10 years later. Shop insurance every year. Your car and RV will both need to be covered and not all insurance companies will cover for full time use of the RV. Be honest when you fill out the application. The insurance company could cancel your coverage or deny a claim if they discover you were untruthful on the application.

■ Extended Warranty

Since we bought a used motorhome, we also carry an Extended Warranty, and it has paid for its cost several times. A towing service is also quite important. We use Coach-Net, and they have been great. The first question they ask when we call is always "Are you in a safe place?". That is a great comfort and peace of mind.

■ Vehicle Registration

Every year your car or truck and rig will need to be registered. Don't forget to plan for this expense.

■ Health Insurance

Health insurance is a key to being able to enjoy the full-time RV lifestyle. If you don't have coverage from prior employment or Medicare, it is available for purchase from many companies. Make sure your healthcare is available across the country. Some plans are only good in the original state of purchase. If you are not yet 62 and on Medicare, you will find that health insurance can be even more expensive than an RV payment.

■ Communication

Cell phones and internet are so important to keep in contact with family and friends. We have Verizon cell service and their air card for internet. Anymore, it is hard to find a pay phone and almost everyone has a cell phone. Most campgrounds will have some form of WI-FI; however, it is not always good. Some use Tengo internet which is a service available in most states at a cost. Almost all public libraries have free internet service and many fast food places offer it free. Just remember that public Wi-Fi is not secure. I would never do my banking or post credit card information using public Wi-Fi.

■ Television

Some parks have cable TV and will charge extra (up to $3.00 a day) for its use. We use Direct TV satellite service and we like it very much. The monthly bill is paid online. If you will be in a park for an extended period and the park has cable services, most satellite TV companies will allow you to put the service to "sleep" for six months.

■ Mail Forwarding Service

How do I get my mail? This is the first question we hear. You will need to get a mail forwarding service which will assign you an address at their office. All of your mail will be sent to this address and then they will forward it to you. There are several companies that provide this service and are listed in the "How Do You Get Your Mail" section. They usually charge a yearly fee and then you will pay the postage to forward the mail to wherever you are located. We have cut way back on our mail. Getting rid of flyers and magazines we do not read cuts the weight of the shipped mail. We do everything we can by internet. Many magazines are available in an on-line version, and generally at a lower cost than the newsstand version.

Variable or Controllable Costs

Variable expenses are those that you have some control over. This is the first place to look when you need to cut back.

■ Fuel

Fuel is probably the biggest variable expense that you will have. Consequently, consider your travel distance and the average price for fuel where you are traveling;

add a few cents to the calculation of the expense and travel accordingly. We plan out 2-3 months in advance and figure out the miles and the cost. To find out how much it will cost for fuel in the different states you will be traveling thru, go on the internet and look at the Pilot/Flying J http://www.pilotflyingj.com/ or Loves http://www.loves.com/ websites. They list the current prices for fuel on a daily bases at all of their stations. There can be as much as ten cents per gallon or more difference between one state and another. Plan your trip based on these variable expenses. Sometimes we stay longer, and sometimes we will do fewer miles. There is no rush to get anywhere, so just enjoy the place you are now for a few more weeks.

Don't forget the LP tank. We use liquid propane for heating water, the stove top, and the furnaces in cold weather, our outside barbeque grill, and the refrigerator if needed. With the motorhome's built-in propane tank, we fill up wherever we find the best price. Except for colder winters, it is usually only two or three times a year. Most of our propane use is for the stove. Because we tend to grill a lot, we have a small LP tank just for the barbeque grill.

■ Camping

Parks range in price from zero dollars to over one hundred dollars a night and more. It all depends on the kind of park you like to stay in. Boondocking (camping without hook-ups) is using the self-contained features of your RV such as water holding tanks, generator, or solar panels for electricity, etc. Boondocking is great fun. We have done it several times and enjoyed it. We don't do a lot, but there are those who will park for months at a time with no camping fees. Staying longer at the campground will give you a better price, and you will have more time to explore the area. Some campers think it is okay to stay at Wal-Mart or other store parking lots for free for an extended period of time. Please don't do this. It isn't fair to the store or the local campgrounds. Belonging to a camping club like Escapees, Good Sam, FMCA, Thousand Trails, RPI or Passport America will give you a discount of some type; usually between ten and fifty percent. We have used them all.

Passport America advertises itself as half-price camping and is more cost effective, but there are restrictions to the length of stay and the time of year. You need to read the fine print.

Camping Clubs like Thousand Trails, Outdoor World, AOR, and Coast to Coast have an initial cost that can be a high, then there is an annual fee, but the only extra you will pay would be for fifty-amp electrical service. All of these clubs can be found online for resale. Be sure to check it out.

Then there are the individual private membership parks that are affiliated with the big clubs. There are many throughout the US. We have been able to camp in many of them as a result of our RPI membership. These are great for a home park near the grandkids, or to visit each year for your annual check-up. Again, there is an annual maintenance fee. Also check if there are reserve funds for any major repairs. You don't want to have a huge unexpected assessment fee.

National and State Parks are a great option. They are beautiful and not too expensive. The only thing we have found is that they do not always accommodate larger rigs. Again, call or go on the internet to check out the restrictions.

The Escapees RV Club has nineteen parks in their system for the use of club members at rates around $20 per night.

■ Food

It is your choice whether you eat out a lot or cook in your rig. This is a major expense that you have total control over. We eat at home and only going out once every 2 weeks. We do a lot of barbequing and grilling, and many times we will cook two meals at a time, so lunch or dinner is all ready for the following day. It's good to have a nice grill and a portable LP tank. This will help keep the heat out of the rig during those long summer days, and there is nothing finer than a hamburger grilled outside. There are grocery stores everywhere and something is always on sale. I have found that planning out meals for a week at a time and taking a list to the store saves a lot of money as well as clipping coupons.

■ Maintenance and Repair

Just like your stick built house, there are regular maintenance and repairs that will need to be done. Getting these done and keeping a record will help to prevent major breakdowns in the future. About every five to seven years you will need new tires on the motorhome. 5th wheels and travel trailers seem to need tires a lot. If you have a diesel engine the yearly oil change and lube can cost as much as $500.00. This is a big expense; plan to put aside a small amount monthly so you are ready. Consider buying an extended warranty to cover major breakdown expenses. We have the Good Sam Extended Service Plan, and it has saved us more that the cost of the annual premiums with engine repairs and replacing our refrigerator cooling unit.

■ Laundry

If you do not have a washer in the rig, this is another expense. It can run about $10 to $15 a week depending on how much the campground or Laundromat is charging.

■ Banking

We do all of our banking on the internet. Most banks and credit unions have websites for on-line banking. Bills and payments are scheduled and controlled through this system. Let your bank know that you will be full timing so they will not be alarmed by charges from all over the country. However, it is your job to check your accounts constantly and keep track of the charges. We have had no problems as of yet. Be careful of public Wi-Fi hotspots for internet connection when banking. These sites are not secure and you don't want your information to be made public. See the "How Will You Communicate?" section.

These are just some of the examples of the expenses you will have. You may have credit card and car payments to handle. If possible, try to pay off everything but the most important and low interest item. Carrying heavy debt can make RVing a nightmare. Be wise and realistic in your finances. Always figure on the high side and you will not run short.

As with everything we have talked about, do your research and talk with others. Talk to your bank or credit union, phone service, TV service and take names for later reference. If possible, get written confirmation of issues you have discussed.

CHAPTER 33

KEEP GOOD RECORDS

This may sound like a no-brainer, but keeping good records can save you a lot of grief as well as money in some situations. We have kept great service records on our motorhome and car, but not so great financial records over the years, We'll break it down.

■ Maintenance Records

Recently, we had to stop at a Cummins Coach Care location with a bad turbocharger. That is quite an expensive repair and thankfully we have an extended service plan to cover much of the cost. When the service center submitted the claim to the warranty company, they wanted to see the last 2 years' records of oil changes before they would approve the claim.

We not only have a record book where we write down the date and time of all RV service work, but we keep a file in chronological order of all receipts from service work as well from accessories purchases. We very quickly came up with the last 2 oil change records and they were submitted. Approval for the service came back within an hour. Otherwise, we would have been out of pocket almost $3500. All because we kept 2 receipts.

Those records and receipts also provide evidence for a potential buyer of what service was done to the rig and when. Looking back through our receipts also lets us know how long things like batteries and tires last. It's an easy thing to make a file folder for rig expenses and another for your toad car or towing truck. These records can also be invaluable when pursuing warranty claims against a manufacturer.

■ Financial Records

In the previous chapter on budgeting, we listed a lot of categories of spending. All of that spending will produce receipts. Some of that may be tax deductible.

You may very well be able to deduct the interest on your RV loan as a second vacation home, or in our case, primary home. Bingo!! You will need good records to do your tax return, or for your accountant to do it. We did not do a good job of personal record keeping when we got started RVing. That's too bad because we can now only imagine what we spent and what we spent it on. Ever since our podcast became a business, we have started to do a better job. Some of our records are our daily travel journal when we are on the road, so we can pick out our travel mileage for later reporting. That journal has a place to record our miles driven as well as fuel expenditures and mileage. At the end of the year, we use that journal to compute our mileage deductions for the year's taxes.

Once our business became an LLC, the need for good records got even greater. Enter bookkeeping software. We had used Quicken before, but we have found that Quick Books is the better choice for our little home based business. Once set up, it allows us to input all spending as well as income. All that can be exported to tax software to make that horrible chore a little easier.

There are many ways to keep financial records. There is always the old shoebox full of receipts you dump on your accountant. Probably not a good idea, especially if you want him to continue to do your taxes. I mentioned software earlier. There are several companies marketing scanners and software to scan and categorize your receipt collection. No matter what you do, you should retain and keep your records in a safe place where you can easily retrieve them when needed.

I have found a great source of information for RVers about taxes is http://www.rvtaxhelp.com/ The site is run by Honey Shellman, a veteran of 30 years of being a tax preparer and she is now a full-time RVer. I have found much useful information here and you can ask generalized questions and get informed answers. Send your questions to honey@rvtaxhelp.com .

Workampers must keep good records of their time in any state other than their domicile state. If you are a South Dakota resident (no state income tax) and work in Pennsylvania, you must pay PA tax on your earned income. If you are there more than 6 months, they may come after you as a full-time resident. Tax strapped states are going after every means possible to raise tax revenues, and we are a possible target. Keep records of when you arrived and when you left. Especially keep good records of your presence in your domicile state. Tax returns if applicable, campground receipts, vehicle registration receipts, driver's license receipts are all good ways to claim your residence. The whole domicile issue is covered in Chapter 28.

■ Medical Records

As folks who travel around the country, we need health care wherever we happen to be. Keep all the summary documents after each doctor visit in a file for each person. Maintain a printed document for each person with all medications taken and the dosages. Keep a record with names, phone numbers, and addresses of all your doctors. Unfortunately, as we get older, that list and the medication list can grow pretty long. We scan most of our medical documents and keep them on a flash drive I carry on my key ring.

CHAPTER 34

PREPARE AN EXIT PLAN

Someday it will be time to hang up the keys and either have a stick built house again, or park the RV and stay in it. Many of you who are reading this are thinking WOW, I haven't even started and you want me to think about stopping. No way! Yes, way!! Planning ahead is very important. Nothing you decide today is written in stone, but you should have an idea of what you will do. These plans will change and evolve. It's up to you, but it is something to think about.

Certainly, financial planning will figure into your exit plan. Some folks sell their house and keep the money in savings for their eventual exit from RVing. Others have a 401k retirement plan or an IRA that will be their exit strategy. Hopefully you have invested so that your savings will increase at the rate of inflation.

Where will you hang up the keys? Will it be close to the kids, or maybe there's a mountain lake or a seaside resort that you really like. You may not have found it yet, but as you travel, keep your eyes open to any possibility. Maybe there's a city you have fallen in love with or an RV park where great friends have been made and you want to spend time with them.

Things to consider are weather, medical facilities, proximity to a city, and of course, is there a Wal-Mart or commissary close by. Is there a church you like? How much will it cost to stay in this area? If it is an RV Park, are you a co-owner or will the rent or fees be going up every year? Does the park have a reserve fund for major repairs, or will there be an assessment fee? Who actually runs the park, a manager or a board of directors? What are the rules? Can you build a casita, and how big? Can water and sewer be added to the shed? How about when you decide to sell; will you get your investment back, or does that really matter to you?

A lot of snowbirds just love the winter time to be with friends and play cards, golf, play dominos, practice line dancing and they eventually buy a park model trailer and stay the whole year. Maybe a stick built house is what you will want.

Where will you settle? Will you buy one and rent it out or live in it part time. Maybe you can afford to have several.

Please remember that life happens. Sometimes life comes at you like a speeding freight train and catches you totally unaware and unprepared. What will you do if suddenly one of you becomes seriously ill or passes away? I believe in the Boy Scout motto "be prepared". If you have a plan, then at the time of the emergency you will know what to do because you have already made decisions.

SECTION V

PART-TIME, WEEKEND, AND FULL-TIME RVing

CHAPTER 35

MEMBERSHIP CAMPING

I guess you could think of membership camping clubs as the "Vacation Condo timeshares" of the RV world. You pay an upfront fee, or initiation fee, or whatever the particular group calls it. In any case, most of these will be in the thousands of dollars. Then there will be a yearly "maintenance fee" or dues. This will probably be in the hundreds of dollars. For that money, you can camp at the properties included in their catalog. Generally there will be conditions such as the requirement to be out of the system for a certain number of days. There may be small daily fees for utilities. All of them require signing a contract that obligates you to pay whether you use the facilities or not.

The recent economic downturn has not been kind to some of these membership camping operations. Many are cash strapped and campground maintenance is deferred in some cases. Our recommendation is to wait at least a year after you set out full-timing before committing to any of these. That will give you time to talk with folks who have these contracts and decide if they are for you.

The only exception is Passport America (PA) http://passportamerica.com/. We suggest you join this club as soon as possible. The dues are currently $44 per year as of 2014. PA has signed up almost eighteen hundred RV parks across the country to give you fifty per cent off nightly rates on camping. There may be conditions such as no discounts during "high season" or discounts only good for one or two nights. No matter what, you will get your money back after only two or three nights of membership camping. We have used PA parks all over the country and we have been quite happy with the membership. PA will send you their large catalog of participating parks. There will be descriptions of the park and directions. There will also be notes about the PA rate and any exceptions. Tell them we sent you. Our membership number is **R-0222567**.

■ **Membership Camping Clubs**

Good Sam, or the Good Sam Club http://www.goodsamclub.com/ , is owned by the Affinity Group, also parent company to Camping World, Coast to Coast, and Motorhome and Trailer Life magazines. The Good Sam Club has a membership camping operation and has signed up several thousand campgrounds that will give five to ten per cent discounts to members. Club membership also includes membership in the Camping World President's Club with ten per cent discounts at Camping World stores. Tell them we sent you. Our membership number is **56780059**.

Coast to Coast http://www.coastresorts.com/ is a membership camping club providing camping for ten dollars a night as of 2015 at over two hundred private resort style campgrounds. You also can camp for fifteen dollars a night at nearly two hundred more Coast Good Neighbor Parks. To become a Coast to Coast member, you first must join any one of the affiliated private membership campgrounds which becomes your "home resort." Once you join the home resort, you are then eligible to become a Coast to Coast member.

Thousand Trails (TT) http://www.thousandtrails.com/ is now owned and operated by Equity Lifestyles Properties, known as ELS. ELS is the owner of several hundred resorts under the Encore http://www.rvonthego.com/ brand.

Gradually these will all be under one roof. At present there are about eighty TT parks around the country. TT has developed a Zone Pass where you can use the parks in one of five geographic zones for $499 every year as of 2014. This gets you thirty nights at no additional charge. Nights over thirty will be $3 per night. This seems like a good membership camping program if you are camping in only one area of the country. Other memberships that include all parks in the system are also available at considerably higher cost but with no nightly fees. Tell them we sent you. Our membership number is **298664930**.

RPI or Resort Parks International http://resortparks.com/ provides access to their network of private affiliated RPI and RPI Preferred RV resorts. **This membership camping club is only available to individuals whose home resort is affiliated with RPI.** You pay twelve dollars per night as of 2014 for an RV site. You may stay at each resort up to seven days twice a year and return to the same resort in as little as seven days between visits. You may stay at any of the affiliated resorts located outside a 125-air mile radius from your home. RPI is owned by ELS, the parent company of Thousand Trails.

Western Horizons Resorts http://westernhorizonresorts.com/ operates 18 resorts and two affiliated camping networks: Sunbelt USA and Adventure Outdoor Resorts http://www.aorcamping.com/. Western Horizons requires a onetime fee and annual dues.

NOTE: We cannot recommend Any of the Western Horizons memberships as the company is in financial trouble and selling off properties.

■ Colorado River Adventures

This campground membership club operates 10 resorts either on or near the Colorado River in the states of California, Nevada, and Arizona. Check them out at http://www.coloradoriveradventures.com/

The Escapees RV Club http://www.escapees.com/ has nineteen campgrounds. About half are owned by the club and the rest are cooperative ventures built and financed by Escapees members. Nightly fees average $15 to $20 per night. You must be a member of the Escapees RV Club to use these parks, and membership is currently about $40 per year as of 2015 which includes a wonderful magazine. This is the premier membership camping RV club for full and long time RVers. They also operate a world class mail forwarding service from headquarters in Livingston, TX. with South Dakota and Florida branches. We love Escapees and are lifetime members. If you decide to join, please reference our member number **88896** on the application.

CHAPTER 36

RV CLUBS

There are many good RV clubs for folks new to RVing, weekend warriors, full-timers, and all in between. These clubs provide information, services, and rallies with activities, entertainment and/or door prizes. These clubs are just that: clubs. A group of likeminded folks who get together to have fun doing what they love. You can meet some great folks that may become lifelong friends.

■ RV Clubs with a Special Interest

These clubs provide a variety of information and services. Most have an annual fee. Most hold rallies, trips and other social events.

Escapees RV Club – http://www.escapees.com Escapees was founded by full-time travelers and grew as a support network and eventually expanded to nineteen RV parks for its members. There are over fifty special interest groups; local, regional and a national rally; and even the CARE center, which is a place you can live in your rig but get assistance with everyday living. Tell them we sent you. Our membership number is **88896**.

Good Sam Club – https://www.goodsamclub.com/ is the largest club with over a million members, and over 2000 local chapters. Good Sam Club provides discounts on campgrounds, fuel, and RV products. They offer members-only rates on insurance and reliable emergency road service. There are national rallies, local rallies, or Samborees, group RV trips called Caraventures, and other trips offered.

FMCA – https://www.fmca.com/ Family Motor Coach Association (FMCA) is a large club for RVers with motorized RVs. They have discounts on campgrounds, fuel and RV products, mail forwarding, and much more. They hold large national rallies as well as local chapter events which are held throughout the year.

NAARVA – http://www.naarva.com/ National African American RV Association promotes the goals and ethnicity of African/American RVers.

SMART –http://www.smartRVing.net/ The Special Military Active Recreational Travelers (SMART) brings military veterans (active, retired, & honorably discharged) together to share camaraderie, travel, RVing, and to support our veterans. They provide information for the military RV family, and support welfare programs while "Seeing the Country We Defend." Tell them we sent you. Our membership number is **12825**.

RVing Women –http://www.RVingwomen.org/ RVing Women is a national network whose members come from across the U.S. and Canada. Established by and for women who are interested in RVing, they have 16 Chapters across the country that offer camping, educational, and social events. They are a diverse group of women who enjoy many indoor and outdoor activities and hobbies.

■ Brand or State Specific RV Clubs

Many RV brands have clubs dedicated to the owners of that particular brand. Most have rallies and other member get-togethers. Most have annual dues. Some of the larger rallies will have factory technicians available to fix small problems with your rig. Check on your manufacturer's web site for more information. An excellent resource is http://www.rv-clubs.us/rv-clubs.html There, you will find links to most of the brand specific clubs, as well as state specific clubs and much more good information.

CHAPTER 37

BOONDOCKING

Kathy and I love everything about boondocking. We haven't, however, done much of it. We know many folks who spend much of their time RVing by camping off the grid in some very beautiful places. Over the years, I have learned quite a bit about this unique style of camping.

I don't want to get hung up in the definition of "boondocking." My feeling is that it means camping without external utilities on either public or private land. Whatever you call it, we are talking about spending nights in an RV without external water, sewer, or power.

■ Why Boondocking?

People boondock for many reasons. For some, it means inexpensive or in many cases free camping. This is where overnight stays at Wal-Mart or other large store parking lots comes in. When you are moving from one location to another, it's easier to spend a night in a Wal-Mart ("Wallydocking") than to book a campground. Another term we read recently is Mooch Docking, or staying at a friend's or relative's place for a while, often hooked up to power.

Many boondockers don't want to be "cooped up" in a campground with its many activities and kids and barking dogs. They crave solitude. Others like the challenge of living "off the grid" for extended periods of time. Many love to be living in beautiful, natural locations where the only sounds are from nature.

Unfortunately, in today's economy, many people camp "off the grid" by necessity as they cannot afford better housing. This brings up the term "Stealth Camping." This is where folks move around from place to place, often arriving late at night to avoid the local authorities. We are not advocates of Stealth Camping.

No matter the reason, it is all about conservation. You must conserve water, as your tanks only hold so much. You must conserve power, or electricity, as batteries only hold just so much charge. You must conserve fuel if you use a generator. You should use good land conservation practices. Leave the spot you are camped in a little cleaner than when you found it.

Solar Power at the Imperial Dam Long Term Visitor Center in Southwestern California.

Living large at Quartzite during the January RV Show and Rally

■ Water Conservation

This is an area where bigger really does mean better. The larger your rig, the larger your holding tanks will usually be. Many small Class C motorhomes have only 20 gallons of fresh water and about 10 gallons of space in the gray and black water tanks. Larger rigs also will have more propane storage ability as well as the ability to have larger battery banks.

In a rig properly set up for boondocking, water holding capacity usually determines how long you can stay in one spot. Obviously, you should arrive at your campsite with empty holding tanks and a full water tank. Now I'm not advocating that you not stay clean, but you will save a lot of water if you only shower every 2 or 3 days. When you do shower, learn how to take a "Navy" shower, so called because Navy ships have to use most of the fresh water to keep the ship running, so water is at a premium. To do this, either start with cold water until the warm reaches the shower head, or collect that cold water for use later for washing dishes or toilet flushing. Get wet and turn off the water. Then soap up and shampoo your hair. Then rinse off as quickly as you can and turn off the water. Many shower heads have shut-off valves, but most will still allow a trickle of water to flow and be wasted. There are aftermarket shut-off valves that will close completely. There, that wasn't so bad, was it?

While you're out shopping for a shower shut-off, you might also want another shut-off valve to put in the water supply line to the toilet(s). This way you can use that water you collected before your shower to flush with. I know several boondocking couples that can live off grid for more than 2 weeks on just a 100-gallon fresh tank and 50-gallon waste tanks. I can't. This is where learning to wash your hair in a cup of water comes in handy. No joke, we know several women that can do this.

Use paper plates and bowls wherever you can as well as plastic tableware to lighten the dishwashing load. Wash your dishes in a plastic washtub and use the leftover dish water for toilet flushing. This is where you will really discover togetherness when you and your spouse share a flush. Saves a lot of flushing water if you can learn to go at the same time.

There are ways to extend your stay beyond your tank's capacity. If there is a dump station fairly close, you can use a portable tank, known affectionately as a "blue boy" and fill it with up to 40 gallons of either black or gray water. You hook it up to your tow vehicle of towed car and take it to the dump station. You will be making multiple trips.

Blue Boy waste water carrier   **Fresh water bladder**

There are large capacity plastic bladders that can hold fresh water for transfer into your fresh water tank. With water weighing over 8 pounds per gallon, you need to plan very carefully where to put one when it's full. The 20-gallon bladder in the picture will weigh 160 pounds when full. These are just suggestions for things I know about. Talk with enough long term boondockers and you'll find many more solutions to extend your water tank capacity.

■ Power Conservation

Your RV's 12-volt battery bank or "house battery bank", is your RV's lifeblood when you are camping off grid. It supplies control power to all your propane appliances as well as power for all the lighting in your RV. These batteries should be the "deep cycle" type that can be discharged to a much lower level than the starting battery and can go through many of these chare/discharge cycles. The vast majority of RV house batteries are the flooded cell type with caps for each cell. This is where you put in distilled water to top off the sulphuric acid based electrolyte that makes the battery work. These can be either 12 volt or 2 six volt batteries in a series configuration. The much more popular six volt batteries will provide more cycles of charge and usually produce more "Amp hours of power output than the 12-volt variety. This measurement tells you how much current can be withdrawn from the battery in a 20-hour period. More is always better with this measurement. Sometimes another pair of 6 volt batteries will be added in a parallel configuration to provide double the output current. There are other types of batteries covered in the chapter on the 12-volt electrical system. I have seen rigs with 8 6 volt batteries in the house battery bank.

The trick is keeping all those batteries charged. Most RVs have a converter that converts 120 volts AC power to 12 volts as well as a battery charging circuit, but they only work when park power is available. Boondockers charge their batteries in several ways.

An on-board generator will provide the power for the converter to work to charge the batteries. Most converters are inexpensive units that do more harm than good as they can boil the electrolyte in your batteries thus killing them over time. The better solution is a 3 stage charger that reduces the bulk charge that does the damage. The next 2 stages bring the battery to full charge safely. There are 3 problems using your generator. They use fuel from your tank, so you only have that much. The second is the noise they can make. Third is that generators emit carbon monoxide that must be closely monitored.

A preferred method depending on local weather conditions is solar power from photo-voltaic cells mounted on the top of the RV. We'll cover that in a later section. Another similar method is wind power.

■ Inverters

An inverter is an electronic device that converts the 12-volt DC power from the batteries to 120 volts AC for your AC powered appliances like TVs, coffee makers, etc. Unfortunately, inverters cannot generate enough AC power to run even one air conditioner. You must decide how much AC power you will need on a daily basis and size your inverter accordingly. They can be as much as 3000 watts, but require a large battery bank to keep them running.

■ Solar Power

Solar power is hugely popular with dedicated boondockers. After your initial investment, it provides "free" power to charge your battery bank from the sun. Obviously, you must be in an area that has a lot of daily sunlight to take full advantage. The heart of a solar system is the solar panels that each contain many individual photo voltaic cells that convert sunlight to DC voltage. The more panels you have, the more amp hours you can put back into your batteries. Between solar panel and batteries is a solar charge controller that converts the voltage from the panels to 12 volts for the batteries. You may opt for a mount for the panels that can be tilted to take advantage of the winter sun which is at a lower angle in the sky.

The initial expense can run into the $3000-dollar range for a 400-watt solar system, so do your homework and calculate just how much solar, if any, you need. If you only boondock occasionally, you may decide it isn't worth the investment.

■ Wind Power

There are wind generators available for RV use that can generate as much as 400 watts if the wind is steady and strong enough. The generator must be raised up above the RV on a mast of some sort. As far as I can tell, wind power just isn't popular enough to get good data.

■ Fuel Conservation

As mentioned earlier, generators run off the RV's fuel tank until the level gets down to about 1/4 tank where the fuel line tap is located for the generator. That gives you enough fuel to get out to get more fuel. There are some generators that use propane for fuel. That means drawing down your on-board propane tank.

That propane is used to power the burner of your water heater as well as the heating coils in an RV absorption refrigerator. It is also used to power the burner in your forced air furnace(s). It is also the fuel for your range and oven if equipped. It is possible to retrofit your rig with an RV Extend-a-Stay device that allows an outboard tank to provide propane for your rig. With 2 tanks you can go to town and refill the empty one.

■ Where to camp off the grid

As you meet other folks who are boondockers and express your interest, they may invite you along to share their "secret" boondocking site. Lacking that, here are some excellent books written about this lifestyle:

- The Complete Book of Boondock RVing: Camping Off the Beaten Path by Bill Moeller
- BOONDOCKING: Finding a Perfect Campsite on America's Public Lands by Bob Difley
- Guide To Free Campgrounds & Overnight Parking Spots by Gypsy Journal
- Snowbird Guide to Boondocking in the Southwestern Deserts by Bob Difley

CHAPTER 38

FINDING A PLACE TO CAMP

Finding RV campsites is probably among the easier parts of this lifestyle. "How do I find a campsite for my RV?" We get this question all the time. There are many books, applications and websites to help you make a selection. A lot depends on what type of campsite you are looking for. If you must have full hook-ups, then probably a private or membership park is for you. If your rig is self contained and you can conserve your resources, you will probably like boondocking on public lands. Public sector campgrounds run the gamut from full hook-ups, to electric only, to bare ground with no facilities. You will need to do a little homework before you leave on your camping trip. We could probably write a separate book just on this subject. We are only scratching the surface here, but in time you will be able to ferret out the very best campsites for you with little trouble.

■ Finding RV Campsites in the Public Sector

Finding RV campsites in the public sector include federal assets like National Parks, National Monuments, National Forests, National Seashores, and National Grasslands. You'll have no trouble finding RV primitive campsites on the lands administered by the Bureau of Land Management (BLM). Find most of these at the National Parks website http://www.nps.gov . A really good App for this is the Ultimate US RV Campground Project. It is around 4 dollars well spent. Find it at www.ultimatecampgrounds.com.

Another Federal entity is the U.S. Army Corps of Engineers, who operate over 400 campgrounds on or near the lakes and waterways the Corps manages. Many of these campgrounds have full hook-ups. Check out all the Corps of Engineers camping opportunities at: http://corpslakes.usace.army.mil/visitors/visitors.cfm

Along with the Federal lands are the parks, forests, and other lands administered by the various States. Almost every state has a camping publication listing campgrounds. These are available at the highway welcome stations.

You will also have no trouble finding RV campsites in many municipal campgrounds in cities and towns. Each State has a website, often many. You should have no problem finding information on camping. A Google search on a town or city name along with "camping" should give you plenty of information. We have spent many nights at county fairgrounds. Many have hookups and dump stations.

Many of the government facilities were built many years ago when RVs were much smaller. The trees in these areas have also grown up quite a bit over the years. Check before you set off to a particular campground to see if your rig will fit.

■ Privately Owned Campgrounds and Resorts

This is by far the largest group of campgrounds available. Finding RV campsites in this group is as easy as reading a campground guide. The large majority of these are open to the public and are "mom and pop" operations. The well-known Kampgrounds of America (KOA) are included in this category. A few are operated by KOA, but the majority fall into the mom and pop category. You can pick up a guidebook at any KOA campground. Another group of campgrounds is the very popular Jellystone Parks. Many of these campgrounds and resorts are listed in the Good Sam Travel Guide and Campground Directory available at half price at any Camping World. Good Sam members will receive 10% off camping at these "Good Sam Parks." Others are private membership type campgrounds and are covered below.

■ Membership Campgrounds

The membership campgrounds may be either member or privately owned. There are usually annual dues in addition to other fees collected. These tend to be quite deluxe and most have full hook-ups and other resort style amenities. Check these out in Chapter 35 Membership Camping.

■ Boondocking and Camping on Public Lands

I believe the most important part of finding a good place to boondock is your personal safety. If a place doesn't look right, or feel right, move on! We will list several sources for finding RV sites in boondocking areas, but the really good ones you see on magazine covers will not be found easily. Those pristine locations and views are a closely guarded secret by those who have been lucky enough to find them. You might try to make friends with boondockers and ask about some sites. Over time you might be invited to one of those secret spots.

I will not cover camping in parking lots of large businesses or any form of what has become known as "Stealth Camping." or "Wallydocking". I'll be discussing camping on public land with no hook-ups.

The majority of federal lands, especially in the west, have areas where you are allowed to camp. Most are free, but some charge small fees. Check with your local BLM (Bureau of Land Management), NFS (National Forest Service), COE (Corps of Engineers) or NPS (National Park Service) offices for locations. Federal agencies call these "Dispersed camping." Finding RV sites in these areas will require some homework and some map reading skills.

Here is a link to an excellent blog post by Bob Difley on finding boondocking sites. I defer to Bob as he is a recognized expert. Check them out here: http://blog.rv.net/tag/finding-boondocking-campsites/

The **Free campgrounds** website lists free or low cost boondocking sites across the country. Check it out: http://www.freecampgrounds.com/

Boondocking.org is an interesting site with a searchable database of known boondocking sites with directions and descriptions. http://boondocking.org/

US Public Lands is an IOS App written by our friends at Technomadia that overlays BLM, Forest Service, NPS and public land boundary maps. It helps you utilize US national resources! Check it out at: http://www.twostepsbeyond.com/apps/uspubliclands/

There are several books that you can purchase at camping stores that list boondock sites.

- 📖 BOONDOCKING: Finding a Perfect Campsite on America's Public Lands by Bob Difley is $9.95 in a Kindle eBook version
- 📖 Snowbird Guide to Boondocking in the Southwestern Deserts by Bob Difley is $6.99 in a Kindle eBook version

■ Apps for Finding RV Campsites

All Stays Camp and RV is our number one camping app for IOS and Android devices. We use it extensively in our travels. It covers finding RV sites in resorts to hike-in spots. Included are amenities, maps, truck stops, rest areas, Wal-Mart and casino parking, low clearance alerts, RV dealers, sporting goods stores and much more. There are two modes. One uses GPS and maps that you can filter. The other is an offline manual lookup mode for when you don't have wifi service. This is not a free app and currently is $9.99. Check it out at http://www.allstays.com/ Campgrounds/

RV Parking Is a free service that has information on every park they can find. We list as much information as we can collect on every RV park we can find. They have detailed information on over 20,000 RV parks. You can filter your search to narrow down results based on what's most important to you. In addition to listing all of the standard information about a park (location, number of sites, etc.), the listings include information submitted by users, such as reviews, photos and travelers' tips. The site can be used from computer, tablet, and smartphones. http://www.rvparking.com/

RV Parky is an RV Park directory built by a full time RVer with the help of the RV community to help fellow RVers on the road. Here you can find information, images, and reviews for over 25,000 RV Parks and campgrounds in the United States and Canada. There is an App for both IOS and Android devices. http://www.rvparky.com/

Ultimate US RV Campground Project This IOS app presents information about publicly-owned, non-commercial campgrounds across the Lower 48 United States. There are over 21,000 facilities, ranging from full-service campgrounds at state parks and Corps of Engineers parks to remote boondocking and backpacking locations with no facilities or services. The App is $3.99 http://www.ultimatecampgrounds.com/uc/index.php

RV Park Reviews This is a highly regarded website with reviews, by campers,

of campgrounds throughout the United States. There is an interactive map and form for submitting reviews. http://rvparkreviews.com/

RVBuddy This website gives visitors the opportunity to post their campground and RV park experiences, good or bad, for other campers. With hundreds of quality reviews covering campground and RV Parks throughout the United States, you should find what you need to know before you go. http://www.rvbuddy.com/

Passport America has Apps for Android, IOS, Blackberry, and Windows Mobile 7. Whether you are a member or not, you can browse all the campgrounds in the Passport America system of half price camping. Members get 50% off at participating campgrounds. http://www.passport-america.com/mobileapps.aspx

KOA (Kampgrounds of America) has extensive apps for IOS and Android devices. You can search on all the KOA campgrounds in the US and Canada. The App integrates with your navigation system for directions to any KOA campground. Reservations can also be made through the App. Check it out at: http://koa.com/get-the-koa-app/

National Parks by National Geographic is an app that lets you explore U.S. national parks easily on iPhone and iPad. There are National Geographic editor's recommendations on park must-dos, as well as photo tips from renowned National Geographic photographers. Some features are Global and interactive map views with filtering by activity and seasonality as well as thousands of points of interest, all tagged with GPS coordinates for easy planning and locating the top must-sees and must-dos for each park. http://www.nationalgeographic.com/mobile/apps/national-parks-by-national-geographic/

There are many other Apps to help you in finding RV sites and evaluating campgrounds, and more are being developed constantly. These listed are the ones we use and can recommend.

CHAPTER 39

SELECTING A CAMPSITE

The RV Campsite selection process determines a lot of the satisfaction of your stay at that campground. We have tried to give you the reader the basics as well as wisdom from many of our RVing friends on site selection.

■ RV Campsite Selection

The first thing you need to determine is whether you need a pull-through or a back-in site. Many parks do not have pull-through sites, while some have them exclusively. Some parks that have both types will charge more for a pull-through than a back-in. For us, a pull-through site makes sense when we are traveling and only need a place to stop and sleep. When this is the case, we don't put out the slide or deploy the leveling jacks. We won't use any hook-ups except electric. We even leave the car hooked up. If we plan to stay in a place for several days or more, we will use a back-in site and set up our rig for comfort.

No matter where you choose the RV campsite, do not pull in or back in until you have walked on the site. It should have adequate utilities such as thirty or fifty-amp power. You should carry and use an AC outlet circuit tester that detects faulty wiring in 3-wire receptacles. These are small inexpensive devices that will detect reversed polarity and other conditions. With the appropriate adapters, it will test a thirty Amp campground outlet at the pedestal. Once you know the power is correct, make sure your power cable will reach the pedestal. If you need a sewer connection, it should be close enough so you can reach it with the hose you carry. Is the hose bib or fresh water connection high enough off the ground to allow you to connect your water pressure regulator? These are basics and should be checked first. If there are problems, ask for another site.

Next you need to check the RV campsite for vertical obstructions. Look up to verify that overhanging trees will not touch your rig and cause paint scratches or worse. Is the approach to the site and the front opening wide enough to accommodate your rig? Are there trees or other obstructions in your path?

Last, but certainly not least, is the question, "Is the RV campsite level? Is the site relatively level front to back and side to side? Will you need to use your whole lumberyard of bits and scraps of wood to make your rig level?" Remember, your RV refrigerator will not work properly when it is not level to within several degrees. We use a four-foot carpenter's level to determine the final positioning so we can manually adjust our leveling jacks. If you have a trailer, purchase two inexpensive bubble levels so you can see how much to adjust.

■ Parking in the Campsite

"OK, I did everything you said, and I'm on my way into the site. What next?" I'm glad you asked. Parking an RV of any kind in a site requires precision maneuvering. This is where you and your partner need to get together on signals you both know and agree on. If you are outside the rig directing your partner, please do not have a dog in each arm and a cigarette in your mouth. I have seen this very thing; it was funny at first, but then it was just plain pitiful. Don't have any distractions when you are directing the parking of your home into the RV campsite. Mistakes can be quite expensive.

Friendly people will come up to you while you are parking and try to help. You must figure out how to tactfully tell them that you would rather do it the way you have practiced. These same people will be there when you are unhooking your car from a motorhome, or your truck from your trailer. If you let them, they will distract you to the point that you will forget a step and pay the price later. Tell them you will be happy to talk with them after you are parked and hooked up.

The key thing to remember is to place the rig close enough to the utilities, but far enough away so basement doors will open. Some RV sites are built with the electric and the water and sewer split apart. Try to get in a place where your power cables and sewer hose will reach. This is when prior practice pays off. You should get several rubber parking cones and practice backing up in a large vacant parking lot. Churches are great places to do this if you can get permission. So are closed Wal-Marts and such. Set up the campsite with the cones or chalk. Keep it up until you both can agree on hand signals. Some folks use cell phones or walkie-talkies to communicate. If that works for you, go for it. Just remember, the driver needs to know whether you are directing the front or the rear of the rig, especially when backing trailers. This is a good time to mention that no matter how good a driver you think you are, it's better to have an outside observer to direct you. Otherwise, sudden, embarrassing, and expensive accidents can happen. We know from painful experience.

■ RV Campsite Setup

Congratulations, you made it into the campsite! There is just a little more work to do and you're ready to enjoy yourselves. No matter whether you have leveling jacks or scissor jacks, you should have jack pads under them. This keeps them from digging into the ground and protects the bottom of the jacks. There are many products on the market to do this. I made mine from a fourteen-foot piece of weather treated two by twelve inch board. I had the store saw the board into one foot lengths and took them home. Then I laid two of them together with the grain running at right angles to one another and screwed them together with three inch galvanized screws. I also purchased six screw-in eye bolts. I put an eye bolt in each assembly to make it easy to reach with an awning rod. We store these in milk crates and use them as both jack pads and drive on leveling pads. Sometimes you just can't get a level site. We also have two sets of plastic leveling blocks. With all that, we can level almost anywhere.

Now we'll hook up the umbilical connections for power, water, sewer, and cable TV if available. Use your AC circuit tester on the power pedestal to make sure there are no problems before you plug in your rig. Turn the breaker(s) off before plugging in. Then turn on the breaker. Be sure to hook up your water pressure regulator first and then the shortest length of water hose that will reach. Turn on the water and check for leaks. The RV park may require a rubber doughnut to seal the sewer connection on the campsite. They may also require the sewer hose be suspended off the ground. This is where you use the plastic "slinky" looking thing you were told you would need. These are probably dictated by local laws and ordinances. This is a good time to remind you to have disposable rubber gloves on hand, (literally). Unless you have a full black and/or gray tank, it is best to leave your sewer valves closed until you need to dump. If cable TV is available, hook this up as well. It's a good idea to have two twenty-five foot lengths of TV cable and a female to female adaptor to use both together.

Now it's time to get the ladder down if you have sunscreens to hang on the windshield. It might be a good idea to clean the windshield first so you don't have to do it when you're getting ready to hit the road again.

From here on out, your personal tastes determine how you fix up the RV campsite. You will probably want a patio mat or other kind of ground covering in front of the entrance door. Lights, lawn ornaments, flags, personal signs and who knows what else will finish up your site. A visit to Camping World will give you some great ideas on this.

CHAPTER 40

RV SAFETY

Every RVer needs to understand that special RV safety precautions must be taken due to the circumstances of our unique lifestyle. Lives are lost annually due to RV fires, Carbon Monoxide poisoning, lightning strikes and other forms of electrocution. Our RVs are built differently from houses and we must be ever vigilant to avoid injury.

■ Electrical Safety

In our opinion, RV safety starts with electrical safety. All RVs should be protected from power surges as well as over and under voltages. A power surge or a lightning strike on power lines can destroy electrical and electronic items in your coach such as stereos, satellite receivers, microwave ovens, televisions and refrigerators. Surge protection is protection against voltage spikes on power lines. Direct lightning strikes are so catastrophic that no device can effectively protect against a close or direct lightning strike. Over or under voltage protection is effective for a gradual increase or decrease in voltage, exceeding the maximum or minimum voltage for which appliances are rated. Over voltage and under voltage protection removes primary power from the RV when the voltage drops below 102V or above 132V (safe mode).

One of the most insidious electrical hazards associated with RVs is "Hot Skin." Basically, this occurs when the RV is above ground potential. There is a most informative article by Mike Sokol that could save your life written on just this condition. http://www.noshockzone.org/rv-electrical-safety-part-iv-%E2%80%93-hot-skin/

There is a wealth of safety information by Mike Sokol available at The No-Shock Zone http://www.noshockzone.org/15/ He discusses how bad wiring at RV parks kills people every year. Mike has also written a wonderful eBook titled «No Shock Zone RV Electrical Safety».

Electrical Management System (EMS) devices are available that can protect from these conditions, as well as power surges and improperly wired electrical pedestals in RV parks. They can be directly wired into the RV or connected to the electrical pedestal and the RV plugged into the protective device. If you have a fifty amp electrical system in your rig, be sure to purchase a fifty amp power protector. A good place to look for these is at Camping World or the RV Upgrade Store www. rvupgradestore.com.

■ Road Safety Equipment

I'm sure you've seen semi-trucks along the side of the road with three triangular reflectors spaced out behind it. They are there to alert people to move over a lane as the rig is disabled for some reason. These triangles are inexpensive and should be in your RV Safety emergency kit along with several flashlights and road flares to signal a night breakdown. You might also want to have an orange vest with night vision strips on it. Obviously, the best piece of emergency equipment is a cell phone to call for help.

■ Fire Safety

Fire safety is a key element of RV Safety. Most RVs come with at least one fire extinguisher, usually of the powder type. This type of extinguisher has a pressure gauge with a red/green indicator. While the gauge may read green, the unit might not function correctly after sitting in one position for a long time as the powder settles and clumps in the bottom of the extinguisher. Pick this type unit up and turn it upside down several times every six months or so to loosen the powder. This is also a good time to check that the gauge is in the green area.

Kathy and I have been to a number of RV safety seminars, including some with live fires to put out. We can't emphasize enough the importance of this vital safety training. It is available at most large rallies. Check out http://macthefireguy.com/ for information on the location and times for this training.

Here are 34 tips on fire safety from Mac McCoy (aka Mac the Fire Guy) that can save your life. **These are reprinted with permission from Mac McCoy**

1. A pinhole-size leak in a radiator or heater hose can spray antifreeze on hot engine parts. Antifreeze contains ethylene glycol concentrate and water. When the water boils off, the remaining ethylene glycol can self-ignite at 782

degrees F. During your monthly fire inspection, check all hoses for firmness, clamp tightness, and signs of leaking.

2. Rubber fuel lines are commonly used to connect metal lines to the electronic fuel injection system, or to the carburetor in older coaches. Check all the lines and connections between the fuel tank and the engine on a monthly basis. If there is any sign of a leak, have the lines replaced and the entire system inspected by a qualified mechanic as soon as possible.

3. A hard-working engine manifold can get as hot as 900 degrees F. The heavy insulation in the compartment reflects the heat back to the top of the engine, and a fire can easily break out. Inspect your radiator and have any problems repaired by a qualified person as soon as possible.

4. Grease, oil, and road dust build up on the engine and transmission, making them run hotter. The grime itself usually doesn't burn, but if combined with a fuel leak or short-circuited wire, a fire could start. Keep your coach's underpinnings clean, and it will run cooler, more economically, and longer.

5. A dragging brake can create enough friction to ignite a tire or brake fluid. Some of the worst fires are those caused when one tire of a dual or tandem pair goes flat, scuffs, and ignites long before the driver feels any change in handling. At each stop, give tires at least an eyeball check. When tires are cool, tap your duals with a club and listen for a difference in sound from one tire to the next. You can often tell if one is going soft.

6. Spontaneous combustion can occur in damp charcoal. Buy charcoal fresh, keep it dry, and store it in a covered metal container. Rags soiled with auto wax or cleaners that contain petroleum products or other oil-based cleaning materials can also spontaneously combust if disposed of in a combustible container. Put dirty cleaning rags in a metal container with a lid.

7. A hot exhaust pipe or catalytic converter can ignite dry grass.

8. Driving with propane on can add to the danger if you are involved in an accident or have a fire. Most refrigerators will keep food cold or frozen for eight hours without running while you travel. Shut the propane off at the tank.

9. If you store your coach, be sure to check the flue before starting your refrigerator on propane. Birds and inspects can build nests and clog the flue, causing a fire or excess carbon monoxide to enter your coach.

10. Batteries produce explosive gases. Keep flame, cigarettes, and sparks away. Be sure your battery compartment is properly vented. Keep vent caps tight and level. Check your battery monthly. Replace swollen batteries immediately. Use extreme care when handling batteries—they can explode.

11. Have any wiring in your coach done by a capable electrician, and use common sense in using any electrical aid. Check all 12-volt connections before and after every trip. Most coach fires are caused by a 12-volt short.

12. Gasoline and propane can pose an immediate, explosive danger. Though diesel fuel is less volatile, it dissipates more slowly, so it remains a danger longer. Deal at once with any leaks or spills, and use all fuels in adequately vented areas.

13. Even if the flame on your galley stove goes out, gas continues to flow and could result in an explosion. A stove should never be left unattended or used to heat your coach. Open propane flames release high levels of carbon monoxide.

14. In a compact galley, all combustibles—from paper towels to curtains—are apt to be closer to the stove, so use even more caution in your coach than you do at home. A box of baking soda—the ingredient in powder extinguishers—can be used in lieu of a fire extinguisher for minor galley flare-ups.

15. Develop a plan of action before a fire occurs.

16. Make sure all travelers know what the smoke alarm sounds like and what to do when they hear it. Test your smoke detector regularly.

17. Have at least two escape routes—one in the front and one in the rear of the coach. As soon as they're old enough, teach children to open hatches and emergency exits.

18. Review with everyone the "Stop, Drop, and Roll" rule so they know what to do when clothing is on fire.

19. Make sure visitors can open the front door. Not all manufacturers use the same lock and latch assembly.

20. Choose a rallying point where everyone will meet immediately after escaping, so everyone can be accounted for.

21. Show travelers how to unhook electricity (screw-on cords can be tricky) and how to close propane valves, in case either of these measures is called for.

22. Practice unhooking your tow vehicle as quickly as possible to avoid spreading the fire to other vehicles.

23. Re-emphasize to everyone aboard that objects can be replaced, people can't. Never stay behind or re-enter a burning coach to retrieve anything.

24. There are plenty of fire and life safety tools that can save lives, but for them to be effective, they must be in working condition and you must know how to use them properly.

25. You should have three fire extinguishers for your coach—one in the galley, one in the bedroom, and one outside of the coach in an unlocked compartment or in your tow vehicle. Make sure family members know how to use the extinguishers and understand which extinguishers are effective on various fires.

26. During your monthly inspection, check the fire extinguisher gauge to determine if there is pressure in the extinguisher. If the gauge indicates empty or needs charging, replace or recharge the extinguisher immediately. To test non-gauged extinguishers, push the plunger indicator (usually green or black) down. If it does not come back up, the extinguisher has no pressure to expel its contents. If you need help testing your fire extinguishers, check with your local fire department.

27. Do not pull the pin and expel the contents to test your powder extinguisher. If you use a portion of the powder extinguisher, have it refilled or replaced immediately. When you have a fire extinguisher refilled, ask to shoot off the charge first (most refill stations have a special place where this can be done safely). This lets you see how far it shoots and how long a charge lasts.

28. Invert and shake your dry-powder or dry-chemical extinguisher monthly to loosen the powder. The jarring of the coach does not loosen the powder; in fact, it packs the powder, which may make your extinguisher ineffective.

29. Deadly, invisible, odorless CO usually results from exhaust leaks or misuse of heating devices. Be sure to put your CO detector in the bedroom. The proper location is on the ceiling or on an inside wall at least eight inches from the ceiling and at least four feet from the floor.

30. Liquid petroleum gas, like gasoline fumes, tends to pool in low spots in the coach until a spark sets it off. Newer motorhomes are equipped with an automatic shut-off for when its sensor detects an LPG leak. If you have a leak, be sure to shut the propane off at the tank.

31. The first rule of RV firefighting is to save lives first and property second. Get yourself and your family to safety before attempting to extinguish a fire. Only if you can do so without endangering yourself or others should you use firefighting aids on hand.

32. Get help. Adults and older children should know how to dial 911 or 0, and how to get emergency help on any CB, VHF, or ham radio available.

33. It's crucial to know your location so firefighters can find you.

34. If you have a quick-disconnect fitting on your water hookup, these hoses can be unhooked instantly to fight a fire. If a nearby coach is burning and you cannot move your coach but can safely stay close enough to keep it hosed down, you may be able to save it.

We were given advice to have a number of extinguishers on hand. You should have one for your car or truck, one for an outside compartment, one in the bedroom, and one near the kitchen area. These small extinguishers will not put out an RV fire that has been going for more than a couple of minutes. You have them to beat down the flames so you can get out of your rig. Even the largest RV can be reduced to a pile of smoldering ashes in five or six minutes. There are many videos on the internet showing this. For that reason, you must get out quickly. Your "stuff" isn't worth your life or your family's life. These four extra fire extinguishers can be purchased for as little as sixty or seventy dollars.

There are automatic temperature activated units for the both engine and the generator compartments. These use a gas such as Halon to displace the oxygen and extinguish the fire. There is also a Halon unit available for the refrigerator compartment to combat refrigerator fires. These units are expensive, but they provide peace of mind as part of your RV Safety plan.

Every RV has at least one emergency exit besides the entry door. It is usually a bedroom window with a hinge on top so the window can be tilted out to allow escape. Check and exercise this emergency exit at least twice a year. Put gasket lube on the gasket to keep it soft and pliable so it will be easy to open when needed. A short stick the size of a broom handle cut to around 18 inches long is a great tool to keep the often heavy window open when using it as an exit. Paint it fluorescent orange and place it where it will be available in case of emergency. Some rigs have breakaway windows. Make sure you know which type you have. In either case, the window edge is usually thin and painful as your body goes over it. There will also be a drop from the window to the ground several feet below. For these reasons, drag your bedding out the window with you to be a cushion over the window edge.

You might consider putting a smaller version of your severe weather "Go Bag" near the emergency exit to take out the window with you.

You and all the folks traveling with you should do a fire drill every year. You need to find all the fire extinguishers, and at least simulate going out the emergency exit. Just remember that the fire extinguishers are to beat the fire back so you can get out quickly, not to put out the fire.

■ Smoke Detectors (Fire Alarm)

Certainly, a key element of RV Safety is early detection. If your rig has a fire alarm, or smoke detector, test it for proper operation and change the battery at least annually. If not, go out and get one immediately. We have found that the alarm is usually placed outside the bedroom and near the gas range. Consequently, it will go off every time you fry bacon. We switched ours to a unit made by Kidde that has a push button switch that turns the alarm off for ten minutes, and then automatically returns the unit to normal operation. We highly recommend it. There is no reason not to install additional smoke detectors in the bedroom and up front in your rig.

■ Gas Alarms

Another aspect of RV safety involves Carbon Monoxide and LP Gas detectors. None of these detectors have a lifespan of more than 5 years. If you have just bought a used RV 5 or more years old, immediately replace these vitally important devices.

Today's RVs have several propane gas appliances including the hot water heater, range top and stove, refrigerator, and at least one gas furnace. Most RVs will have a propane gas alarm mounted near the floor by the kitchen. This is because propane is heavier than air and will sink to the floor. These alarms may be battery operated or permanently connected to twelve volts from the RV battery. In either case, test these units twice a year according to the manufacturer's instruction book.

If your rig does not have a carbon monoxide alarm, get one immediately and place it in the sleeping area near head height. Carbon monoxide or CO is odorless and colorless and will displace oxygen. Carbon monoxide gas is produced by combustion such as from a generator set or even an engine running outside your rig. CO can kill you and your loved ones. Don't take a chance without having a functioning CO alarm. Check and replace the alarm battery annually with the smoke detector battery.

■ Weather Safety

We consider our weather radio an essential piece of RV Safety equipment. We turn it on and tune to the one of seven frequencies that is strongest, and we get National Weather Service (NOAA) forecasts and severe weather alerts for our area. Our radio also can use the Specific Area Message Encoding (SAME) system. A programmed NWR SAME receiver will turn on for the alert message, with the listener hearing the 1050 Hz warning alarm tone as an attention signal, followed by the broadcast message. At the end of the broadcast message, listeners will hear a brief digital end-of-message static burst followed by a resumption of the National Weather Service broadcast cycle. To program NWR SAME receivers with the proper county(s) and marine area(s) of choice, you need to know the 6-digit SAME code number(s) for that county(s). Once you have the number, follow the directions supplied the manufacturer of your NWR SAME receiver for programming. The number is available either online at the http://www.nws. noaa.gov/nwr/indexnw.htm , or by telephone at 1-888-NWR-SAME (1-888-697-7263) for a voice menu. Your campground management will have information on the name of the surrounding counties. We use a Midland Model WR 120, which has the SAME technology. It retails for about fifty dollars but can be found at many stores for around thirty. We don't always program our radio as it will give broad area information including severe weather alerts constantly. Our radio is on constantly, so we check its internal battery often.

We also use weather apps on our Android smart phone. These are "The Weather Channel" and my favorite, "Radar Now" which uses the built-in GPS and shows live weather radar in your area.

All these apps and radios will only alert you to the fact that you must find a safe place when severe weather is imminent. Ask the campground personnel at the front desk where the severe weather shelter is located. If there isn't one designated, look for a building of block construction. Most bath houses fit this description. The worst place to be in this type of emergency is in an RV which can be blown over by strong winds, or set afloat during a flood.

What do you take with you when evacuating to a shelter or out of the area? Good question. The answer to this RV Safety issue is a "Go" bag. A go bag will contain the essentials to get you through a stressful period away from your rig. Any bag will do, but a zippered gym bag is probably the easiest to grab and go if it is ALWAYS in the same place and constantly filled with up to date items. Here are some of the essentials:

- Photos of labels from medicine bottles and packages
- photocopy of eyeglass prescription(s)
- Photocopies of Driver's Licenses, credit cards, and Passports
- Photocopies of Insurance policies
- A printed page or two with phone numbers and addresses of family members, doctors, pharmacy, lawyer, broker, insurance agent, and other people you may need to contact
- Pet information and vaccinations

Note: All the above items can be placed on a flash drive to save space

- several days' worth of essential medications
- Cell phone(s) with car charger(s)
- A small flashlight, preferably one with an LED lamp and extra batteries
- An extra set of vehicle keys
- Several bottles of water and perhaps a few protein bars
- Change of clothes, especially if going out of the area

What you take with you in that bag may well be all you have until the threatening weather passes. Choose wisely and give it some thought. I would never consider bringing a laptop computer, but I have a large capacity flash drive on my key chain with up to date copies of all my important files. RV Safety is serious business and preparation and knowledge can save your life.

■ Financial Safety

Let's face it, most of us use credit or debit cards because we don't want to carry large amounts of cash with us. Here are some great tips to keep you from getting ripped off using plastic.

1. Do not sign the back of your credit cards. Instead, put 'PHOTO ID REQUIRED.'

2. When you are writing checks to pay on your credit card accounts, DO NOT put the complete account number on the 'For' line. Instead, just put the last four numbers. The credit card company knows the rest of the number, and anyone who might be handling your check as it passes through all the check processing channels won't have access to it.

3. Put your work phone # on your checks instead of your home phone. If you have a PO Box use that instead of your home address. If you do not have a PO Box, use your work address. Never have your SS# printed on your checks. (DUH!) You can add it if it is necessary. But if you have It printed, anyone can get it.

4. Place the contents of your wallet on a photocopy machine. Copy both sides of each license, credit card, etc. You will know what you had in your wallet and all of the account numbers and phone numbers to call and cancel. Keep the photocopy in a safe place.
    You might also carry a photocopy of your passport when you travel either here or abroad. We've all heard horror stories about fraud that's committed on us in stealing a Name, address, Social Security number, or credit cards.

5. We have been told we should cancel our credit cards immediately. But the key is having the toll free numbers and your card numbers handy so you know whom to call. Keep those where you can find them.

6.   File a police report immediately in the jurisdiction where your credit cards, etc., were stolen. This proves to credit providers you were diligent, and this is a first step toward an investigation (if there ever is one).

But here's what is perhaps most important of all:

7.   Call the 3 national credit reporting organizations immediately to place a fraud alert on your name and also call the Social Security fraud line number. I had never heard of doing that until advised by a bank that called to tell me an application for credit was made over the Internet in my name.

The alert means any company that checks your credit knows your information was stolen, and they have to contact you by phone to authorize new credit.

Now, here are the numbers you always need to contact about your wallet, if it has been stolen:

1.   Equifax: 1-800-525-62851-800-525-6285
2.   Experian (formerly TRW): 1-888-397-3742 or 1-888-397-3742
3.   Trans Union: 1-800-680 7289 1-800-680 7289
4.   Social Security Administration (fraud line): 1-800-269-0271 or 1-800-269-0271

■ Personal Safety

A key aspect of RV Safety is personal safety. You must be aware of your surroundings. Are you comfortable with those around you? When you check into an RV park, ask where the storm shelter is located. You should know how to get to the nearest emergency room. A question that always comes up is "should I have a gun?" I'm sure you've been waiting for us to talk about guns. Well, here it is. We are reprinting with permission from Nick Russell an essay he wrote on just that question.

The Armed RVer used by permission of
Nick Russell
Gypsy Journal RV Travel Newspaper www.gypsyjournal.net

A frequent question posed by Gypsy Journal readers is whether or not they should carry a firearm in their motorhome or trailer for personal protection, and if so, what kind. It is a question that does not have one answer that fits every situation. There are too many variables.

As a long time gun owner, shooter, and advocate of personal protection, I have always said that every American who can legally own a firearm should have the right to do so. But I always qualify that statement with the addendum that just because we should all have that right, it does not mean that all of us should exercise it. A firearm is a dangerous weapon, and in the wrong or untrained hands, it can cause far more harm than it ever can good.

Gun ownership carries with it a terrible responsibility. Only you can decide if you are willing and able to accept that responsibility. Before you make the decision to carry a gun in your RV, you must understand the legal ramifications that come with gun ownership and use. Understand that the possibility of ever having to use a firearm for self-defense is very remote, and that if you ever do, you will probably find yourself facing criminal prosecution to prove you were justified in your actions, as well as civil litigation from whoever you used the weapon against, or their heirs. You can be completely in the right and still face a prison sentence and years of legal battles and mountainous legal fees. Be aware also that the emotional impact of using deadly force will stay with you the rest of your life. Are you willing to shoulder that responsibility? Only if you are completely aware of the consequences using, or even possessing a firearm can bring, and are completely willing to deal with those consequences, should you have a gun in your RV.

Nobody should own a firearm unless they are well trained in its safe handling, as well as the circumstances where it can be legally used for defense. The laws vary from state to state, and you must comply with the rules where you happen to be at the time.

In some states, firearms laws are fairly easy to understand, and many states will issue concealed carry permits to residents who meet the legal criteria, pass a background check and training class. In other states, the mere possession of any firearm, even unloaded and cased in your vehicle, can lead to stiff penalties. Know before you go.

In several years on the road, and many nights spent boondocking in out of the way places, truck stops, roadside rest areas, and shopping center parking lots, we have never felt threatened enough to feel the need to put a gun in our hands. That said, we also have a firearm or two within reach, and that has probably added to our sense of security. But long before I would ever consider using a gun against a threat, I would drive away from the situation if at all possible.

Having a firearm presents problems whenever you have children or grandchildren visiting your RV. Make sure that it is unloaded and locked away out of sight. Likewise, whenever strangers, such as service technicians or mechanics have access to your rig.

The first rule of firearms ownership is safety, while the second is discretion. Nobody has to know you have a gun, and the fewer who do, the better. Never display your weapon except when you feel a real threat to your life or safety. The fellow who brandishes a gun to "scare away" suspicious characters is looking for trouble and will more than likely find it. That person you find suspicious may well be a fellow RVer or truck driver out for an evening stroll to work the road kinks out of his back, or possibly even a police officer checking on the welfare of people parked in a roadside rest area. Even if someone is busily engaged in taking the tires off your tow car, they are not a threat to your life. Drive away, call the police on your cell phone, honk your horn and flash your headlights, cry for help on the CB. But whatever you do, do not get into an armed confrontation. There is not a material thing in this world worth a human life. The only time I would consider using deadly force is when somebody is actually entering my motorhome or directly threatening the lives of myself or someone else.

The type of firearms best suited for RV use are varied. A short barreled shotgun, loaded with bird shot is very effective at close range, and the lighter load will not penetrate a neighboring vehicle like buckshot will. Often the mere sound of a round being chambered in a pump shotgun will ward off trouble.

Handguns, while easiest to maneuver in the close confines of an RV, carry the most severe penalties if discovered in states with strict gun laws. While you may be able to convince a policeman or judge that you have a shotgun for sport hunting, it's hard to explain that you go after squirrels or ducks with a short barreled .38 revolver.

The type of handgun also varies with the user. What works for me may well not work for you. For a relatively inexperienced gun owner, my first recommendation would be a .38 revolver with a two to four-inch barrel. It makes a combination that is easy to point and accurate at close range. The four-inch model would be the one I would suggest, since the shorter barrel revolvers lose some accuracy and bullet velocity.

I feel that any handgun less than .38 caliber is too small for defense, while most heavier caliber handguns are either too hard to control in inexperienced hands, or have the risk of over penetration that can harm innocent people nearby. Magnum calibers run too much risk of over penetration to be considered in RV situations.

Semi-automatic handguns are the favorite of the military and most modern police agencies, and the high capacity models are the current rage in all of the shoot-em-up Hollywood movies. That may be fine on the big screen, but in real life if you can't get the job done in two or three shots, you're probably dead anyway. Semi-autos are harder to master and their safety features can confuse inexperienced shooters. Those who may have become familiar with semi-automatics in the military would probably feel more comfortable with their use than first-time gun owners.

I recommend the use of Glaser Safety Slugs in handguns. They are designed to provide maximum stopping power while not penetrating walls to endanger people in neighboring homes or vehicles. If Glasers are not available, my next recommendation would be hollow point or round nose bullets. Some people have told me they carry snake shot in their handguns for defense. Their feeling is that the small BB sized shot will ward off an intruder while not being lethal. To me, this is foolish thinking. If things get so bad that I have to use a firearm, I want it to stop the threat, not make somebody mad enough to do me even more harm.

Whatever you decide, if you do feel the need for a weapon, do your homework first. Go to a good gun shop and look over the selection. If possible, find a shooting range where you can try and compare several different firearms before you make your purchase. Then enroll not just yourself, but anyone you travel with, in a firearms safety course to become comfortable with your weapon.

And if worst comes to absolute worst, and you find yourself reaching for your firearm, first ask yourself if there is any way to avoid its use. If there is, choose the alternative.

CHAPTER 41

TECHNOLOGY FOR RVers

Full-timers and even weekend campers need technology to stay in touch with our families, friends, business and banking interests. All I can say is, "Thank God for the new technology that brings us cellular communications and the World Wide Web!" I'm not sure how this absolute dependence on fast communications developed, but we are addicts. When we can't get cell phone service, we are almost lost and devastated. Something might happen and we won't know it within three minutes. OMG!! Sorry, I got carried away a little. It is true, however, that we desire the fastest and most reliable access to communications media. So then, how will we do this?

■ Cellular Technology on the Road

In my opinion, this is a primary need. We use cell phones to contact emergency services either by dialing 911, or to call a towing and/or repair service after a breakdown. A motorhome with a towed car doubles the chance that you might need to call for assistance. Of course, we also desire to talk with our family members and friends for birthdays, anniversaries, and just to chat. Occasionally we use the phone to contact our bank, credit union, and credit card company if problems develop. I could go on, but you get the point. We need cellular coverage.

Most cellular communication technology in use today is 4G or Forth Generation. This refers to the technology used to move calls along a long string of cell towers. 4G technology is also referred to as LTE. An enhanced and faster version of LTE is becoming more prevalent in the more densely populated cities. This is a much faster service and is capable of streaming video content without slowing down, depending on the area and high or low usage. Hopefully, 4G will roll out to many more rural locations soon. In the meantime, there are a lot of cell towers that also support the older technology 3G, or Third Generation, which provides connectivity to the internet, but at a much slower rate than 4G.

Three companies are the most popular among full time RVers. They are AT&T, Sprint, and Verizon. At the time of this writing, AT&T is stronger in the cities and Verizon has the best coverage nationwide. Sprint is gaining and may soon be equal to the others. All three have available electronic bill paying via the internet. We prefer that to getting bills sent through the mail and possibly arriving late.

What happens when you don't have a strong enough cellular signal to make and receive calls? I'm glad you asked. Enter the cell phone amplifier. The purpose of a cell phone amplifier is to boost the signal it receives from its own antenna and feed that signal into your cell phone with a cable or wireless cradle. That is fine as long as your phone has an external antenna jack, which many don't. What to do? Enter the wireless cell phone amplifier. Now the amplifier has both an exterior antenna to communicate with the cell tower and an interior antenna to communicate with the cell phone. We use a cellular amplifier and antennas from Wilson Electronics, now known as weboost, the biggest and most well-known supplier of this type of equipment. Go to https://www.weboost.com/us/ This technology works great if you are in a fringe area, or have buildings or hills between you and the cell tower. Unfortunately, there are areas in our country without cellular service of any kind. We have been in a few of these areas. The only thing to do is drive until you get to an area with enough signal strength to make calls. These areas are mostly in the unpopulated areas of the western states. Check the map of your cell phone provider to find these "dead zones".

New rules from the FCC went into effect on May 1st of 2014 outlawing sales of old booster models and paving the way for a new generation of cellular boosters designed to reduce the potential for causing interference to wireless networks. Fortunately, our friends at Technomadia have figured out how to do this registration and you will find it on their website http://www.technomadia.com/

Over the last several years, "Smart Phone" technology has dominated the sales of cellular phones. These are cellular telephones that can be connected to the internet and are GPS enabled, so they know where they are. Besides having internet access, the coolest thing about smart phones is applications. You must have heard the catch phrase "There's an app for that". Applications are mini programs that accomplish a specific function and run on smart phones and tablet devices. This technology started with the Apple iPhone and iPad, and quickly migrated to other manufacturers' operating systems such as Android and Blackberry. It's hard to believe, but there are hundreds of thousands of applications such as games, finance and banking, business, navigation, and so many more. A search using the letters "RV" in the Apple App Store returned more than 250 different apps. It's a little overwhelming, but we have settled on a few app's we use a lot. "All Stays RV" is an application that uses GPS and your current location to find campgrounds along the way with descriptions, contact information, and even reviews. "Gas Buddy" gives the current fuel prices at either stations near you, or at a location you select. We use two weather apps frequently. One is "The Weather Channel" for current weather and forecasts. The other is called "Radar Now". This one gives us the weather radar picture of our location using GPS. Lately we have been using WAZE, which shows the traffic conditions ahead of you and alternative routes. A lot of these apps are free, and most are less than ten dollars. New apps are being introduced constantly for all the various platforms. We make driving decisions based on the weather apps.

■ Connecting to the Internet

Next to a working cell phone, internet access has the highest priority among the communications mediums. There are several ways to get on the internet, including a wired modem providing high speed DSL, often available to folks staying 2 months or more at a campground so equipped, Wi-Fi, cellular data, and satellite connection.

■ Wired Connection

Wired internet service can be available at your campsite if there is an active phone connection available. Connected through the telephone jack installed in most later model RVs, this can be a very fast and reliable reliable method of internet connection, but you must enter into a short term contract with the provider. Many folks do this when they winter someplace for an extended period of time.

■ WI-FI

According to the internet encyclopedia Wikipedia, Wi-Fi is a popular technology that allows an electronic device to exchange data wirelessly using radio waves over a computer network, including high-speed internet connections. Currently, this is a popular method to connect to the internet. It is used by laptop and desktop computers, new technology smart phones, tablet devices such as the Apple iPad, and others. Wi-Fi adapters of various capabilities have been standard in laptop computers for several years. The speed of the connection is dependent on many variables, including the strength of the received and transmitted radio signal, the capability of the installed Wi-Fi adapter, obstructions such as trees and buildings in the line of sight between antenna and computer, and primarily the bandwidth of the park's connection to the internet. It is possible to have a five bar signal at the computer, but slow or no service due to too many users on a less than capable system. This happens frequently at larger parks. At first, campground Wi-Fi was free, but more and more campgrounds and resorts are installing pay-as-you go systems. This does not guarantee fast uninterrupted service, however.

■ Cellular Data Connection

This is the method Kathy and I use to access the internet. The simplest way is to have a smart phone, such as an Apple iPhone, or an Android smart phone. These are capable of internet connection and retrieving e-mail. Small screen and limited battery life are concerns. The Apple iPad and other tablet devices has overcome the small screen and battery life issues. Kathy can get by with nothing but her iPad for all her internet use. Of course, being a techie, I need more. It is possible to tether a data capable cellular phone to a laptop computer with the addition of some inexpensive software. This could be great if you have a cell phone with an unlimited data account. Those account features are going the way of dinosaurs. The next possibility is an air card, which is essentially a cellular phone optimized for data. This requires a separate plan from your cellular phone provider which is priced according to the amount of data you expect to use each month. It is a small device that connects to a computer's USB port. With the proper software and activation codes, you will be able to have high speed internet access whenever you have a cell signal. The Mi-Fi device seems to be the device of choice as it can simultaneously connect up to five devices such as computers, tablets, and wireless printers to the internet.

We have added a wireless router to our home network. This device will accept either an air card or a Wi-Fi signal and transmit it with an onboard radio. This is similar to your own Wi-Fi hotspot, but with a hardware firewall to provide security for your data. It can handle many more devices than I will ever own. When there is no cellular signal, it will default to the strongest Wi-Fi signal available.

Now that we have added a wireless cellular amplifier to our arsenal of communication devices, we have both a cell phone "cloud" within our rig and a secure Wi-Fi cloud as well. Probably the very best book written about this subject is "The Mobile Internet Handbook" by Chris Dunphy and Cherie Ve Ard. Check it out at

▶ http://www.technomadia.com

■ Satellite Connection to the Internet

Prior to cellular internet connection, satellite internet systems were the best and most reliable way to connect to the internet. Hughes Corporation, which provides internet connectivity by way of the HughesNet Company, operates a constellation of communications satellites accessed by dish antennas mounted on houses and other structures. The Datastorm Company has made this technology portable. They provide a roof mounted collapsible dish with automated raising and pointing electronics for motorhome or trailer use. The system costs around five thousand dollars and installation can add another thousand. Monthly service fees start at about sixty dollars a month. This works great in Alaska and Mexico where cell service is spotty to non-existent. Unfortunately, internet signal speeds at best are slower than cellular internet for the same monthly rate. Another drawback is that the bandwidth on the particular satellite you are subscribed to may be oversold. This means that when many users are online, the speed can drop as low as dial-up slow. There is a tripod mounted satellite dish available for around fifteen hundred dollars, but the monthly fees are the same and the same speed roadblocks apply. Unless you are stuck in an area with no cell service, I cannot in good conscience recommend this type of system when cellular internet is so easy and affordable.

■ Technology Training for RVers

No discussion of Technology for RVers would be complete without mentioning our friends Jim and Chris Guld, otherwise known as the Geeks on Tour. We met these folks early in our RV journey and we have learned so very much from the excellent seminars they do at RV rallies and RV shows across the country. Kris had her own business as a computer software trainer and Jim was a hardware and network guy. They married, hit the road full-time and now they give hundreds of seminars about software and hardware RVers need to know about. Some of their seminars are on Blogger, Facebook, Google Maps, Microsoft Movie Maker, the Picassa photo program, Microsoft Streets and Trips, and general topics like smartphones, Microsoft Windows, and more are coming on line every year. Check out their website at: http://www.geeksontour.com/

■ Technology Products RVers Need

Some other friends are Eric and Tammy Johnson, and their business is called Techno RV. They are a presence at many RV Shows and Rallies along with the Geeks on Tour. They sell such things as Wifi boosters, cell phone boosters, electrical protection systems, tire pressure monitoring systems, and many other products using modern technology to enhance our RVing experience. Tell them John and Kathy sent you. Check them out at: http://www.technorv.com/

■ Communicating on the Road

I would also like to mention again the folks at Technomadia, Chris Dunphy and Cherie Ve Ard http://www.technomadia.com/ They are the authors of the excellent book "The Mobile Internet Handbook" This has become the go to source for information on cellular communications on the road.

■ Television

I have included television because it is a form of one-way communication. We love to watch TV, but having The Weather Channel can be a necessity during severe weather. It must be important because almost every RV we see has a crank-up "Bat wing" antenna installed. We have one, and we use it wherever we have adequate local channels available. These antennas are also capable of receiving High Definition (HD) signals if you have a newer television set with an HD receiver. If you absolutely "must" have TV, satellite reception is the answer. Satellite service is available from Direct TV or from DISH Network in the US, and there are several Canadian providers. We have had both and I see little difference in either content or service. Customer service can be difficult because most of the agents do not understand the fact that our antennas move around, but eventually you will convince them. There are many packages of satellite service you can order with increasing monthly subscription costs.

If you have a roof mounted dome satellite antenna, bear in mind that if you desire HD programming, you are limited to DISH Network. Direct TV HD broadcasts require the acquisition of at least three satellite feeds. Consequently, a larger antenna than what will fit in a dome is needed. Also remember that your dome could be blocked by trees in your campsite.

Our rig came with a crank-up satellite dish. We used it for five years with our Direct TV subscription. At the same time, we had another dish we used on a tripod when we were parked where trees would block the satellite signal. Now we have upgraded to a High Definition technology TV, so we needed an HD compatible dish. It is larger and heavier than the standard dish. We had to find a heavy duty tripod for it, but it works well and we are quite pleased with it. I recommend a website that I found when searching for the tripod. Go to http:// www.tv4rv.com . They have a monthly newsletter with plenty of valuable advice for setting up and pointing satellite dishes.

CHAPTER 42

WINTER RVing

Winter RVing can be a lot of fun. Although most folks prefer to use their RVs during the warmer times of the year, there are circumstances when you might want or need to do some winter RVing. There are less people at campgrounds (if they are open at all), you may enjoy winter sports like cross country skiing, ice fishing or snowmobiling. Perhaps a family member is sick and you need to be near them. No matter the reason, there are a number of things you must know in order to have a safe and comfortable winter RV experience.

You must concern yourself with keeping your fresh water line from freezing. The same goes for sewer lines. You must concern yourself with how to keep your holding tanks from freezing. You must learn how to conserve propane and the best way of connecting it to your rig. Winter camping will require you to figure out the best way to add insulation and wind protection to keep comfortable. How will you handle snow and ice accumulation on your RV? You will also need to control condensation that forms inside your RV.

■ Driving an RV in Winter Weather

There are also considerations for driving or towing an RV during winter weather conditions. Some folks use chains for the RV. That isn't a choice I would make as they are heavy, need to be stored, and sometimes difficult to put on. Stay in camp until the weather clears sufficiently so chains are not needed.

If you must drive your RV in winter weather, stay on the main, well traveled roads, especially during bad weather. Use winter tires if applicable. Carry all the emergency materials you would use for any type of extreme weather, including a weather radio, blankets, water, flashlights, extra batteries, a GPS unit and food in case you do get stuck. Stay with your rig as hypothermia can set in quickly in cold, wet conditions. Notify someone of your location in case you get in trouble. Carry your cell phone. This might be a good use for a CB radio.

■ Preparing the Fresh Water System for Winter RVing

You must prepare your RV for winter RVing. If you will be in a campground with a working (and hopefully heated) shower house, you might winterize the water system and not use it at all. I'm not sure I would like to get up and go to the shower house in the middle of the night to use the bathroom. Assuming you will use all the facilities of your rig, we will start with the fresh water system.

You will want a heated water hose to connect to the park water system. Year round parks often have heated pipes from deeply buried water lines so they won't freeze. You will plug in your heated hose to the regular hose bib. You can insulate the exposed part of the hose bib with bubble wrap wrapped over with duct tape. If you can't afford a heated hose, you can purchase a length of electric heat tape. Lay the heat tape out along the length of the hose. Secure it at 1 foot intervals with electrical tape. Then cover the hose and heat tape with foam pipe insulation. Secure it with duct tape. Plug it in to a thermostatically controlled outlet and then into the 20 Amp connection at the park electrical pedestal. So far so good. It is a good practice to place a drop light with a 50 watt bulb in the wet bay where the water hose is connected. This will keep the bay with all its water plumbing warm and frost free.

If your rig has heating pads installed on the bottom of the fresh water tank and the gray and black water holding tanks, you are good to go! If not, you must run your propane furnace(s) occasionally to keep them from freezing. I would suggest keeping the sewer hose stored until you need to use it. Heat tape will probably melt the plastic material and cause a leak in the sewer hose. Once used, drain the hose and store it away until you need it again. This means keeping the cap on the park sewer opening. You might want to mark its location with a wire coat hanger if snow is expected. I wouldn't want to go searching for it after a new snowfall. Isn't winter RVing fun?

■ Insulating your RV for Winter RVing

This is probably the best thing you can do to stay comfortable for winter RVing. Windows and doors are a constant source of air leakage. If your rig has dual pane windows, great! Just remember that the windshield on motorized units is not dual pane nor is the window in the entrance door on side door models. The windshield can be covered with pleated foil available under the Reflectix brand name and available in hardware stores and RV supply shops. Cut it to fit and tape it in place, then pull the curtain closed to add another barrier. An excellent way to insulate single pane windows is with plastic storm window kits also available at hardware stores. This lets you see out of the windows.

There are thick cut-to-fit foam insulation products available at RV supply shops to place inside the vents to prevent heat loss there. Home style insulating tape can be placed in loose fitting doors to keep them weather proof. You might consider insulated Styrofoam panels to go inside the cabinets on the outside wall. This is another place cold air enters. Many people leave cabinet doors open so the insides get heated. There are water lines inside many cabinets.

Wind is a big reason RVs get cold in winter. They are up on wheels so the wind blows right under. This is the reason bridge roadways freeze up first. The cure for this is skirting for motorized and towable RVs. Custom skirts can be purchased made of a vinyl material with snaps. They must be held to the ground with rocks or other weights. You can make your own skirting quite inexpensively with plywood held in place with stakes. Make sure to put skirting all the way around all four sides. Some folks will be tempted to use hay bales. This has several drawbacks. It is an extreme fire hazard around propane fired appliances. Secondly, it will attract mice and other rodents. There has been much material written on protection from mice and other critters. Some folks use moth balls, some essential oils, some commercial dryer sheets. Use whatever works for you, because mice want to be warm too.

Here is a link to a company that makes skirting for RVs that are easy to put on and roll up for storage. http://rv-skirting-solutions.com/

This is an example of the product from the above company's website

■ Handling Condensation in an RV

Now that you have your rig well buttoned up and as air tight as you can, you need to consider condensation. It will form especially on windows, but also on ceilings as well. It's part of the price you pay for being warmer than the outside air. A wonderful product called Damp-Rid can help quite a bit as well as providing some small amount of outside ventilation. A dehumidifier can be helpful as well, but must be emptied constantly.

■ Using Propane Appliances in Winter

Propane is the fuel of choice for most RV appliances. It powers refrigerators, stove tops and ovens, as well as RV furnaces. Unfortunately, the typical RV forced air furnace is very inefficient, and blows a lot of heat outside. Using just propane fired forced air furnaces can empty an RV propane tank within 2 days. We are forced to use them some of the time to keep basement compartments and holding tanks from freezing for winter RVing.

There are several solutions. One is to use electric space heaters to supplement the furnace. The ceramic disk units are small and produce an amazing amount of heat. Another is to use a propane fired catalytic heater. These are almost 90% efficient and warm gently. We use a 6000 Btu unit that keeps us warm inside with occasional use of the furnace.

Under no circumstances should you use your propane oven for heat. If propane is burned in this way for just a few hours, levels of carbon monoxide (CO) can become deadly. Use the furnace or a propane heater rated for RVs. Always clear away snow and other obstructions from water heaters, refrigerators or vents. Make sure your CO detector is less than 5 years old and is operating. Even with a catalytic heater, some ventilation is the smart way to go. Just a small opening in a vent and another window is enough.

The best thing we have done is install an "Extend-a-Stay" valve in the propane line just on the downstream side of the pressure regulator. This allows connection of another propane tank to supplement your RVs on-board tank. There is a valve to isolate your tank while using the outboard tank. This way, you don't need to move your rig, just go get the outboard tank filled again. This makes winter RVing almost easy.

■ Snow is not your friend

You have probably heard that snow is a good insulator, and it is, for igloos. For winter RVing, the snow will melt and refreeze as ice next to the roof or walls of your RV. Show on the roof will quickly exceed the rated roof weight load and should be brushed off after the storm stops. It is especially important to remove it from slide tops and slide top awnings. It's OK to have it lap up against the skirting, as it will help to insulate that.

I hope you try winter RVing at least once. You will see a side of nature rarely seen. You can follow and identify animal tracks, enjoy the silence only a cold winter day brings, and return to your warm secure RV to warm up. You will also experience a season most RVers do not even try.

CHAPTER 43

WORKAMPING

Are you interested in Workamping? To quote from the home page of Workamper News, "Workampers are adventurous individuals, couples and families who have chosen a wonderful lifestyle that combines any kind of part-time or full-time work with RV camping. If you work as an employee, operate a business, or donate your time as a volunteer, and you sleep in an RV (or on-site housing), you are Workamping"

Do you want to RV but need a little extra income? Well, we are in the same boat. Or, you may want to do volunteer work. There are enough workamping opportunities to work and volunteer out here on the road that we don't see any unemployment problems. Many folks have left a lifetime of work and in retirement, want to give something back. There is a world of volunteer opportunities available to them. You may want to be on the road full time but need some additional income. There are many, many paying jobs you may have never thought about. Lots of RVers are willing to trade a few hours of work for a campsite in an area they wish to visit. We have done all of this, and we are the richer to have chosen Workamping.

There are, however, some basic principles to remember when you decide that Workamping will be part of your RV lifestyle. The main thing is: you are not starting a new career. These are part-time seasonal jobs. The pay, if any, will be at or near minimum wage. Secondly, unless you have been hired as a manager, do not try to be one. This can quickly lead to problems between you and management, and can just as quickly lead to dismissal. If you can keep these basics in mind, and keep a good work ethic and attitude, you will be successful.

■ What is Workamping?

Workamping typically means trading your labor for an RV site. The electricity may or may not be included. This type of job is usually in a campground in one of their departments. You could work in the office, maintenance, grounds, food service, security, or perhaps in the activities department. These are quite typical jobs that RVers may take. You should receive your site and utilities for perhaps ten hours of work each, or maybe a little more. You may not be asked to do any more than that; or you may be asked to work more hours for pay (usually minimum wage for the state). This is how the bulk of workamping jobs are offered. Some places will offer pay for all hours worked but you pay a discounted rate for your site. Many high end resorts do this. You might even be fortunate enough to find work where you are paid for all hours and receive a free site.

There are many other types of Workamping jobs out there for RVers. You might work at an amusement park such as Adventure Land in Iowa where they have a campground for workampers. Maybe you want to work at Disney World? They do not have housing for you, but you will receive passes to the park for your family. You could work at Dollywood in Tennessee and get health insurance while you are working. Most of this type of job requires a seasonal commitment. This means the whole summer or winter season. Some positions even offer an end-of-season bonus for staying to the end. If you don't want to commit so much time, consider something like the sugar beet harvest in North Dakota. It lasts between two and four weeks and pays quite well. Maybe you have the stamina to work for Amazon.com in one of their warehouses for the eight to twelve weeks leading up to Christmas? This job could require you to walk as much as fifteen miles a day while lifting heavy packages. They do not have campgrounds for you but they will recommend some in the local area and will pay for your camping.

My best advice is to go to Workamper.com and sign up with them. For a very reasonable fee, you will have access to their Awesome Applicants resume database. Once you complete your resume there, it will be made available to employers signed up with Workamper. Kathy and I have found all but one of our jobs through their service. We receive e-mail daily with new job postings. We submitted resumes to those employers we wanted to work for, and sometimes we received multiple offers and got to pick and choose. That's a good situation to be in.

Other sources for Workamping jobs are:
▶ http://www.happyvagabonds.com/
▶ http://www.work-for-rvers-and-campers.com/

far the best place we have found is http://www.workamper.com. It is
we have gotten most of our jobs, and we have found them to have all kinds
ormation on their web site. They have quite a bit of advice for those just
ting out working on the road. Their resume database is scanned by many,
y prospective employers. A bi-monthly magazine, the Workamper News,
ains job listings in every state as well as general information. Daily e-mail
ices of newly posted jobs are available as an option. We support Workamper.
n because they provide complete service for the workamper. As such we
ccupy a Concierge position with them which allows us to offer a free issue of
he magazine if you join through the posting on our website. Otherwise, please
se the code **hugg4019** in the "referred by" space on the application. We are
compensated by Workamper.com for generating new members.

Workamping Tips

We got some great workamping tips after we were able to interview the manager
our last campground job and there is some real gold in this interview from
the perspective of the employer. They had worked very hard at selecting their
workcamping team, and they looked at over 5000 applications. Here are some of
the thoughts that they had, and what they are looking for:

Workamping Tips for Preparing the Resume

These workamping tips are all about the workamper resume, which is
completely different from any you may have seen or written before. This workamper
resume focuses only on skills that the campground manager can use to operate
the campground or other business using workampers. You are not applying for
a career position. It is a part-time seasonal position. It is extremely important
to remember that when preparing a workamping resume. The workamping tips
below come right out of the mouths of hiring managers.

- Demonstrate good people skills. This will help catch the eye of the manager.
- Because managers have so many resumes to look at, it's good to have a
  bullet list of your skills and the talents that you have. It makes it a whole
  lot easier for the manager to pull out your resume and look it over.
- Don't forget: if you are looking for an office job and have a lot of spelling
  errors, it will not help you. Use spell check.

- If you use the phrase "open to all possibilities" then make sure you are. It will get you through the first group of reviews.
- The average manager will look at thousands of resumes every year – you will want yours to jump out at him or her.
- If you are looking for a paid position, do not apply where pay is not being offered. It is a waste of time for you and for the manager.
- Read the posting and make sure it offers everything that you are looking for. Don't throw out your resume to the world hoping that if you don't get a paying job, you will take one that doesn't. It's not fair to the hiring manager or to you.
- Employers are registered with workcamper.com and they can put in key words to bring up resumes that would fit the positions that they have available. Use the words that are in the posting for this reason.
- Keep your resume up to date. Revise it every six months to be sure it is current. There is nothing more frustrating than having to look at a resume that is 10 years old.
- If you are looking for a job in the northwest, put that in there so those campgrounds looking for workers will know that you will be a good fit.
- Be honest about your physical abilities; if you are unable to do outside work anymore, learn how to do office work. There is no reason a man can't work in the office or a woman can't do maintenance work.
- Make sure the pictures on your resume are up to date.Workamper.com offers a class to help you write a resume.
- Remember, this is not a regular job; it is a seasonal part-time job, not a career.
- If you need to make money, be sure to express this up front.
- Make all your desires known. You might not get everything you want, but ask.
- Do not print your resume in blue text. It is hard on the eyes.
- Put info the employer wants up front. These are the things specified in the ad posting.
- Keep it short; 1 page is more than adequate.
- Give them something to remember. A short memorable story about you will be remembered years later.

- Campground managers look though a lot of resumes and the first important thing is the introduction to your resume. Make it eye catching, not just: "we are John and Kathy", but "we are full of life, and we are friendly and outgoing. We are people persons."
- Don't concentrate on what you did before you retired unless it would pertain to the job you are applying for at the campground.
- If you have workamped before, put that at the top of the resume.
- Did you work with a specific campground reservation system? Which one?
- Specify if you have a special skill such as builder, office work, electrician, or anything that will pertain to the position you are applying for.
- You should bold the specific skills you have such as campground master, or CPO certificate.

■ After You are Offered a Job...

These workamping tips also came from our campground manager interview.

- They expect you to be both on time and who you have claimed to be. If you said you know Campground Master and you don't, then you have lied.
- You are not the only new employee. There may be as many as 200 or as few as 2 and everyone needs to be brought up to speed on all the systems and how that particular campground uses them.
- Download the reservation program used in the campground and practice if it has been a while since you have used it. Then you can relax and enjoy the experience.
- Once you have been hired, change your status to not available until the next season if you use the Awesome Applicants feature at Workamper.com.
- Get a commitment from the employer as to the particulars of the work in writing, and give a written commitment back to the employer. This is called a Workamping Letter of Understanding. Click for a sample.
- Don't take the first job that comes along just to have a job. You will most likely be disappointed.

■ A Few More Workamping Tips

These are some more workamping tips to help you land the job of your dreams.

- If you are looking for work, talk with the manager at the park you are interested in, and talk with the other workampers. Network and talk to people.
- If you need experience, go to the park during the off season. The managers will have time to work with you, and you will have time to learn and become an asset to the campground.
- Work on the cleaning crew and take an hour or two on your own time to learn how to work in the office.
- Understand the area you are going to. If fly fishing is your thing, don't apply for a job in Arizona where lakes and streams are scarce. If surfing is your thing, there are plenty of jobs near the California coast. Go where there are opportunities to enjoy your particular interest.

There are many good articles on workamping in the Viewpoints section on the workamper.com website, although you must be a member to see them. Check out Workamper.com

These books are also loaded with workamping tips.

- Roadwork II: The RVers Ultimate Income Resource Guide by Arline Chandler
- Support Your RV Lifestyle! With CD by Jaimie Hall Bruzenak
- Work Your Way Across the USA by Nick Russell
- and of course our book So, you want to be a workamper? by John and Kathy Huggins

■ Campground Jobs

There are probably more workampers working at campground jobs than any other venue. The overwhelming number of help wanted postings are for campground work. In a lot of cases, one spouse, usually the wife, works at the desk/campstore taking reservations and answering the phone. The other works maintenance and grounds. There are many other possible campground jobs depending on the size of the campground. We'll look at each of these. Bear in mind that at smaller campgrounds, one person may be asked to assume several tasks.

■ Reservations

The person doing reservations will need to take phone, mail, and electronic reservations. Systems for this range from file cards in a card box, electronic spreadsheets, to computerized reservation systems. More and more campgrounds are using these computer based systems. Digirez, Campground Master, and Campground Manager are 3 of the more popular systems, although the KOA properties use a proprietary system unique to KOA. You can download demo versions of some of these to get experience before actually using it on the job. This and maintenance are two of the most prevalent campground jobs available.

► http://www.campgroundmaster.com/free_demo.html
► http://campgroundmanager.com/

■ Front Desk

The front desk is where the customer gets his or her first impression of both staff and facilities. Manning this area will require good customer service and communications skills. You will be asked questions about local stores and restaurants, as well as directions to nearby attractions. There will also be a cash register for taking camping fees and possibly camp store purchases. Often, computerized reservation systems will also have a point of sale (POS) module to control the register and maintain store inventory. This job is often combined with reservations in smaller campgrounds.

■ Camp Store

The Camp Store clerk rings up store purchases, helps customers with purchases, answers their questions, stocks shelves and rotates stock. This position is also combined with Front Desk and Reservations in small campgrounds. Many campgrounds with a digital reservation system will have a point of sale (POS) terminal as the cash register. You may also be tasked with periodically taking inventory.

■ Maintenance

The campground maintenance department is responsible for maintaining buildings and other infrastructure including fresh water and sewer systems as well as the park electrical system to include individual campsite pedestals.

Plumbing, electrical, painting, and carpentry experience is a plus for obtaining a position in the maintenance department. There are campground jobs in maintenance during the off-season because that is when major projects and upgrades are completed.

■ Swimming Pool

If a park has a large pool complex, especially with lifeguards, there will usually be a separate department. New Federal laws concerning public swimming facilities are making it prudent for campgrounds to hire a Certified Pool Operator (CPO) to maintain safe and sanitary conditions at the pool. Smaller campgrounds usually have operation of the pool facility fall under the Maintenance Department. I have been hired for 2 workamping jobs because I hold a current CPO certification. This was among my most favorite campground jobs. This can be obtained by attending a 2-day class overseen by the National Swimming Pool Foundation. Here is a link to the training site http://www.nspf.org/en/cpo.aspx

■ Grounds

The Grounds Department is responsible for keeping the grass cut regularly as well as trimming trees and shrubs. They will also be responsible for any flower beds and other plantings around the campground. If the campground is open during winter in snow prone areas, snow plowing is their responsibility. Experience using mowers, weed eaters, tree saws, edgers, etc. Small parks will usually have the Maintenance Department handle grounds as well.

■ Security

Members of the Security Department are responsible for making sure campground rules and regulations are enforced. Large campgrounds with many campers will possibly have 3 shift 24-hour coverage. Sometimes security personnel check in new arrivals and man an entrance gate. The Security Department, along with management, will coordinate emergency situations such as threatening weather, lost children, and personal injuries.

■ Housekeeping

Housekeeping personnel clean park facilities including bath houses, cabins, and other public buildings. They will also be responsible for laundering towels and bed linens for cabins. Cleanliness of park bathroom and shower facilities is a primary measure of quality for a campground. The bathrooms are where campers judge how clean a campground is. Our very first workamping job was cleaning a comfort station at a large campground. We enjoyed it.

■ Campground Jobs in Activities

The Activities Department puts the fun in spending time at a campground. These folks plan and set up children's activities as well as those for adults. The Activities Director previews and books entertainment as well as caterers for meals. Activities folks decorate for dances, holiday dances and meals, as well as sell tickets for them. This can be a really fun job. Kathy and I worked Activities at a 55+ park one winter and we had a ball.

■ Sales

Campgrounds that sell lots and/or timeshares will have one or more salesmen that attract new customers and close sales. These salesmen may require a real estate license in the state where the campground or resort is located.

■ Management

All the above positions report to management for directions and resources. The park manager should have experience in personnel management as well as budgeting and fiscal planning. Managers take direction from the park owners. A successful manager will combine personnel and material resources to make a good camping experience for the customers. They are his real boss.

■ Oilfield Gate Guard

Perhaps you might want to work as an Oilfield Gate Guard. Here is some great information on that job.

There are many opportunities for Oil Field Gate Guarding as a result of the rapid growth of oil exploration and production in this country, and more and more positions are being created. Oil and gas companies hire contractors to sign in vehicles that pass through the gate of an oil drilling operation. The landowner or the oil company have requirements that must be met on all vehicles entering the site. Sometimes there will be inspections for weapons, cameras, etc. The prime directive for oilfield gate guarding is to log vehicle information such as the type of vehicle and license plate number, as well as have the driver and passengers identify themselves, who they work for and sign their name on a check-in sheet. Your oilfield job will not be exciting, but it can be a stable position that can last up to a month or more as the well is drilled and then put into production. Then you move on to the next one.

At this time, most gates pay $150 per day going up to $300 a day for a very busy gate with multiple wells in various stages of production.

■ Where are the Gate Guard Jobs Located?

There is a lot of oil and gas drilling activity in South Texas because of the Eagle Ford shale oil discovery. A lot of RVers travel to South Texas each year to stay in the Rio Grande Valley. The Eagle Ford shale discovery is about 200 miles north of that area, but winters are usually somewhat mild in South Texas. West Texas also has much new drilling activity. There are also Oilfield Gate Guard positions in Louisiana as well as some in the Baaken area up in North Dakota and Montana.

■ The Gate Guard Set-up

The oil company should provide a generator and fuel as well as a septic tank that is attached outside your RV and emptied weekly, as well as a water tank for bathing and other needs. Both of those will be on trailers. You should have your own generator and a supply of propane tanks to run your heater in case the big generator goes out.

If you are working as an independent oilfield gate guarding contractor, you may have to furnish these things yourself. They are tax deductible, along with your RV if you make it a full time job. In most cases you must furnish your own travel trailer or RV, but in some cases a private security company may provide one for you.

■ Daily Gate Guard Life

While a well is being drilled and brought to production, you will see the same rig workers and oilfield company men throughout the course of the drilling of the will. You might meet some interesting people, but for sure you will watch lots satellite TV, and if you are a reader, you will likely finish more books in a week than ever before. Most gates ate manned 24 hours a day, seven days a week until the drilling company starts production on the site. You will have to figure out the distribution of work hours between you and your spouse. Two 12 hour shifts leave little time for being together. It is probably best if both work 2 shifts. On most gates, one of you must be awake and ready to sign in vehicles at any hour of the day or night. Although most traffic will occur in the early morning and late evening when the oil rig crews change shifts, other vehicles will come during your day. This is not an easy life, and you will definitely earn your money.

The type of traffic is18 wheelers hauling drilling mud and water, rig crews, oilfield salesmen, (you may be told not to let them in), oilfield "company men" or consultants, and oilfield service employees.

You should not discuss anything about what is going on or even exactly where you are. These new wells are on secret locations. An oilfield gate guarding employee could well get fired and never hired again for this type of work for leaking company information. Be careful when blogging about where you are or the state of the drilling operation.

■ Tips for Gate Guards

AT&T is the strongest carrier for South Texas, while Verizon should be your choice for gates in the Permian Basin and New Mexico.

Get a cellular amplifier for your phone and/or cellular internet connection. Be sure to get one authorized according to the 2014 FCC regulations for cellular amplifiers. Wilson Electronics is a good source. You might want to consider a directional cell antenna as well to get the strongest signal.

Look professional and look the part of a professional Gate Guard. Keep the clutter under and around to a minimum. Slobs usually do not get another oilfield job.

Do not let the wrong person in the gate. You can be fired for admitting unwanted visitors. Some may be just looking around, while some may be from rival oil companies. This is another way to get fired. Your "Company Man" can help you with some of these decisions.

Unless you like waiting in line to do your laundry in a Laundromat, have your own washer/dryer. It will save you a lengthy weekly trip.

Find your exact GPS location and post this on the wall of your RV, along with other indications of your exact location, such as highway reference marker number, mile marker, and distance from landmarks. Keep emergency numbers such as the Border Patrol and Sheriff handy. 911 often rings to the wrong county, especially when using a cell phone booster in the middle of nowhere. For emergencies, dial the nearest Highway Patrol, or sheriff's office directly.

■ **Gate Guarding is not for Everyone**

By now, you should have figured out that oil field gate guarding isn't for everyone. You will not be able to go off together. Only one of you can go and do the shopping, and it could be 50 miles or more to the nearest store. You will find most gate guards do not get but 6 hours of sleep on average. Your rig may have seemed large when you bought it, but those walls close in when you are cooped up in it.

You are expected to log a vehicle in as soon as it crosses the gate line. You won't last long if you have to wake up and stumble outside for every vehicle. Many experienced guards set up a shelter outside and sit outside waiting. The wind blows constantly in southwest Texas, often cold in Fall and Winter and hot in Summer. All day and night. With that wind come a fine powdery dust. The wind blows it into every nook and cranny and you will be cleaning it constantly. When it rains, that dust becomes a sticky, gooey mud. When the wind blows everything dry, that mud turns to almost concrete, from which the dust blows off.

I don't want to make this sound too horrible, because you can get used to almost anything, but there are critters. Critters such as rattlesnakes, scorpions, and other slithering things. The snakes like to lie on the warm road in front of your rig on cool nights and are also attracted to the vibration of your generator. You will want to keep lights on all night.

■ **Companies that Hire Oilfield Gate Guards**

There are quite a few companies that hire gate guards and as contracts change, so do those companies. The best way to find them is to get on the internet and

Google Oil Field Gate Guards.

■ Application Process

You have to complete the following paperwork in order to obtain work as an Oilfield Gate Guard.

1.   Independent Contractor Agreement (most of the companies)
2.   W-9 for taxes
3.   Agreement for Workers' Compensation
4.   Application cards for fingerprints and Registration application
5.   Level II Security Officer Exam for the Texas Dept. of Public Services
6.   Passport size photo

There is a fee of approximately $70 per person to obtain the security license. The company you are applying to may or may not pay this fee.

■ Oilfield Gate Guarding Blogs

▶ http://www.ourrvadventures.com
▶ http://www.wanderingwendels.com/adventures-in-gate-guarding-in-south-texas
▶ http://www.theforkintheroad.wordpress.com
▶ http://www.myoldrv.com
▶ http://www.memorymaker11.com/blog
▶ http://www.bounderrv.wordpress.com
▶ http://www.kitandjerry.com
▶ http://www.blueheron98.wordpress.com
▶ http://www.travelinterriers.wordpress.com
▶ http://www.doris-and-dave.blogspot.com
▶ http://razzchronicles.blogspot.com
▶ http://workampingstories.blogspot.com
▶ http://readytogofull-timeRVing.blogspot.com
▶ http://turnwhentheroaddoes.com
▶ http://www.roadworking.com

■ Annual Sugar Beet Harvest Jobs

American Crystal Sugar Company is a Minnesota agricultural cooperative corporation owned by about 3,000 sugar beet growers in the Minnesota and North Dakota portions of the Red River Valley. It also owns Sidney Sugars, located in Sidney, Montana. American Crystal is engaged primarily in the agricultural production, manufacturing and marketing of sugar from sugar beets. Every year the companies hire over 1300 workers stationed at 45 sugar beet receiving stations. These seasonal employees are an integral part of making yearly sugar production a great success. These short term positions offer excellent compensation and attract applicants from all over the United States and Canada. Locals and travelers alike come to make a hefty paycheck while being able to enjoy various outdoor attractions and company paid camp sites.

The Sugar Beet Harvest ground operation is generally comprised of three main roles:

Helper and Sample Taker – Collects beet samples and assists Pile Operator in cleaning. Helper will also communicate with drivers to ensure safe and accurate unloading of trucks.

Pile Operator – Maneuvers pile control switches, orchestrates repair work and supervises and assists in the clean-up of daily operations.

Skidsteer Operator – Operates skidsteer. Must be able to lift 50 lbs.

RV/CAMPERS please contact us with your address and telephone number. You will need to fill out applications and mail them into our Express Employment Professionals office by July 1. To request an application please contact us with your home address and telephone number. A Sugar Beet Representative will mail you an application packet. The web address is http://sugarbeetharvest. com/index.cfm

■ Amazon Camperforce

The Amazon CamperForce program brings together a community of enthusiastic RVers who help make the holidays bright for the customers of the world's largest online retailer, Amazon.com. As a CamperForce Associate, you'll begin this seasonal assignment in early Fall and work until December 23rd. For 2015, the locations are in either: Jeffersonville, IN, Campbellsville, KY, Murfreesboro, TN or Haslet, TX. The cities will change from year to year depending on the needs of the company. Amazon offers great pay, a paid completion bonus, paid referral bonuses, and paid campsites for its CamperForce Associates.

Amazon is seeking hardworking and dedicated seasonal campers for the CamperForce program. The program lasts 3-4 months in the winter and your responsibilities will be in the areas of picking, packing, stowing, and receiving.

Along with the chance to build lasting relationships with coworkers, the CamperForce Program also provides the following benefits:

- Paid campsites
- Paid good wages, plus time & 1/2 for overtime, plus shift differential
- Paid completion bonus when you work until released
- Paid referral bonuses

To apply, go to http://www.amazonfulfillmentcareers.com/opportunities/camper-force/

■ Become an RV Inspector

Why become an RV inspector? More and more potential RV buyers are wanting the rig they have chosen to be inspected so they know exactly what if any issues are involved with that RV. In the past, dealerships have offered Pre-Delivery Inspections (PDI) that were not only expensive, but biased towards making a sale. Private sellers can't even offer that.

Recent statistics show that over 65% of RV sales are from private seller to private buyer with no RV dealership involved. That usually means the buyer has no warranty and has no idea of the true condition of that particular rig. Enter the independent RV inspector.

This should be a person with no connection to the selling dealer or private seller. He will provide, at a predetermined fee, a totally unbiased inspection report to whoever requests his service, known as the "Client."

How does someone get to become an RV inspector? Actually, there are no requirements or licenses required for someone to hang out a shingle as an "RV Inspector." This opens up a real can of worms for the client who expects a professional to do the inspection.

My feeling is that the best way to do this is to become very familiar with all types of RVs and RV systems along with a general knowledge of RV problem troubleshooting. The job can certainly be done by both men and women, but it is not for the faint of heart. You will be climbing on RV roofs as well as scrambling underneath to examining frames and running gear. The inspector should have an inspection report template for each type of RV inspected from Pop-up to diesel pusher. An inspector should follow some sort of code of ethics to ensure his unbiased position. He should also develop a set of standard practices so every inspection is done the same way.

The person wanting to become an RV inspector should also learn all about forming his or her own small business, probably doing this first. There is so much to starting your own business I can't cover it here, but great help is available from the US Government Small Business Administration. www.sba.gov .

Fortunately, a recent organization has been formed called the National RV Inspection Association (NRVIA). They have written up both a Code of Ethics for RV Inspectors, and an expansive Standards of Practice document. There is an exam in order to become a Certified RV Inspector as well as an annual fee to join this organization. I hope all prospective RV inspectors will join with the NRVIA and proudly advertise that they are NRVIA Certified inspectors.

Now that you are certified and have become an RV Inspector and set up your own business, how do you get clients? It's called marketing! You should have a website for your business where you will have an internet presence. Local newspapers might be a source as well as bulletin boards in local businesses. What if you are an RVer yourself and are traveling full-time? That website becomes more important yet. While you are waiting on clients, perhaps you can do some RV service work in campgrounds. Yet another small business possibility!

Searching the internet will turn up a few RV inspection companies that are looking for inspectors. This is where you need to really do your homework on those companies. Can they get you work across the country, are they truly independent and unbiased, do they offer training?

I have found one I particularly like called the RV Inspection Connection. These folks hold training sessions all over the country. Their first course is a 5-day RV Technician course with heavy emphasis on small business formation and also on RV inspection. They also offer a 5-day Advanced Inspector class covering inspection software and doing several graded mock inspections. This company has developed an excellent suite of inspection software available to their technicians.

They also will handle all of the incoming calls, billing, preparation of finished inspection reports, and much more "back office" tasks for the technician. Once you notify them of your location, they can schedule inspections for you in your area. They do require someone be NRVIA certified and pass several examinations as well as the advanced inspector course before they bring someone on as an independent contractor. Contact them at http://rvinspection.com/.

I believe the RV inspection business is a real up and coming business opportunity that can make you a decent living on the road. Along with owner to buyer transactions, there are a growing number of dealers that want their used trade-ins inspected so they can offer a "Certified Pre-Owned" rig at a premium price. What about inspecting park model trailers for resale? This business is just beginning to take off. This is a good time to become an RV inspector and get in on the ground floor.

■ Volunteering

While Workamping was our goal, in our first year RVing, we joined an Escapee group of Red Cross Disaster Volunteers. Almost immediately after training, we found ourselves in San Antonio, TX, working in a shelter for victims of Hurricanes Katrina and Rita. That was an amazing three weeks. We also did two stints of volunteer work at the Escapee CARE (Continuing Assistance for Retired Escapees) Center in Livingston, TX. I've never washed so many pots and dishes, and at the same time been so happy about it in my life.

■ Volunteer Jobs

Many of the volunteer jobs for RVers are with Federal, State, and local government agencies. Check out http://www.volunteer.gov/ . You can search for positions by state, zip code, and by the type of job you would like to do. Most of these jobs will not include an RV site. Type RV Site in the keyword box for those. Make sure you are in agreement with all the requirements of the position you want. Better to decline now than to make a commitment and drive a thousand miles only to find out you don't like the job.

We know a few folks who love to do volunteer work at various fish hatcheries. Another volunteer job involves setting up a spotting telescope to help tourists to observe wildlife. We have met several volunteer docents at Pacific Coast lighthouses who come back year after year. Having an RV site perched atop a bluff overlooking the Pacific Ocean in Oregon might be part of the reason. How cool would it be to live and work at your favorite National Park like Yellowstone, or Glacier? Some of the National Parks even have paid positions.

The Escapees RV Club has two particularly outstanding volunteer job opportunities for Escapees members. One is Continuing Assistance for Retired Escapees (CARE) that was mentioned previously. Volunteers here help operate the facility by cooking and cleaning up after meals, driving participants to doctor's appointments and shopping, and being on-call during staff off hours. The other is Disaster Operations Volunteer Escapees (DOVE) which was also mentioned earlier. After provided training, DOVE volunteers participate in Red Cross disaster operations when and where they may occur.

Another type of volunteer job is with various charitable organizations. These might include:

- **RV Care-A-Vanners** is a volunteer program for anyone who travels in a recreational vehicle, wants to build Habitat for Humanity houses, and have fun doing it. RV Care-A-Vanners welcomes people of all ages, from all walks of life who want to pick up a hammer and help change lives. http://www.habitat.org/rv

■ Church Volunteer Jobs

Numerous church denominations have volunteer job organizations that participate in building and maintaining churches and church properties. Some are:

USMAPS (Assembly of God Mission America Placement Service) USMAPS was formed to help meet the need for construction and renovation of churches, Assemblies of God colleges and universities, and other facilities. Another goal is to strengthen the arm of evangelism of U.S. Missions ministries by encouraging and facilitating non-construction RVers and church teams' involvement with U.S. Missions evangelism outreaches. http://usmaps.ag.org

SOWER (Servants on Wheels Ever Ready) this ministry is primarily a physical labor ministry. While there is an occasional need for office-type work, on most projects the men are involved with the construction or remodeling of structures and associated utilities, repair of vehicles, or landscape installation using their skills in carpentry, electrical, plumbing, roofing, masonry, mechanics, etc. Women have helped with office work, tutoring, sewing, painting, kitchen work, cleaning, etc. There are opportunities for everyone of reasonably good health to contribute. http://www.sowerministry.org

NOMADS (Nomads on a Mission Active in Divine Service) provide volunteer labor for United Methodist organizations. NOMADS demonstrate God's love through their work and by listening to the people with whom they work. They do new construction, remodeling, and repairs for churches, children's homes, camps, colleges, outreach missions and disaster rebuilding. Team members do maintenance, cleaning, painting, electrical, drywall, sewing, and flooring. http://www.nomadsumc.org

SECTION VI

RV TIPS

Everyone considering using an RV will want RV tips from those who have gone before; and who have made mistakes the newcomers do not want to make. We have picked some of the best from our experience and others who are willing to share them in this section.

- ▶ **Chapter 44 RV Inspections**
- ▶ **Chapter 45 RV Buying Tips**
- ▶ **Chapter 46 Financing Tips**
- ▶ **Chapter 47 Finding RV Insurance**
- ▶ **Chapter 48 Essential RV Accessories**
- ▶ **Chapter 49 RV Trip Planning**
- ▶ **Chapter 50 RV Driving and Towing Tips**
- ▶ **Chapter 51 Camping with Pets**
- ▶ **Chapter 52 Solo RVing**
- ▶ **Chapter 53 Staying Fit on the Road**
- ▶ **Chapter 54RV Show Tips**
- ▶ **Chapter 55 Refurbishing Your RV**
- ▶ **Chapter 56 Storing Your RV**
- ▶ **Chapter 57Lessons Learned**

CHAPTER 44
RV INSPECTIONS

With used RV prices increasing at the same rate as new prices, it is often difficult to know if you are getting good value for the hard earned dollars you are paying for your new to you RV. Even new RVs have problems that must be fixed by the dealer before you can use the rig. With 65% of used RV sales happening between a private owner and a prospective owner, you don't even have the sometimes dubious assertions by a dealer that the rig you are buying is in good condition. The search process for the ideal RV for you is tedious enough without having to worry about unseen problems cropping up. What is the used RV buyer to do?

■ **The RV Inspection**

The answer is an RV inspection. Many dealers will provide you with a pre delivery inspection or PDI for anywhere from $500 to $1500 dollars. They say they check out every system and make sure everything is working properly. Don't you suspect the seller is going to make sure that the inspection comes out okay? Of course it will, because they have a vested interest in selling that rig without further expense to them.

Who, then, should do the inspection you ask? An independent trained RV inspector, that's who. You want someone who is not connected with the seller in any way and who has no interest other than to do a thorough inspection and deliver a concise and accurate inspection report. With that report in hand, you will have leverage with the seller if there are issues with the RV. You can ask for a price concession to cover problems found during the inspection. This actually works both ways. A prospective seller who thinks his rig is in good condition can get top dollar with a good inspection report to back up his claim. It might be a good idea to suggest that buyer and seller share equally in the cost of the inspection. The seller will get a better price and the buyer will know the true condition of the RV they are buying.

■ Contents of the RV Inspection

What should be inspected during an independent RV inspection? The first thing the inspector should do is compare the VIN number displayed on the plate in the RV with the Inspection request to ensure he is inspecting the rig that the prospective buyer is paying him to inspect. Hard to believe, but unscrupulous sellers will do a "bait and switch" to get rid of a problem plagued RV.

Next should be safety items that affect your life. All installed fire extinguishers should be checked for pressure and dry powder units should be shaken to stir up the powder. Installed alarms including fire and smoke, LP Gas, and Carbon Monoxide should all be checked for proper operation. The electrical system should be checked for a "hot skin test" so entering or touching the outside of the rig will not result in electric shock. The emergency exit(s) should be checked for proper operation. All wall receptacles and GFCI outlets should be checked for proper polarity and operation. A timed leak test should be performed at the gas cook-top. All these items are to ensure that the RV is safe to operate.

After the ID and safety items have been done, the inspection should include a thorough look at:

- the roof, looking especially for points of water intrusion and possible damage to rubber roof membrane if so equipped. Special places to look are any places where things like vents, air conditioners, etc come through the roof. All caulking must be inspected. Any suspicious points found on top should be looked at inside.
- front and rear caps
- slide-outs
- awnings and slide toppers
- chassis turn signal and running lights
- 120-volt AC electrical system
- generator (if installed) (possible oil and coolant analysis)
- inverter (if installed)
- battery system
- fresh water system
- waste water systems (gray and black)
- propane system and tank(s)
- refrigerator

- water heater
- furnace
- cook top
- air conditioner(s)
- washer/dryer (if installed)
- microwave
- dishwasher (if installed)
- exhaust fans
- cabinets
- furniture
- entertainment system
- shower
- chassis and undercarriage
- leveling system

If the rig is motorized:
- steering
- engine (possible oil analysis)
- radiator (possible coolant analysis)
- transmission (possible fluid analysis)
- Running gear (axles and tires, etc)
- hitch system/hook-up.

Wow, that's a lot of stuff! How long will something like this take? That depends on the type of rig. Obviously a large diesel pusher will take as much as 8 hours while a Travel Trailer could be done in 2 or 3. It also depends on the level of inspection you order.

■ Making the inspection happen

Obviously, all this activity will require the rig being inspected to be in a place where full hook-ups are available and an electric hook-up to the capacity of that rig. The inspector needs access for the entire time of the inspection as well. You, the inspection client, must arrange for that as well as for payment of the inspection, usually in advance. The inspector or his company will prepare the inspection report and provide you with either an electronic file or both that and a printed inspection report. If fluid samples are involved, this could take as much as 5 or 6 business days.

I can't emphasize enough how important this inspection can be to give you the buyer the peace of mind that you are getting a rig in a known condition, as well as giving you some leverage in the buying process. If a seller refuses to allow an inspection, don't walk away, run! There are plenty of used rigs and your perfect one will be out there if you look long enough.

■ The NRVIA

The National Recreational Vehicle Inspection Association (NRVIA) has been formed to provide a code of ethics and standards of practice for RV inspectors that qualify for membership. I highly recommend that any inspector you hire be an NRVIA certified inspector. He should have credentials to prove that.

■ Inspection Connection

We also recommend the RV Inspection Connection for all your inspection needs. They only hire NRVIA inspectors and they are located across the country. Check them out at https://rvinspection.com/

CHAPTER 45

RV BUYING TIPS

We wrote these RV buying tips because the buying process can be a relatively good experience if you have done your homework, chosen the right rig for your lifestyle, and are armed with knowledge about the process itself. Some folks we know have likened it to torture. We had quite a different experience. We knew exactly what we wanted in a rig and we knew we wanted a late model diesel pusher. We had researched brands and product lines within brands. After having lived with that first (and only) RV for more than 10 years, we are still satisfied with our buying decision.

We were armed with "The RV Buyer's Survival Guide" by Bob Randall and had read it several times. I can't emphasize enough that this small book is an RV buying "Bible" and is available on Amazon.com. The sections on figuring MSRP and understanding trade-in values are worth the current $14.95 price of the entire book.

By the time you are ready to enter into the buying process, you should have decided on no more than two rigs, preferably one. You should then only discuss the buying price of that RV. If you have a trade, you must save that negotiation for later. Unfortunately, many RV dealerships use the "four-square" method of figuring a price. They will divide a piece of paper into four squares and one will be your trade, one will be the RV you want, one will be the finance details, and the last will have the final price based on all of those details. Don't fall for that. If you are asked "How much can you afford each month", do not answer. Instead, insist on a selling price somewhere between the initial asking price and your initial purchase price based on your homework.

One important RV buying tip is that RV dealerships, like every for-profit business, must make a profit in order to stay in business. They must make money over and above their original purchase price on the unit. My feeling is that five percent is a good figure, considering this will be a major purchase. As the negotiation progresses, you should get to an acceptable purchase price that you are willing to make a buying decision on the spot. After all, you have done a ton of homework to get to this point.

■ RV Buying Tips for the Trade-in

Then you will have to deal with your trade-in. The best possible solution is to sell it yourself. When you trade at a dealership, you add a middleman, the dealer, who will have to profit from the transaction. That's more money out of your pocket. You must realize that you will want more than the dealer will give. Here again, homework is key. There are tools available for evaluating the price of used RVs. Remember that the dealer will want to give you wholesale instead of the higher retail value. This is why you want to avoid mixing the rig price and the trade-in price.

So, now you have a purchase price you can live with and there is handshaking all around. Not so fast. We have another RV buying tip. You must demand that this price is only valid upon a satisfactory PDI (Pre-Delivery Inspection). This is a thorough inspection of every aspect of the RV from the roof to the basement, headlights to tail lights. All equipment such as air conditioners, refrigerators and other appliances, slide rooms, driver controls and all water and electric systems must be operated and work as if new. The PDI should be performed on both new and pre-owned units. Some less than scrupulous dealers will try to charge you for this vital service. Don't fall for that, it's a deal breaker. You must demand this be put in writing on the purchase contract. If discrepancies are found during the PDI, the dealer must fix them prior to purchase. Once past this hurdle, you have finished the "front end" of the deal.

■ The Back End of the Deal

Now you are entering the "back end" of the deal. This is where the dealership really makes money. You will be moved to another office to talk with the Finance and Insurance Manager. Are we having fun yet? The finance manager will explain the various means of financing your RV and introduce several banks and finance companies that he works with. Please remember, we are now introducing another "middle-man" into the transaction that will ultimately be paid by you, the RV buyer. Is it time for another RV buying tip?

Part of your homework is to obtain pre-approved financing. Remember that in addition to the price of the RV, there will be taxes and licensing fees. This is also a good time to remember that not all finance companies will loan to full-time RVers without a permanent "sticks and bricks" address. Usually banks won't, but some credit unions will. This is all part of your advance preparation and RV buying tips. The next chapter will have much more information on financing your RV purchase.

The next thing on the Finance Manager's agenda will be the extended warranty. He will have at least one company that will offer several levels of extended warranty coverage on your RV. Because we drive a diesel pusher with lots of on-board electronics and expensive appliances, I recommend an extended warranty. Here's a must do RV buying tip. Get an Extended Warranty. We are on our second one and we have gotten our money's worth. There are, however, some considerations. I would also do some homework to investigate several of the warranty companies and compare both prices and coverage. Visit some RV forums and ask about other folks' experience with different companies. We should have done this, but I didn't. When renewal time came along, we had done the investigation and I believe we picked a good one.

The Finance Manager will now try to sell you a roadside assistance plan and/or towing insurance. We have found through tough and expensive experience that the best company for this is Coach-Net. They are RV pros. They will also know what equipment is required to tow your particular RV. Next up for the Finance Manager will usually be insurance. Some larger dealerships have in-house insurance agents. Once again, you should have already picked an insurance company for both vehicle insurance and the extended warranty. This is a good time to remind you that not all insurance companies will write coverage for full-timers. Now he plays his last card to get more of your money, paint and upholstery protection. This will be another $500 to $900 of your hard earned dollars for a "treatment" of some kind or another. Again, this is an expensive and unnecessary add-on. At long last you have jumped through all the hoops and are ready to take delivery on your new (to you) RV.

It's time for another RV buying tip. If you are trading in a rig, there should be a space set aside for that with both rigs side-by-side to facilitate moving all your stuff from one to the other. There should also be an opportunity for a technician to come over to the new rig to explain all the various features and systems as well as point out all the documentation you will receive. You must insist on this step. Spend a night at the dealership so you can then try all this stuff out for yourself. Make sure you are hooked up to electric, water and at the end of this process, you will want to dump the holding tanks. Make a punch list of items for the dealer to fix. Don't leave the dealership until you are satisfied. This is your last, best chance to get things fixed to your satisfaction. Are you tired yet? Buying a rig can be an exhausting experience, but immensely satisfying if you have done your homework and end up with the RV of your dreams. That's the reason for RV buying tips.

CHAPTER 46

FINANCING YOUR RV

You are entering the final stages of your RV purchase. You've done your homework on what kind of rig you want and you understand that this is a lifestyle change. At the end of the day, it always comes down to money. Lots of questions must be analyzed and answered.

Many folks of retirement age have 401K plans or other retirement savings to fall back on for large purchases. Many RVs are bought as cash purchases. Is this the right move for you? Can you afford the large cash outlay and still have enough money to finance your new lifestyle? This is all part of the homework you must do before you buy any rig. If you want to full-time RV, check out Chapter 32 on Budgeting.

Any RV you buy, especially new units will depreciate, sometimes at an alarming rate. Banks know this and charge higher rates for RV loans. This is where you need to make some important decisions about how much money to put down if you are financing. Too little and you will be upside down on the loan (owe more than the unit is worth) within the first year. RVs deprecate the fastest during the first 5 years of their life. For that reason alone, it might be worthwhile to look at older high end rigs.

Now that you have made the decision to finance, you need to pick a lender. Bear in mind that if you are a full-time RVer, your choice of lender is very limited to mostly credit unions and a few banks. Lenders like to know where their borrowers are. We financed in 2005 when the banks were much more RV friendly. The trick was that we still had a house and jobs. The loan went through without a problem. This could be a major concern for someone already on the road full-time replacing their RV. I would suggest you buy the rig before you quit your job and sell your house if you can swing it as you will get much better terms and more options in who you choose to finance with.

RV dealers love to have you finance your RV purchase. They have relationships with many lending institutions and usually they get a kickback on the loans the dealer sends to them. That's money that could be in your pocket if you find a lender and get pre-approved before you walk onto the dealer's lot. Search the internet for RV financing and you will find many, many lenders until you tell them you intend to travel full-time in the RV that you want them to finance.

We can't emphasize enough the importance of obtaining financing before you sign a purchase agreement. You need to know what it is going to cost each month and you need to know all extra fees up front. Use a loan calculator and plug in the rate of the finance company you have chosen. That can help you decide what is affordable.

It is possible to get almost any kind of RV loan if you have good credit. You will pay more interest if your credit score isn't 700 and above. There are lending institutions that won't lend money on low end RVs because of the rapid depreciation. The same thing applies to rigs older than 7 to 10 years old. Tell the loan officer what type and age of an RV you're considering before you fill out the application. Keep in mind that every application you submit will affect your credit score from 5 to 10 points. Don't bother with companies that will not loan on your chosen RV type.

You can get several finance quotes, but do not pay an application fee. If they want money up front, walk away. All the reputable companies can complete your loan application within an hour or so. They may want to work out the terms later. Don't fall into this trap! Get all the numbers and know exactly what you will pay up front in down payment and exactly what the monthly payment will be. Also insist on no pre-payment penalties in case you decide to pay off the loan early or make larger payments.

Look for a simple interest loan and you will pay interest only on the principal which is reduced every time you make a payment. Be sure to reject any company that inserts clauses into the loan contract that limits your range of travel, especially out of state. The whole idea is to travel isn't it? Try to avoid long term loans over 10 years as the depreciation will eat up any equity you have and send your loan under water.

Now that you've done your homework, you can shop with knowledge and confidence.

CHAPTER 47

FINDING RV INSURANCE

Let's face it, we have a lot invested in our RV, whether it is a trailer or a motorized unit. Even a pop-up trailer costs in excess of $10,000 these days, and choosing RV insurance to cover damage is a wise move. In the case of use of a motorized unit, insurance coverage is required by law. If you have financed your RV, the financial institution will require insurance to protect their investment.

■ RV Insurance

We are going to discuss several different types of RV insurance here. In addition to standard RV insurance, we will talk about Full-time RV Insurance, RV Towing and Roadside Assistance, and Special RV Medical Insurance. We will also briefly mention extended warranty or service plans.

There are some basic insurance terms we need to understand to be able to discuss coverage with an insurance agent. They are:

- **Deductible**: is the amount you must pay up front, **for a claim**, before the insurance company pays up to the limits of the policy.
- **Collision**: pays for covered repairs caused by a collision with another vehicle, person, or object.
- **Comprehensive Coverage**: pays for any damages caused by fire, a theft, falling objects, animals, wind, hail and other weather related damages.
- **Liability**: Covers damages to a person, vehicle or property that you are deemed liable for. There are 3 types: Bodily Injury, Property Damage and Personal Liability.
- **Premium**: insurance speak for what you pay for insurance.
- **Seasonal Coverage**: is where the insurance company only charges you for certain coverage during the time you use the rig. This is usually only offered by companies that specialize in insuring RVs.

Most automobile insurance companies will also cover RVs. The coverage is not well regulated, and almost every company offers differing coverage at different rates. This is where you will have to educate yourself to get the coverage you want and need at a good price. Shopping for RV insurance on price alone could cause you big expensive problems later on if you have damage that isn't adequately covered, or not at all. Think about towing. Many automobile policies cover towing. An automobile insurance company will not know about how a large motorhome must be towed nor will they cover the complete cost which can go into the 1000's.

Many companies do not cover "attachments" to your RV. This could be awnings, satellite dishes and TV antennas among other expensive items to replace or repair.

Some that do cover it, do as at a depreciated value. Others cover it at replacement cost. Ask! You will want "trip interruption" coverage in case your rig is damaged while you are on vacation or otherwise away from home and must stay in a hotel or other lodgings. In the case of a motorized unit, ask if a rental car is part of the coverage.

If you tow a vehicle behind a motorhome, are both vehicles covered by the same policy? Usually this is not the case. Folks fall in love with the low cost insurance they have used for many years on their car, but find some other company to insure the RV. In case of an accident, usually both vehicles will sustain damage. Now you have 2 accidents with 2 deductibles and 2 separate claims. Using the same company for both units will fix that issue.

In the case of a total loss, are you adequately covered so you can replace your RV? I certainly hope so if it is financed! Many companies offer some type of replacement coverage. The best is where you will receive a brand new rig in the case of a total loss. This coverage is usually only offered for rigs in their first five years of life. The best you can get after that is to receive full purchase price for a total loss. You must nail down this coverage in writing at the time of policy purchase. Read the fine print!

What about your personal possessions carried in your rig? Many companies only cover up to $3000 worth. You can purchase more at additional cost. Now is the time to inventory everything in your rig. Take pictures of everything and keep receipts for everything over $500. Keep this information on a flash drive in a safe place. This will get you a far bigger settlement than if you can't even remember what was in the rig. You may need to have special riders written into your policy for things of high value such as jewelry and high value electronics.

One way of saving money on RV insurance is selecting a higher deductable. Moving from $100 to $1,000 deductable will save you money, but also increase the risk you are willing to take.

All this being said, you still should shop around for RV insurance. Ask for Better Business Bureau ratings on different companies. Ask people you consider knowledgeable about RV insurance. Ask this on Facebook and you will get the entire list of every possible insurance company. You know what I mean. The very best thing you can do is to speak with a knowledgeable RV specific insurance agent who understands the special circumstances of damage to RVs.

Here are some questions you should ask the agent when shopping for RV insurance:

- *What is the minimum coverage required in my state?*
- *Will I have full-replacement-value coverage?*
- *Will I need personal liability coverage?*
- *How much of my personal belongings are covered?*
- *Does my homeowner's insurance cover personal property inside the RV?*
- *What is the deductible, and how much can I save by raising it?*
- *Do I have towing coverage for my RV?*
- *Can I pay for full coverage only when I use my RV?*

■ RV Insurance for Full-time RVers

If you are a full-time RVer, you will have some other considerations to think about in obtaining adequate RV insurance. Insurance rates vary widely by state and even to a part of a state. A full-timer can choose a domicile state in which they get their mail, pay their taxes, vote, get their drivers licenses and pay for RV insurance. Our Florida insurance rates were almost double those in South Dakota when we switched there for our domicile. Most Insurance companies can write coverage in multiple states. Research what state is best for you.

Full-time RVers will by nature of the lifestyle gather more "stuff" than casual or weekend RVers. You must ensure all your belongings are covered. "Full-time coverage" will provide higher limits of personal item protection. Make sure it is enough.

A full-timer will require personal liability similar to what you had in your sticks and bricks house. Someone can slip on your top step and sue you as a result. This alone could wipe you out without adequate liability protection.

Because of the additional cost, you might not tell your RV insurance company that you are living full-time in your RV. Please do not do this. The liability issues alone could cause you to lose your rig and other assets. It's just not a good idea to falsify an insurance document. Some full-timers rates are actually lower!

There are very few options when choosing an insurance company for full-time RV protection. They understand the special nature of our lifestyle and our rigs. Here is a list of the best of them:

- AIS RV Insurance endorsed by Escapees RV Club
  http://www.aisinsurance.com/rv
- National General Insurance is the former GMAC insurance company and is also one of the carriers for Good Sam Insurance as well as our personal choice. http://www.nationalgeneral.com/
- **FMCA RV insurance** is offered through several RV insurance agencies, as a coalition, with policies offered by several different RV insurance companies.
  http://www.fmca.com/benefits/fmca-rv-insurance.html
- Foremost Insurance
  http://www.foremost.com/
- Progressive Insurance
  https://www.progressive.com/rv/
- Explorer RV Insurance Agency, Inc.
  http://www.explorerrv.com/

■ Towing and Roadside Assistance Insurance

There are many Roadside Assistance plans offered by automobile insurance companies. Since RVs are a completely different animal, you really need to have an RV specific towing and assistance plan.

None of the Roadside Assistance companies own any towing equipment, They have contracts with tow companies across the country to service their customers. A key consideration is does the towing company that shows up have the proper equipment to tow your particular type of rig? A large Class A motorhome will require a very large and expensive tow truck with the proper towing attachments to prevent damage to your rig.

In our opinion, there are really only three choices of companies for this type of insurance. They are:

- AAA RV Plus
  www.autoclubmo.**aaa**.com/memberse**rv**/**plus**RV.html
- Good Sam Roadside Assistance
  http://www.goodsamroadside.com/
- Coach-Net
  http://www.coach-net.com

We have had Coach-Net for 7 years and have used their services for towing as well as roadside assistance. They also have qualified RV technicians available to help talk you through troubleshooting on your own.

■ Extended Warranty or Service Plan

Another type of RV coverage is the extended warranty. This type of policy covers mechanical breakdowns once the regular manufacturer's warranty has expired. There are many companies in this business. Many policies or contacts are sold by the RV dealer at the time of purchase. The number of these companies are only exceeded by the number of complaints against them. Unfortunately, many of these complaints are because the customer did not read the exclusions clause in the policy. This is a list of what is not covered. Is it written into the policy that new factory authorized parts will be used? How much diagnostic time is covered by the policy? Once again, it is up to you, the RV owner to read the fine print and ask good questions.

I had a recent trip to a shop to replace a faulty turbocharger, an almost $4000 issue. My warranty company wanted to see the last 2 year's maintenance records to ensure oil changes had been done. Probably a pretty fair request. Keep good records because failure to do required maintenance can void the policy. I had less than good experiences with the extended warranty company that has since gone out of business that I received when I bought our rig. Since then I have been using the Extended Service Plan from Good Sam with great results. These are the only two companies I have heard good reports on.

- Good Sam Extended Service Plan
  http://www.goodsamesp.com
- Wholesale Warranties
  http://www.wholesalewarranties.com

■ Special RV Medical Membership Plans

We RVers can travel pretty far afield and even to foreign countries. Unfortunately, medical emergencies do happen. Your health insurance may cover you, but what about returning you to your home hospital and doctors. You could be in a place where medical assistance is inadequate and you must be transported. Enter special RV medical evacuation coverage. This is not actually insurance, but a membership in one of these companies. All the companies have different benefits and rates, but some will return you and a spouse to a place of your choice (or your home address) where you can obtain care or recuperate. This can require the use of air evacuation by a specially equipped aircraft. It can also be ground transportation by ambulance. Most will arrange for or pay for the return transport of your RV and pets as well. I have listed the major players in this very specialized but important service.

■ Skymed

SkyMed is an essential service for anyone who travels more than 100 air miles from home. If, during your travels within the SkyMed UNIVERSE you become critically ill or injured, SkyMed will return you home by air ambulance. Only SkyMed *TAKES YOU HOME* guarantees to transport you home, to your own doctors and loved ones.

Your SkyMed Traditional membership includes:

- Hospital-To-Hospital Emergency Air Transportation
- When a SkyMed member is critically ill or injured more than 100 air miles from home, SkyMed will arrange and pay for medically equipped air ambulance transportation, by fixed-wing aircraft, to the hospital nearest their US or Canadian home. Ground ambulance to and from each hospital is included.

■ **MASA Assist – Medical Air Services Association**

Platinum

Single $540.00 per year + $60.00 – onetime fee

Family $720.00 per year + $60.00 – onetime fee

Based on rates and services for residents of USA

- Emergency Air Ambulance / Medical Evacuation
- Non-Injury Transportation
- Commercial Air Transportation
- Repatriation/Recuperation
- Return Transportation
- Escort Transportation
- Vehicle Return
- Mortal Remains Transportation
- Organ Retrieval
- Organ Recipient Transportation
- Ground Ambulance – Unlimited
- Helicopter Transportation
- World Wide Coverage

■ **FMCAssist**

FMCAssist, an emergency evacuation/repatriation and emergency medical reunion benefit, is an association-paid member benefit. No sign-up required. Just join FMCA and you are covered.

FMCAssist is included as a portion of the annual dues for all full members (F), life members (L), and family associate members (A). FMCA is the only RV club to offer such a valuable benefit to its membership.

Highlights of FMCAssist include:

- emergency evacuation/repatriation
- emergency medical reunion
- return of mortal remains
- return of dependents
- RV/vehicle return (limited to North America)
- pet return.

■ Good Sam Travel Assist

Sometimes, the first healthcare facility you're taken to can't provide the quality of care that you need for your personal medical emergency. Once you arrive at a healthcare facility, contact Good Sam TravelAssist, and if the first location isn't adequate, we'll arrange to have you medically evacuated to one that is... free of charge! Considering that an air ambulance service can cost from $10,000 – $50,000, how can you afford not to have this support?

Transportation to Home Area After Stabilization

If necessary while you're hospitalized at a medical facility for an unexpected injury or illness, we'll arrange your return to your primary residence or to another medical facility nearby.

Coverage for Family Members

In addition to coverage for you, your spouse, and dependent children, Good Sam TravelAssist Premier will cover your other family members when traveling with one of you. That includes adult children and their spouses, grandchildren, parents, and grandparents.

Transportation to Join Hospitalized Family Member

Good Sam TravelAssist will provide two tickets home if your family member who is not traveling with you will be hospitalized for three or more days or passes away while you are away from home.

Transportation Home due to Natural Disaster

If a natural disaster damages you or your traveling companion's home, Good Sam TravelAssist will pay for two economy-class tickets so you can get back home immediately.

CHAPTER 48

ESSENTIAL RV ACCESSORIES

This is a list of our favorite products that we have either in or on our RV. I have tried to include links where available to make these items easier to find.

■ **Electrical Management System (EMS) Surge Suppressor**

We bought the Surge Guard 50A Hardwire – Model 34560 Rated 120/240V, 50A. We got it less than a week after we picked up our rig. This will protect all the sensitive electronics in your rig from surges and brown-outs. It and other recommended units from Progressive Industries are available on-line. There is a thirty-amp model available, as well. This can be installed by someonewho understands electrical wiring. We bought it at Camping World, but youcan check out the company's offerings at http://www.trci.net/ What follows is from the manufacturer's data sheet. This 50 amp Surge Guard product monitors shore power continuously and shuts off when it detects excessive voltage or open neutral conditions that could damage electronic equipment in your coach. Like its thirty-amp partner, the 50 amp hardwire unit is permanently installed within the bay of your coach, preventing potential theft and damage from the elements. Some additional features include: The unit provides automatic reset on power restoration. Automatically shuts off the power when the following is present: Open neutral, Low (<102V) and High (>132V) Voltage Caution indicator light indicates: Miswired pedestal, Reverse polarity, Elevated ground voltage 2 minute 15 second reset delay protects A/C compressor. 1750 Joules of power surge protection.

EMS Surge suppressors from both Surge Guard and Progressive Industries are available on-line. Here are the company websites: Surge Guard http://www.trci.net/products/surge-guard-rv and Progressive http://www.progressiveindustries.net/.

■ Battery Watering System

The first time I tried to check the water level in the battery, I almost had to remove all the large gauge wiring from the battery tops to open the cell covers. Then it was hard to see the level in the cells to the back of the battery compartment. Enter another favorite product, the Pro-Fill RV battery watering system. All the varieties of the Pro-Fill system and accessories are available on-line. Here is some material from the manufacturer: Pro-Fill On-Board Battery Watering System, 6-volt RV Edition, provides the most convenient and accurate means of filling and maintaining proper battery water levels. Hard to reach batteries are just as easy to fill as batteries on a workbench. Several batteries can be filled safely and simultaneously from a single remote position without ever having to touch a battery or remove a cap. Pro-Fill's automatic control valves ensure each cell is closed when the precise level is reached. Here is the company web address https://www.flow-rite.com/battery-watering/pro-fill .

■ Three Stage Water Filter

During our homework period before we bought our rig, I learned a lot about water quality and different methods of filtration. The best information I got was from The RV Water Filter Store at http://www.rvwaterfilterstore.com/ . These guys know their stuff. They have a store during the winter months at the Yuma, AZ, flea market. You can also order online. I decided to build a three stage filter that could later be upgraded to a reverse osmosis unit. I bought three Culligan brand canisters at a hardware store along with all the brass fittings needed to complete the project. The first has a twenty-micron sediment filter; the second has a one-micron sediment filter; and the third has a carbon block filter inside the canister. A painted steel top from the RV Water Filter Store completed the project. I've been using this setup since 2005 with no problems. Just change the sediment filters when they get discolored and the carbon filter quarterly. This system is also available completely assembled as part number Code B2304. The 2014 price is $93.95 plus tax and shipping. check it out at http://www.rvwaterfilterstore.com/WCStandardCanisters.htm

■ High Capacity RV Water Pump

We had not lived in our rig for more than a couple of months before we decided the original twelve-volt water pump was inadequate. Mainly it didn't pump enough water at a high enough pressure. It was also noisy and irritating, and it would cycle during low flow conditions. It was hard enough to try to take a shower with it, but run the sink at the same time and forget about it. The Aquajet RV was a direct replacement for our old pump and produced 5.3 gallons per minute (gpm) at sixty-five pounds per square inch (psi) of pressure. This is sufficient to give full flow with several fixtures in operation. We added a pair of two foot hoses to quiet down the operation and it hasn't given us any trouble for the five years we have had it, so it definitely made the favorite product list. It was a little expensive; they are now about $170. It is available on-line.

■ Water Pressure Regulator

Excessive pressure can cause your plumbing to leak or even rupture. It doesn't take long at high pressures to cause damage; even a fairly brief "spike" can do it. Pressure regulators are installed in your water supply line to limit the water pressure going into your RV. RV plumbing is normally tested around one hundred pounds per square inch, but you certainly don't need to use that much. Fifty to sixty-five pounds per square inch is a very comfortable pressure for faucets and showers. Parks don't always have that much, but when they do, having a regulator designed for good flow and pressure adjustability will allow you to take advantage of that better pressure without creating a problem with standard RV plumbing systems. I built my first one from a household regulator and some brass fittings. I still have it, but it is heavy. I purchased a Valterra model A01-1117VP several years ago and it's great. It is lightweight and compact. I have had to replace the pressure gauge. Other than that, it has been trouble free. The problem with these is that you have to remember to disconnect it and take it with you. I paid to have the old heavy one shipped to our next campground. Available on-line, here is the company website http://www.valterra. com/product-category/rv-products/aftermarket/.

■ Heavy Duty Sewer Hose

I have used several brands of sewer hose through the years, but none are as good as the Rhino Flex model from Camco. It has among the thickest outer coverings in the industry and the only leaks I have had were caused by me. It is certainly one of my favorite products. Don't use a weed eater anywhere near your sewer hose. Trust me on this one. I bought mine from Wal-Mart for a little over $25 and I added a ten-foot extension hose to reach out to twenty-five feet. There is a new model of the Rhino Flex out now that is crush proof, but I haven't tried it. I also have two older ten-foot sewer hoses from another manufacturer that I use when I need the extra distance. These are usually available at Wal-Mart Superstores or on-line.

■ Oxygenics Shower Head

I have no idea how we lived without this marvelous shower head. It is a favorite product of both of us. We have probably bought three or four others and they all had the same problem. When there was low camp water pressure, it was almost impossible to have a good shower. When we got this one, we couldn't believe the difference. Depending on park pressure, we had to turn it down a few times. It comes in white, chrome, and brushed nickel. Be sure to use the included wand holder too. It is made for the Oxygenics and will hold it at a great angle. These are available on-line. The company website is http://oxygenics.com/.

■ Heavy Duty Satellite Antenna Tripod

We purchased a tripod from the TV4RV Company. Their heavy duty model was designed to handle large HD dish antennas in up to fifty mile per hour winds. The legs are adjustable and there is a built in bubble level to make set-up easy. Once leveled, a compass fits in the top to orient the tripod. Then put the dish on and you will be plus or minus two degrees from the optimum signal point. Dish setup and aiming has been reduced to less than five minutes. Check them out at: http://www.tv4rv.com/

■ Catalytic Heater

We bought this heater six years ago with boondocking in mind. It turns out we use it almost exclusively instead of our gas furnaces. The unit uses no electricity and is super-efficient on gas usage. We put in a tee from the range top and ran a gas line down to the floor by the refrigerator with a quick disconnect fitting. There is a twelve-foot gas hose attached to the Wave 6 so we can position it anywhere to get good coverage. This six thousand BTU heater has kept us warm every winter since we bought it. During very cold weather, this certainly becomes a favorite product. The feet and the 90-degree gas fitting must be ordered separately. All three models of the Olympian Wave are available on-line. The Camco website is http://www.camco.net/Products/Item?prodID=10320#.VJnD9P843I.

■ Tire Pressure Monitoring System

We bought the TST Model 507 with 10 sensors to include our car. At the time we bought it, this was the only system I found with replaceable batteries. They use the button style batteries used in watches and last around 2 years. This system has provided us with peace of mind about our tire pressure and temperature while rolling. I believe a TPMS is a necessity for both motorhomes and 5th wheel and travel trailers. We have had this system in use since 2009 with no problems. We have changed the type 1632 batteries twice. This and other TST systems are available from Techno-RV Company website is http://www.technorv.com/default.asp

■ Emergency Weather Radio

Midland Consumer Radio WR-120EZ NOAA Weather Alert All Hazard Public Alert Certified Radio with SAME, Trilingual Display and Alarm Clock Public-alert certified monitor receives 7 NOAA channels with flood, tornado, thunderstorm, and other warnings SAME(Specific Area Message Encoding) alert programming sounds an alert only when specific counties are threatened 25-county memory system; 90 dB siren, voice alert, and flashing LED warning systems Uses three AA alkaline batteries for emergency power back-up in the event of power outage Built-in clock with alarm and snooze; measures 6.0 x 1.5 x 5.0 inches (W x H x D); 1-year warranty Receives 7 NOAA channels with flood, tornado, thunderstorm, and other warnings SAME programming sounds an alert only when specific counties are threatened Trilingual (English Spanish French) Compact alert monitor for weather, civil emergency, and other hazards. We bought ours at Wal-Mart and it is available on-line. Here is the Midland website https://midlandusa.com/.

■ Select Comfort Sleep Number Mattress

We decided very early on that the mattress that came with our motorhome was not going to be satisfactory for full-time use. We had a king size sleep number bead in our sticks and bricks home before we hit the road, and I'm afraid we were addicted to it. We called up Select Comfort and found out they had an RV model that met all the RVIA fire codes. We ordered it and it arrived in four boxes. We were able to wrestle the old mattress out of the rig and the new air mattress went together in less than a half hour. We love it still since it was new in 2005. The company stands behind it and sent a replacement air bladder when one of them leaked. Great, fast customer service. No question that it makes the favorite product list. We bought ours direct from Select Comfort because we wanted the fire retardant RV model. Check them out at http://www.sleepnumber.com//

CHAPTER 49

RV TRIP PLANNING

Besides the actual travel, RV trip planning can be a lot of fun. After we decide on a destination, I lay out the route in the DeLorme Street Atlas software. Then I adjust the route to include particular stops we want to make as well as particular roads we want to be on. We like to stay off the interstate highways. Then I put in the miles per gallon and the average price of fuel to get total fuel cost for the trip. I input miles per day and size of fuel tank and marks are put on the map for approximate fuel stops and overnight stops.

Next, we look at membership campgrounds along the way to save money on campground fees. At the end of this, we know our total mileage for the trip as well as fuel cost and campground nights. Obviously, all this will probably change along the way, but we have a basic budget and route.

Each evening, I input the next day's travel into the Rand McNally GPS APP running on our iPad so whoever is navigating can follow our route and see what amenities are along the way.

I've included information on the books, paper maps, APPS, and other items we use when both planning and traveling. There are hundreds and hundreds of APPS and websites you can use. I have included the ones we have found to be particularly useful.

■ RV Trip Planning Software Programs

DeLorme Street Atlas ($39.95) This is the first place I go for RV Trip planning. Although it is GPS enabled with an outboard GPS receiver, I only use it in a static mode to lay out routes and waypoints. Features include planning aids that put markers on the route for overnight stops and fuel stops according to miles per day and miles per gallon figures that I input. I bought my software as a download from DeLorme direct at http://shop.delorme.com/OA_HTML/DELibeCCtpSctDspRte. jsp?section=10120&minisite=10020 There are numerous free overlays available from the Discovery Owners Group that put icons on the map for such things as Particular brands of fuel stops, campground associations such as Passport America, and many other places RVers will be interested in.

Microsoft Streets and Trips (no longer sold or supported by Microsoft) Streets and Trips was a very popular program among RVers for travel Planning. It is very similar to the Street Atlas program and there is a Mega File of overlays containing all the Discovery Owner's Group overlays in a single file.

■ Global Positioning System (GPS) units

While there are many, many GPS units available, the best fit for RV trip planning is the RV or Truck specific models. With those, you enter your rig length, width, height, and weight. With that information stored in memory, the unit should route you over roads that can accommodate your particular rig. Unfortunately, the map database installed in these units will not be up to date. This can cause the unit to route you on roads you really do not want to be on. That is why we keep our paper maps close by. Here are some of the units available that have RV specific features:

- Garmin RV 760LMT GPS (Vehicle, 7" LCD) $350-$400 https://buy.garmin. com/en-US/US/cOnTheRoad-c518-p1.html
- Rand McNally RVND 7730 7-Inch RV GPS $355 http://www.randmcnally. com/category/rv-gps
- Magellan RV 9365T-LMB 7-Inch RV GPS $299 http://magellan. premiumstore.com/?cid=2885&chid=1600

All these and more are available on-line.

■ Paper Maps

While GPS is a wonderful technological advance, they can miss route you. This is usually due to the installed mapping being out of date. That is why we keep our paper maps close at hand. Here are the ones we use most.

Rand McNally Large Scale Road Atlas We have both the Wal-Mart and Good Sam editions of this must have publication. The Good Sam edition has colored dots for Good Sam Campgrounds. The Wal-Mart edition has several pages listing all the Wal-Mart stores.

Family Motor Coach Association North American Road Atlas This is a large scale atlas with colored markers for many campgrounds including FMCA member campgrounds. There are also marks for Wal-Marts, Sam's Clubs, Cracker Barrel restaurants, and Flying J Fuel and Travel Centers. http://www. fmca.com/home-mainmenu-1/shop-fmca-store.html

Motor Carriers Road Atlas This Rand McNally product is the map with all the low clearance bridges listed and marked. It is available at most truck stop stores as well as on-line.

■ Books for Trip Planning

We have all these books either in a basket close by the passenger seat, or in an overhead bin above the cockpit. They all get used at one time or another in the RV trip planning process and especially on the road.

The Next Exit tells you what services are available at every exit in the Interstate Highway System across the country. Here you will find fuel stops, restaurants, and all other businesses at interstate exits. Listings in red print identify big rig friendly places. available on-line.

The **Good Sam RV Travel Guide and Campground Directory** is our main source for campground listings along our routes. Number of sites, site lengths and widths along with available hook-ups, prices and amenities tell us what we need to know to select a place to spend a night or two. Available at Camping World stores.

Mountain Directory East and West is an essential source of information about mountain grades along most big rig accessible roads. The listings tell the grade length, other items such as switchbacks, and vehicle length restrictions. I use these in the initial route planning stage. These are available from the publisher at http://www.mountaindirectory.com/shop/

We also have the books from our affiliate campground associations close at hand. Most helpful is the **Passport America Catalog** of over 1800 campgrounds we can stay for half off most times. http://passportamerica.com/

■ RV Trip Planning APPS

We run all these APPS on our iPad because of its larger screen size and availability on this platform. Some folks place the screen so the driver can see it. We think that is unsafe as the driver's attention is diverted from the road. We keep the iPad in the passenger seat, or as we call it, the navigator's seat.

All Stays Camp and RV ($9.99) This is our personal favorite as it runs on our iPad using its GPS to find campgrounds and services along your route without an internet connection. Get it at http://www.allstays.com/apps/camprv.htm

Co-Pilot Live ($29.95) is another trip planning app using device GPS. It can be used without internet connection as all maps are downloaded into memory. Get it at https://copilotgps.com/us/

Camp Finder ($3-$4) makes it easy to find the right campground or RV park for you. It has information on over 18,000 campgrounds, RV parks and RV resorts across the US including National Park, National Forest, State Park, County Parks and all the privately owned ones too. You can use it at home to plan your future trips or on the road as it uses your GPS location to pinpoint campgrounds nearest to you. You can search by amenities, camping clubs and park types, read reviews, view photos to quickly find the perfect place. It is available on both the iPhone and Droid. Get it at http://www.campingroadtrip.com/camp-finder-app

iExit (free) What's coming up on the next exit? Days spent on the highway waiting for a convenient exit might have been a mystery in the past, but this app takes the guesswork out of your trip. **iExit** gives you a rolling list of available services for any interstate you are on so you can easily figure out if you have enough gas to get to the next town or is there a bathroom coming up any time soon. You can even use it maps to scroll around to find specific restaurants in the area not just the ones on your highway. This is a seriously useful app for the road tripper. The app is available on iPhone, iPad and Droid. it is found at https://iexitapp.com/

■ **Some Additional RV Trip Planning Websites**
  - Trip Advisor
    http://www.tripadvisor.com
  - Historical Marker Database
    http://www.hmdb.org
  - Bridge Hunter
    http://www.bridgehunter.com

- America's Byways
  http://www.fhwa.dot.gov/byways/
- US 101 Mile by Mile
  http://www.oregoncoasttravel.net
- Legends of America
  http://www.legendsofamerica.com
- Discover Historic Travel
  http://www.discoverhistorictravel.com/destinations/historic-sites/
- Civil War Battlefields
  http://www.civilwar.org/battlefields/
- Discover America
  http://www.discoveramerica.com/usa/states.aspx
- Landmark Hunter
  http://www.landmarkhunter.com
- Rules of the Road
  http://www.woodalls.com/articledetails.aspx?articleID=1195129
- The Milepost Alaska
  http://www.milepost.com

CHAPTER 50

RV DRIVING AND TOWING TIPS

Driving an RV is certainly much different than driving a car. The principles are the same, but the added size adds a big level of uncertainty to a novice driver. Whether you drive a motorized RV or pull a fifth wheel or travel trailer, there are many things to learn to become a safe and confident driver.

The very best advice we can give a first time RV owner is to consider driving lessons. There are several RV driver training schools around the country. The best thing is to use a web search tool like Google to check them out. We received our training at the *Lazy Days* dealership in Steffner, FL where we bought our rig. This one-day course is outstanding. One thing every driver school will emphasize is proper adjustment of your side view mirrors. Once you learn this, check for proper adjustment each day.

Now that we are trained, we're ready to hit the road, right? Not so fast neophyte RVer! There are some very important first steps to do before we head out.

■ First Steps

All important fluids should be checked before starting out on a trip. Engine oil, transmission fluid, and coolant should be at the proper levels. Learn where the dip sticks are and do this properly. If you have a generator, oil and coolant levels are important there as well. Don't forget the windshield washer fluid, too.

Next you do the walk-around. Start outside near the entry door and walk all the way around your rig starting by looking up to make sure all antennas are down and secured along with awnings and slide-out rooms. Now look at the cargo doors and be sure they are securely closed and latched, locked is best. Next we ensure the leveling jacks are totally up and stowed.

■ Tire Check

Last outside step is your tires. Check tire pressure in the morning when tires are cold. All should be within 5psi of the optimum pressure dictated by tire company charts and individual axle weight. Don't know the weight? Many folks don't. Have all axle corners weighed either by an RVSEF team or at an Escapee RV Club event or park where they have scales. This should be done as soon as you have your new (to you) rig loaded for travel. It should be done again a year later to check for overweight on any particular axle corner or side-to-side.

Do the tire pressure check with a tire pressure gauge appropriate to your tire's pressure range. It is very important that all the valve caps are in place and tightened. A great accessory is a non-contact infrared thermometer. These are available everywhere tools are sold. When you stop for gas or lunch, do a walk around and point the thermometer at each tire. Any one tire significantly warmer than the others is probably low on air. A simpler method is to invest in a Tire Pressure Monitoring System (TPMS) that reads pressure and temperature. This is a great peace of mind instrument that reads on the fly. Get sensors for every tire on truck and trailer or motorhome and towed car. Another tool I believe every RVer should have and use is a torque wrench with the proper socket(s) to maintain proper torque on the tire lug nuts. This check should be done before each trip. I got my torque wrench at a Harbor Freight store.

■ Tow Gear

There is a separate chapter on towed cars, but be sure to check out the towing gear at each stop. Look for disconnected cables and loose connections. On a towed car, check the auxiliary braking system for proper operation at this time as well.

■ Brake Check

OK, now you can go inside your truck or motorhome. Leave your partner outside for brake checks. Start the engine and cycle the turn signals and get confirmation from your outside observer. Apply parking brake only and make sure it will hold the vehicle by shifting into a lower gear and gently pulling against the brake.

For hydraulic brake equipped vehicles, do the following:

- With the engine running, apply firm pressure to the service (foot) brake pedal and hold for five seconds. The brake pedal should not move (depress) during the five seconds.

- If equipped with a hydraulic brake reserve (backup) system, with the key off, depress the brake pedal and listen for the sound of the reserve system electric motor.
- Check that the warning buzzer and/or light is off.
- Check the service (foot) brake operation by moving the vehicle forward slowly (about 5 mph) and apply the brake firmly. Note any vehicle "pulling" to one side, unusual feel or delayed stopping action.

For air brake equipped rigs, here is the procedure:

- With a fully-charged air system (typically 120 psi), turn off the engine, chock the wheels, release (push in) the parking brake button (all vehicles) and trailer air supply button (for combination vehicles) and time the air pressure drop. After the initial pressure drop, the loss rate should be no more than 2 psi in one minute for single vehicles and no more than 3 psi in one minute for combination vehicles.
- Turn the key to the on position. Rapidly apply and release the service brake pedal to reduce air tank pressure. The low air pressure warning signal must come on before the pressure drops to less than 60 psi in the air tank. If the warning alarm/signal doesn't work, you could be losing air pressure without knowing it. This could cause the spring brakes to activate suddenly. Only limited braking can be done before the spring brakes come on.
- With parking brake, (all vehicles) and trailer air supply button (for combination vehicles) released (pushed in), apply firm pressure to the service brake pedal. Watch the air supply gauge and listen for leaks. After the initial pressure drop, the loss rate for single vehicles should be no more than 3 psi in one minute and no more than 4 psi in one minute for combination vehicles. If the air loss rate exceeds these figures, have the air system repaired before operating.
- Continue to rapidly apply and release the service brake pedal to further reduce air tank pressure. The trailer air supply button (if it is a combination vehicle) and parking brake button should pop out when the air pressure falls to the manufacturer's specification (usually between 20 to 40 psi). This causes the spring brakes to come on.

- When the engine is operating at 1800 RPM, the pressure should build from 85 to 100 psi within 45 seconds in dual air systems. (If the vehicle has larger than minimum air tanks, the buildup time can be longer and still be safe. Check the manufacturer's specifications.) If air pressure does not build up fast enough, your pressure may drop too low during driving, requiring an emergency stop. Don't drive until you get the problem fixed.

- Wait for normal air pressure, release the parking brake and trailer air supply button (for combination vehicles), move the vehicle forward slowly (about 5 mph), and apply the brakes firmly using the brake pedal. Note any vehicle "pulling" to one side, unusual feel, or delayed stopping action. This test may show you problems which you otherwise wouldn't know about until you needed the brakes on the road.

The observer should see the wheels rolling freely on whatever you are towing and see the brake lights come on. Now it's time for the wife/partner/observer to come inside as well, unless you need them to spot you while you maneuver out of your parking space.

■ Cruise Control

There are times when you should not use cruise control. One of the main ones is when it is raining and the roads are wet. After the rain starts, the fine layer of oil and grease from passing traffic will lift and make the road slippery. A second rain issue is when you have very heavy rain and too much water on the road. Both these conditions make hydroplaning a possibility.

Your tires can only handle so much water on the roadway and a heavy downpour only makes it worse. Oil and grease on the road surface cancels the friction coefficient that makes tires grip the road. In either case, your rig can start spinning out and heading off the road.

Usually, we deal with these conditions by backing off the gas, not using the brakes, and steering into the skid. If the cruise control is switched on and your rig hits one of these perilous conditions, it is programmed to maintain your set speed. If the driving wheels slip because of the road conditions, it will try to increase speed to compensate. This is where very bad things can happen. How do I turn off the cruise? Tap the brake usually does that...don't do it! That can only help cause a skid. Try and be patient enough to turn the cruise control switch off. The very best thing to do is turn it off when you see that you will be coming into a rain situation.

■ Driving

A great lesson we learned is to take the long view in front of you. If you look just in front, the tendency is to constantly correct steering causing a lot of sway, or "tail wagging the dog." I try to look out about a quarter mile and see the larger picture. This will minimize steering corrections.

Driving an RV on the highway is probably the easiest thing you will do. Keep your distance from the vehicle in front of you and know your stopping distance and highway driving is a breeze. Turning on to surface streets is another thing altogether. Left turns are easiest because you can see much better where you are going. If two lanes turn, use the outside lane, it will be much more forgiving. In a motorhome, pull forward straight until the lane you are turning into is even with your left hip, then do your turn. That little towed vehicle behind you will follow along every time, don't worry about it.

■ Turning and Tail Swing

An old joke reminds us that the way to Carnegie Hall is practice, practice, practice. The same thing goes for making turns in an RV. Practice putting your RV through turns before you get in a difficult traffic situation. Use an empty parking lot, an assistant, and rubber cones to mark the pavement. Some cardboard boxes set up to simulate obstacles can help you see how easily it is to make corners. The real big issue with RV turns is tail swing.

Tail swing occurs when you steer one direction and the rear end of the rig goes the other. How's that? We can illustrate it with a pencil. In a car, tail swing isn't as big an issue. In a motorhome the rear wheels can be quite far away from the back bumper, and the effect of tail swing is multiplied. Think about getting fuel. You park close to the pump to let the hose reach, but if you don't pull forward enough, your tail swing can cause the rear of the rig to contact parts of the fuel island. Not a good way to keep your insurance premiums down. The same tail swing effect can affect towed trailers as well.

In a motorhome, your side mirrors can help you see the extent of your tail swing. Towing a travel trailer, you'll be blind on the right side as you make a left turn and vise-versa. This is where all the practice comes in. Drive your motorhome in the parking lot with a spotter ensuring you haven't "hit" your obstacle boxes. If you're towing a trailer, the only way to see what your rig can and can't do is to have someone else drive it while you stand outside and see the tail swing effect for yourself.

I hate right turns. You must pull far enough ahead so that your rear tires don't go over the curb. This takes a lot of practice, and using cones in an empty parking lot can help quite a bit.

■ Backing up

Oh boy, now the fun begins! My advice to you no matter what type of rig you have is to have an observer/spotter outside to help you back into a campsite. This will require you to have a system of communication that you both understand and will use! Kathy and I use hand signals we have practiced over the years we have been on the road. Some folks like walkie-talkies, others cell phones. No matter what, once you two are in sync with your communications, the driver must follow the spotter's instructions. The spotter can see many things the driver can't. Once again, lots of practice with cones in a parking lot can make this much easier.

Once you are in your space, driver, get out and look things over with the spotter. Make sure you are not so close to the utilities that you can't open basement doors. If there is a patio slab, make sure your tires are not on it. Have you backed up enough to park your towed vehicle or tow truck? Now get back inside and lower your jacks and open slide rooms and then turn off your noisy engine. I love the deep throaty sound of mine, but nearby campers probably don't.

I've just scratched the surface here, and we recommend you take a driving class like the RV Driving Confidence class that Lazy Days gives in their Steffner, FL location. They will teach you how to adjust your mirrors so you know where your rear tires are and other key metrics.

CHAPTER 51

CAMPING WITH PETS

Do you already have a pet, or are you considering getting a pet? It's an important decision to make. You must consider just what kind of pet(s) you have, how they will travel with you, and how you will care for them. We have seen people traveling with dogs, cats, birds, and even heard of someone who has snakes (not my favorite); but whatever you now have, it takes some consideration to travel with your pet. Not every dog or cat enjoys traveling.

There are new laws coming that may require that your pet be restrained or buckled up when traveling. We think a cage with plenty of room inside is probably the best way for both you and your pet(s) to travel. Make sure the cage is secured so it won't fly around if you have to stop quickly.

What is the right pet for you? If you are looking for one, consider whether you have any allergies or if you have a strong preference for one type or another. Make sure your current pet will be able to travel comfortably. If not, there may be a lot of friction and neither one of you will enjoy the experience. Do not take a pet with you unless you have strong feeling towards him or her. Does your pet have a great personality? Does it like traveling? Size is a big consideration. Two seems to be the limit at most RV parks. Some parks are very strict, and some are lenient. You don't want to be asked to leave a park because of your pets. What about special needs for your pet? Can you get the special food or the right medication for them while traveling? If you leave your pet in your RV for any length of time, consider having an automatic generator start installed. That way, if the power goes out, which can happen when it is very hot, your pet will have air conditioning and stay healthy.

Cats tend to be very independent and do not bark, so they could be easily left in the air-conditioned RV while you are out exploring. They do however, need a litter box, although I have seen cats being walked on a leash. That was an eye opener. Where will you put the litter box? Some have used the shower stall for the litter box and go to the bathhouse at the park. What will be your solution? Ask yourself these questions before you travel, or before you buy your RV and obtain a cat.

Dogs are easily accommodated in most RVs and RV parks. There may be some restrictions on the breed or size of the dogs. When you call for a reservation be sure to let them know you have a pet, what kind, and how much it weighs. When you check in, bring your vaccination records with you. It just saves time. I have only had 2 or 3 parks ask for the records, but it shows the manager of the park you are a responsible pet owner. Some dogs get anxious when you are not with them and will bark a lot. This is very inconsiderate to your neighbors, and it is important to keep everything friendly at the park. Bring your dog's kennel or bed and it will help with the adjustment to camp life. It will be a little taste of home for your pet. While actually traveling, it will help keep your pet safe. Grooming can be another issue. Does your pet need to be groomed, and where will you have it done? We have found that by talking to fellow RVers in the park, they will recommend a good groomer, or they will let us know if the local one is not so good. We found a great groomer in Benson, AZ, that only charged $25.00, and a pet center that charges $65.00. So, ask around to get the best one for you and your pet. Usually the park employees can also recommend someone to take care of your pet, whether you need grooming or veterinary care. Ask around before you have the need of one of these professionals.

There are many dogs and cats at your local shelter, so please consider getting an older pet from one of the local shelters. All of our dogs have been found at the local shelters, and they have been a real blessing to us.

■ Park Pet Rules

Keep your pet on a leash at all times. No matter how good your pet is, they may see some other dog or person and take off after it for no real reason. Even the best trained pet may bolt for no apparent reason. I have had this happen twice in parks. Both times, it really scared me. I was just walking my dog, and a German Sheppard was off leash in an open field, being trained. He took one look and me and my dog, and came after us. Fortunately, I turned my shoulder and he did not injure either of us. That owner threw the dog in his rig and was packed up and out of the park in about 5 minutes. I was so shocked by the whole thing I didn't report the incident. The next time, as I was walking my dog, I saw an owner who had two standard poodles off leash; when I mentioned that the dogs should be on a leash, she said that that was not a problem because her dogs never left her side. So, as I was returning from my walk and passing her RV, those two dogs came running at full speed up to me and were jumping all over me. I know they meant no harm, but it was a very unpleasant experience, especially since the first incident really frightened me. Please keep them on their leash.

Do not allow your pet to continually be barking all the time. It is so unpleasant to try and have a meal outside or to be sitting outside just enjoying the evening and there in the next camping spot is this aggressive barking, growling, and snarling dog.

Please do not leave your pet unattended for long periods of time. Dogs get bored when left alone for long periods of time and they start barking and becoming a nuisance. We leave the TV on or you could leave a radio playing. It gives the dog some sense of comfort, and makes them feel like they are not alone.

You absolutely must always pick up after your pet. You would not like to step in poop, so don't leave your dog's poop for others to step in. We keep plastic grocery bags and use them as a poop bag. Some parks will have a dog run and will have bags you can use. Please don't take a whole bunch of bags, they are for everyone to use. Leave some for others. It is so nice of the parks to supply these bags, don't abuse the privilege.

■ Here's the Scoop on the Poop

Microorganisms like whipworm, roundworm, hookworm, and coccidian thrive in your dog's poop. If the poop isn't picked up and disposed of properly, these organisms can infect the land and water, causing sickness and infections. People and pets can be affected by storm water that has been contaminated, and at some beaches the rise in bacteria levels are so high that everyone must stay out of the water. Fines for not picking up the poop can range from $100 to over $750; over 3.6 billion pounds of dog poop are produced in the United States every year. I have no idea who or how they measured this. A single gram of dog waste can contain 23 million fecal coli form bacteria. It's a simple process to pick it up. Get a plastic bag, bend over and pick it up, then tie it up and put it in the trash. I always carry two bags just in case he does a double duty. Campgrounds are becoming so fed up with pet owners who do not pick up after their pets that some are no longer allowing any pets in their parks. Please pick up after your pet.

Make sure you have some kind of ID, whether it is a tag, microchip, or a photo of your pet. They can easily get lost or forgotten. I know you are saying, "I would never leave my pet." Well, we were in a park and found this really cute Shih-Tzu up by the front office. The owners have 3 of them and thought all of them were in the fifth wheel. They had already left the park. Fortunately, there was a tag on the dog, and we were able to call the owners before they were too far down the road. The dog had slipped out the door as the couple was unhooking their rig; they pulled out, thinking all the dogs were in the rig.

■ Pet Health Records

Bring all of your records with you, in case your pet becomes ill on the road. The emergency vet you will see then knows that at the last check-up your pet was okay. Also, having the shot records is a huge help because the vet will be able to rule out some things and get right to the heart of the problem. Also, you will need this information when you are crossing the borders into and out of the United States. When crossing the borders, be sure to have the receipt of where you purchased your pet food with you. Coming back to the United States, all pet food from Canada is prohibited because of Mad Cow disease. So, if you have Canadian food just donate it to a shelter and get new as soon as you cross the border. Also, when crossing into Canada, some pet foods containing meat products (even in cans) are not allowed.

■ Aggressive Dogs

I don't want to enter into an argument about breed specific problem dogs The old rule that a dog is allowed one bite is no longer true. One study found that a dog bite can cause the owner over $16,000.00 in penalties. It's no fun for the owner or people around you to be worried about your dog biting someone. Maybe now is not the time to start RVing if you have a dog with this issue. Campsites are much closer together than homes. Some parks have banned certain breeds. You know you have a great pet, but the park does not; they may have had trouble with pets of that same breed. So be sure that the park you want to go to has no restriction, or if they do, what are they? It would not to fun to pull into a park and be turned away because of the breed of pet you have is restricted in the city or county.

Campground insurance rates are directly affected by the types of dogs accepted. Those breeds considered dangerous can raise a parks rates many thousands of dollars. Again, I don't want to get in the argument about "Dangerous dogs". This is a fact and campground owners can ill afford to have these animals in their campground no matter the specific dog's disposition. You just can't argue this.

Another issue is tying a pet outside of your rig when you are not there with the pet. This one can get you in trouble not only with fellow RVers, but park management and local animal control authorities. This may well be what you do at home, but it's not appropriate in an RV park or campground.

We love having Charlie with us. He's a 10-pound Poodle and Bichon Frise mix and what a joy; but there are times, especially when it is raining, that I wonder: is this a good idea? Going out in the thunderstorms to walk the dog can be unpleasant, but the joy of having him in our lives far outweighs that. He also has given us an excuse to meet people. If you have a friendly, well behaved animal, people love to come and pet them; then there's a chance to make a new friend. We were just in a park with a Poodle and a Bichon Frise, and Charlie is a mix of the two. It was fun to watch them run and play together. But, we have been in parks that had pets running loose and have become a real detriment to everyone's enjoyment of the campground. We have seen people kicked out of parks because they did not pick up after their pet, or the pet had become such a nuisance that the park could not allow them to remain. So, choose your pet wisely, and take care of their training and medical needs.

CHAPTER 52

SOLO RVing

Many questions are asked in social media about RVing alone. Often, someone has lost a spouse and wants to continue the traveling lifestyle. I have not seen any demographics on solo RVers, but I know there are many of them out there. When we attend an Escapees RV Club function, the Solos group is always large and quite active.

The questions that are asked are usually by women trying to decide if they can actually be a single RVer. The answer is an emphatic "Yes!" I know the idea of driving a large RV is probably intimidating, especially if the husband did most of the driving. This is where one of the many hands-on RV driving schools can help with confidence. Some things may be physically challenging, like loading a car on a tow dolly, or perhaps hooking up a fifth wheel trailer. While many singles still travel in the large rigs they used when still married, many move to smaller, easier to drive Class B motorhomes.

The common campground chores like dumping holding tanks and hooking up and leveling the rig remain and must be learned by aspiring solos. Enter the awesome RVer community that will step in and help train someone to do these things.

There are several RV clubs devoted to single RVers, including the Escapees RV Club Solo group. The Solos are a Birds of a Feather (BOF) group with special interests that is a part of the larger Escapees RV Club. Check them out at https://www.escapees.com/fun/bofs?id=323

Loners on Wheels is a club dedicated to single RVers and has members across the USA, Canada, Mexico, and other countries. The only requirement for membership is that you be legally single. The club is now in its 45th year and operates the LoW-HI RV Ranch campground in Demming, NM. Check them out at http://www.lonersonwheels.com/

RVing Women is a National network whose members come from across the

US and Canada. The group was established by and for women who are interested in RVing. Check out their website at http://www.RVingwomen.org/

The Wandering Individuals Network is another singles group interested in travelling together. This 28 year old group has no age restrictions and you don't need to own an RV. Check them out at https://rvsingles.org/

CHAPTER 53

STAYING FIT ON THE ROAD

Well, you bought the RV, sold the house and stuff, and you are now on the road to adventure. However, now you seem to have more time on your hands. It only takes a short time to totally clean the RV and you are wondering what to do next? This can cause you to get very lazy. It's so easy to start the day with a cup of coffee outside and watch everyone getting up and starting their day; there may even be some wildlife giving you morning entertainment. WOW, what a life; but you still want to stay healthy and active, and this will require some planning. Every day it is so important to do something. Walk, ride your bike, hike, jog, swim, jump rope, dance, or do yoga. Being active is a necessity; some authorities recommend 30 minutes, 3 times a week, to maintain your health. This doesn't seem like much, but with so much to do and so much to see, planning is essential. I like to get up and take a walk every morning. I am usually up by 6AM – the campground is quiet, and the sun is coming up. What a great time of the day! However, if I don't get it done then, I don't seem to get it done at all. I have seen campers doing yoga in the morning sun, riding bikes, riding a stationary bike, lifting weights, jumping rope, swimming laps, roller blading, and jogging. What will work for you? If you don't like to be outdoors, try exercise videos.

Maybe going for a hike will fill the need? Parks will usually have a list of hikes in the local area, and they are rated easy, medium, and strenuous. The National Parks are great for this; the newspaper you get when you enter will list all the hikes, rate them and then give a description of what is involved. The trail might be 3.2 miles round trip with a rise in elevation of 250 feet. Campgrounds will also have a walk laid out around the campground, so you can judge the distance and keep a record if you want. They can also recommend local hikes, and state and city parks that will fit the bill. If you are not in good shape, check with your doctor first to make sure it is okay to start some kind of program.

When I first started walking 40 years ago, the best I could do was to walk down the driveway and go one house down; but I kept at it, and each week would add one more house. Then, I started adding blocks. Today, it is easy for me to walk 3-4 miles a day. Just get started, and every week add a little more. You will feel better, and if you have a partner with you, the walk is a great chance to spend quality time together. Talk about your plans for the day, or talk about the day you had together. As you can see I love to walk, but you can find something else to do no matter what it is; as Nike says "just do it."

Eating right is really easy. Although the kitchen area is small, there is still plenty of room to prepare food. Farmers markets may be close, and since you have time, enjoy the wonders of farmers markets. Different areas of the country have different specialties. Eastern Washington State has an abundance of wonderful fresh fruits and vegetables, corn on the cob in the Midwest, tomatoes almost anywhere, and fresh shrimp along the Gulf coast. Just take a few minutes, ask and look around, and you will find everything you need to have a healthy and delicious meal. There are many wonderful cookbooks just for RVers, and going online to find a great recipe is fun. I just put in the ingredients that I have on hand, and several great meals will come up. I like the ones that recommend barbequing. That's John's job, so I (Kathy) can just sit and watch. If you have a special diet, make sure that what you need is available in the area you will be in, or if possible, order it online. Most campgrounds will accept UPS or FedEx deliveries; just be sure and ask before you have anything sent to the campground. Stock your RV with single serving healthy snacks so you are not tempted to get fast food. If you do stop for fast food, try the salads or the healthier version rather than the same old hamburger. Remember, when you are in travel mode: be sure to stop every couple of hours, get out and stretch. We go with the 3,3,3 plan: no more than 300 miles a day, stop every 3 hours to stretch, and stay at least 3 days. Of course this is the plan, sometimes it's more, and sometimes it's less. And last but not least, make sure you get plenty of rest. We try to get at least 6-8 hours of sleep a night. I don't know about you, but I get cranky when I am tired. A little planning will make the full-timing adventure fun and exciting. Keeping fit will help the adventures last longer and be much more enjoyable. See you on the trails!

CHAPTER 54

RV SHOW TIPS

We love RV shows! They are a wonderful venue in which to get information on many different brands of RVs, and on lots of RV products and services. Depending on the size of the show, there could be well over a thousand RVs of every type and hundreds of vendors all vying for your attention. Without some up front preparation, your show experience could be quite disappointing. It is easy to get lost among multiple brands and models with salesmen trying to tell you all about the virtues of their particular rig or service. If you are looking for new RVs, make sure the show you have picked will have all new rigs. Otherwise, dealers will have used rigs of many different brands all together in one location.

Would you like to attend an RV show and make the most of your precious time? We discuss strategies for before, during and after the show. We show you what to look for in an RV besides the glitz. We include a list of RV shows around the country with live links to their websites. After reading and implementing our show strategies, you won't ever come home from a show and wonder what you saw.

■ Before the RV Show

When you make plans to attend an RV show, check out the dealers and brands that will be represented. Decide early on which ones you want to look at. Most shows will have a website with show maps. Usually the particular brand will be located on that map. Print a copy and circle the areas you definitely want to visit. This will save you a lot of time and keep you focused on the types and brands you want to concentrate on. If it is a very large show and you don't have a narrow focus, you should plan on visiting the show on more than one day. This might be your only chance to see so many rigs all together for another year.

This is also the time to look up any particular vendors of RV related products you want to investigate. The show map should also have vendors listed and booth numbers indicated. Try to plot out a walking route through the show ground that will take you to all of the brands and types you have pre-selected. This will maximize your time and eliminate wandering through areas in which you have no interest.

If you are considering a towable RV, you must know the capacity of your tow vehicle, its hitch system, and the tongue and towing weight of the trailer. There are many factors at work here, and most salesmen are not competent to give you advice. We have found a wonderful website that can help you to know what will work and what will not. The site is called Fifth Wheel Safe Travel. Check it out at http://www.fifthwheelst.com/index.html . Knowing all your towing information can save you a lot of both money and grief later on. The site also has links to the towing information on most trucks sold in this country as well.

If you have already decided on one or two rigs that you might buy, make sure you have your finances set before you visit the show and start negotiating. You should have your bank or credit union pre-approve you for the financing you will need. This way you will not be swayed by the many possible finance options offered by the dealer. All this being said, we do not recommend making a buy decision in the high pressure environment of an RV show. A "Show Special Price" will be just as special back at the dealer's lot after the show. Rigs bought at a show must return to the dealership for "Prep" anyway. An RV purchase is probably the second largest thing you will buy in your life after your house. Why rush into a decision at a show when you can take your time and mull it over for a few days at home and then do the deal at the dealer's lot?

If you are a senior, the first day of many RV shows is designated as "Senior Day" and there is discounted admission. Occasionally there will be coupons at RV dealers and in newspapers for discounted admission. Try to take advantage of these cost saving measures.

Just a quick word about pets. We have seen lots of folks with dogs at RV shows, usually in wheeled stroller type carriers. I cannot imagine that a pet would be comfortable at an RV show with large crowds of people. Do your pet and yourself a favor and arrange for care for your pets on RV Show day. Pets won't be welcome in RVs displayed at the show anyway.

■ What to Bring to the Show

In order to make the most of your time at the RV Show, you should bring a few things along with you. First and probably most important is to wear comfortable shoes as you will be doing a lot of walking and climbing into and out of many RVs. At least one of you should have a backpack to carry all of the rest of the stuff you need as well as the brochures and other paperwork you will pick up during your time at the show. You may want to have a small umbrella for each of you if rain is in the forecast for show day. Bring along a small digital camera to take pictures of special features of rigs as well as a shot of the name and model number. You will see a lot of RVs in a short time, and details run together and are easily forgotten. Bring a small notebook and a pen to jot down details, prices, and other things about particular rigs. Some folks even bring a small digital recorder to make voice notes and observations.

A great addition to your "Show Kit" would be a pocket sized tape measure to determine the sizes of drawers, lengths of furniture, and many other things you may want to measure. Another small item that will come in handy is a small bright flashlight for looking into compartments, closets, and such.

Food and drinks are usually quite expensive at an RV show. Recently, we attended a show where a hamburger was $9.25. Drinks, including water, were $4.00. To avoid this, prepare snacks and bring bottled water.

If all this is too much for one person to carry, each of you should have a backpack.

■ During the Show

If possible, attend the show on a weekday. The crowds will be smaller. We try to be as early as possible and arrive early enough to get a good parking space close to the gate. This is where a strategic plan comes into play. Plan to see the RVs you are possibly interested in purchasing first before the crowd gets too large. That way you will have the salesmen's attention and get the best information while both you and the sales folks are fresh. Next you want to look at RVs you are less interested in. If you have no intention of buying and only want to see what's new, all bets are off. Wander around and have a ball. Do remember to use the camera and notebook, though. We usually are looking at things we can implement in our own rig. For that reason, we always visit vendors of RV furniture and accessories.

Use the camera and notebook to record details you might otherwise forget after looking at many similar rigs. Make sure to gather brochures on the models you are most likely to buy. If you don't see any literature, look in the storage compartments above the sink. That is a favorite storage place. If you still can't find what you want, ask the salesmen from that particular brand or dealership. At larger RV shows, there will probably be representatives from the RV factory there to answer questions. I have found these folks to be much more helpful in answering specific questions about that particular brand than the dealership sales force. We have even met 2 company presidents at RV shows.

■ Looking at RVs

Usually, the things that attract immediate attention are the floor plan and exterior styling. I'll start with the exterior. Look for the type of roof material. Rubber, or EPDM, will require more maintenance than fiberglass or aluminum. It will also only have a service life of about 10 years. Look at the outside access to storage. Are the doors easy to open and close, and do they latch securely? What about access to batteries, leveling systems, and inverter if so equipped? If it is a motorized rig, is there easy access to service items such as air, oil, and transmission filters and dipsticks.? Can you reach the electrical inverter if so equipped? How about the amount of exterior storage? Pass-thru storage compartments hold much more than the molded plastic bins on most rigs. Look closely at the fit and finish of all exterior body panels and other items such as mirrors and awnings. Look at how easy (or difficult) it will be to access and service the generator if there is one.

Above all, the layout or floor plan should work for your family's needs and camping style. If you cook most meals inside, make sure there is plenty of usable prep space. You will need plenty of pantry space to store food items. If there is a gas oven and a convection/microwave, will you use both? Storage is king. Does the galley area provide enough space to store all your pots, pans, and utensils? Pretend you are cooking a meal. Go through the steps and determine if the layout will work for you. Does the refrigerator have enough space as well as freezer space? Make sure the dinette is large enough for everyone who will be eating inside.

Look in the bedroom for storage. Are there enough drawers and wardrobe closets for your clothes? Look at the mattress. Is it a standard size? A normal queen bed is 60" x 80". Short queens or beds with rounded corners are very hard to find sheets for. Each of you should lay on the bed. How much room is there to get up and get dressed? Look at the bathroom space. Have the tallest member of the family stand in the shower to see if he or she can get a comfortable shower. Ensure there is enough medicine cabinet space for your needs.

Is there enough comfortable seating in the living area? If the unit is motorized, can the driver's and passenger's seats be turned around and be used while parked. Look at the TV from the living room seating. Do you have to turn your head to see it, or can you look straight ahead at it?

The best advice we can give is to try to envision you and your family actually living in the rig. This is much more important than how big the TV is or aesthetic things. After all, you are buying it to use, not just to look at.

Try to avoid discussions with sales staff about price and financing. This can be quite time consuming and should be left for a dealership visit. Your main job at an RV show should be to sort out the many similar brands to determine the one that will fit your needs and budget.

Once you have explored all the rigs you are interested in, stop for refreshment and check your notes. Make sure you haven't forgotten any brands or model numbers before moving on.

■ Vendors

Now it's time to see the vendor area and look at all the stuff they have to offer. This is where the backpack will really come in handy. If you buy heavy and/ or bulky items, most vendors will be able to assist you in getting the articles delivered to your car. Visit the vendors in which you are most interested first to conserve time. Be sure to check out the campgrounds and campground companies for special promotions. We have landed numerous free 1 week stays as well as a month in Florida in December for $199, a really awesome price. Many of the larger shows will have almost a complete Camping World set up in the vendor area. If you are time constrained, skip this area as you can always visit a Camping World Store or shop there on-line. It goes without saying that any time you fill out a form to win something, you are putting yourself on a mailing or other contact list. Do not be surprised to get email from vendors you did not even visit. The lists are often sold.

■ Seminars

Many shows offer seminars on all aspects of the RV lifestyle. A lot of these are excellent and you will learn much. Take notes, especially website information for later use. Other seminars are really infomercials about the speaker's product or service. These can be interesting, but remember that the presenter has competition with similar products. The seminar schedule should be available on the website with show information. Part of the strategic plan is to fit the seminars into your now very busy schedule.

If you have any time left, you could visit the rest of the vendors or even a few more RVs. Sometimes there will be entertainment scheduled for the afternoon or evening.

■ After the RV Show

Once you get home you will probably be quite tired after all the walking and climbing in and out of numerous RVs. Wait a day and then lay out all the material you collected. Separate it by brand and floor plan. Dig through it all until you narrow your choices down to 2 or 3 rigs. Look at all the specifications as well as the layout. Make sure the rig has the cargo carrying capacity to haul all your stuff without exceeding the vehicle gross weight rating. If you are looking at towable RVs, make sure your tow vehicle and hitch can handle the weight

Go to the manufacturer's websites of the rigs you like. That is where you will find detailed specifications on each model number and floor plan. This is also where you will find the all important weight limits. Check out the glossary of towing terms for definitions of the important measures.

At this point, if you are ready, you can go to a dealer with confidence that you know which rig you want to buy that will fit your family's camping style.

■ A List of Major RV Shows

- Chicago RV Show
  http://www.chicagorvshow.com/
- Florida RV Shows
  http://www.frvta.org/rv-shows/
- San Francisco Bay Area RV Show
  http://www.rvshow.net/RV_show.html
- Hershey, PA RV Show
  http://www.prvca.org/default.aspx?tabid=59
- York, PA RV Show
  http://www.yorkrvshow.net/
- South Texas RV Show
  http://trva.org/
- Michigan RV Shows
  http://www.marvac.org/marvac-rv-shows.html
- Recreational Vehicle Industry Association (RVIA) shows 85 shows listed
  http://www.rvia.org/?esid=rvshows&all=1

CHAPTER 55

RV UPGRADES

No matter what RV you have, there will be things you will want to change, or improve. Many folks buy older RVs with the intention of changing everything in them to make the RV work for them. There is a growing movement to totally gut out older Airstream trailers and being them back to modern tastes. No matter what the reason, RV upgrades can change your RV from awful to awesome.

■ Flooring

Changing RV flooring is probably the most popular of the RV upgrades done to older RVs. With the introduction of luxury vinyl and wood laminate flooring materials, the job is well within the reach of the do-it-yourselfer. There are however, some considerations to take into account.

Color selection is very important. If your rig has dark cabinetry such as a dark cherry, a dark wood floor might make the rig seem too dark. The same thing applies with light cabinetry and light flooring. Try to find a pleasing balance.

Many rigs use sliding pocket doors. The bottom latches must be modified for the additional floor height so the doors will latch properly again.

When the new floor is higher than the original, things may not fit without adjustment. You must be aware of the clearance required by slide-out rooms so they operate smoothly.

Once the original floor covering is removed, check the subflooring very carefully for wood rot from water leaks. Any soft spots will have to be replaced. The subfloor should also be level before installing the new floor material. If you are doing vinyl or wood planks, ensure the lines are perpendicular to the length of the rig. This is the time to be doubly sure you have removed the hundreds of staples the RV manufacturer put in with a staple gun.

Be very aware of the total weight of the removed material vs. the weight of the new material. You must have enough gross vehicle weight rating available for the upgrade. This is especially important when you are installing tile.

If you are installing new carpeting, be very careful of how it fits around the edges of slide-out rooms where they move in and out so they do not bind. Adding thicker carpet padding will also mean adjustment to sliding door latches.

There are many, many videos on YouTube all about RV floor material replacement. Here are a few:

▶ https://www.youtube.com/watch?v=b5MgGW9gfYc
▶ https://www.youtube.com/watch?v=B6O9z_cG-jQ
▶ https://www.youtube.com/watch?v=jp9wKK0wuhQ

■ TV Replacement

TV replacement is up there with floor upgrades among the top RV upgrades. Older rigs have older tube type televisions that cannot receive current digital over-the-air signals. We can thank the electronics industry for coming up with the light weight flat screen TV to make our life easier doing the change out. Once the old TV is out, there will be a pretty large opening to be filled. Many folks make a hinged door and mount the new TV on it. That gives them some much needed bonus storage space. If you are doing a furniture upgrade as well, you might consider putting the TV on a lift called a "televator" that resides behind a cabinet or sofa only to rise majestically when needed as a TV. I hope you or a friend have good carpentry and cabinet making skills for that one. You won't run into a weight problem with this upgrade either as the flat screen TV's weigh far less than the earlier Tube TV's.

■ Mattress Replacement

Let's face it, most RV mattresses are not very high quality and some are downright lousy. Even the memory foam mattresses that come with some higher end rigs need some help to be comfortable. The trick here is to know the size mattress you have already. Many rigs have "RV Queen" beds that are only 75" long instead of the standard 80". Some have rounded corners to allow you to move around the bed. Just remember whatever you get, you will need sheets that fit it.

We were very fortunate to have a standard 60x80 queen bed in our rig. We replaced it with a Sleep Number bed by Select Comfort that was designated for an RV model because it has a flame retardant cover. Then we added a 4" memory foam topper and we both sleep like babies.

NOTE: Air beds will inflate at higher altitudes, so you might think about letting some air out before you head up into mountainous regions.

I have read where folks have cut memory foam mattresses to accommodate rounded corners, but you still need sheets to fit it.

■ Curtains, Shades and Window Treatments

Many RVs come with curtains and window treatments that only a designer could love. Here's where the RVer who's handy with a sewing machine can make a huge difference in how your rig's interior looks. The side windows usually come with the dreaded "Day-Night shade." These things are almost always too tightly strung and are hard to move up or down. Two or three times up and down can cause a string to break and now you have a 2-foot-tall shade that just became six feet long and must be restrung. The day-night shades are also horrible dust collectors and are as hard to clean as they are to adjust.

Enter the roller shade. You can buy common roller shades from any hardware store and install them yourself. The more elegant solution is to get specially made RV roller shades with dual rollers, one opaque for no-see-in nighttime use and daytime privacy shades on the other roller. We replaced several of our day-night units with roller shades from the MCD Corporation. http://www.mcdinnovations.com/ The measuring instructions on their website made it quite easy to order what we wanted and the installation was very easy using videos from the same website.

Often the shades are mounted inside a fabric covered wood backed valence with contrasting side pieces called "lambrequins". We removed the lambrequins and it opened up the entire look of the windows. These valences can be recovered quite easily with the material of your choice. If you like the all wood look, valences constructed of fine wood are also available.

■ Kitchen and Bathroom RV Upgrades

Many newer RVs have nice tile back splash areas around the stove top and sink and even in the bathroom sink areas. This is a popular option in houses as well. There are several products available to help you get that custom look in older rigs.

Ceramic wall tiles come in an extensive array of styles and colors. To use ceramic wall tile, you must take the added weight into consideration as well as the backing material. Most conventional wall board cannot accommodate the weight of the heavy tile and added grout. You can use standard drywall material and add the tile over it, but the added thickness may not work in all applications.

A quick and easy solution is the Smart Tile stick-on wall tiles, made of a plastic material that is light weight and wipes clean with a damp cloth. These come in squares approximately 1 foot on a side. They can be cut with a scissors or craft knife and make a very professional looking installation. These Smart Tiles are available at many hardware stores.

Here is the company website
► http://www.thesmarttiles.com/en/
Here are step by step directions from one RVer
► http://www.doityourselfrv.com/installing-smart-tiles-smart-way-real-tile-look/

A quick and easy upgrade (if you have a very basic understanding of plumbing) is to replace the kitchen and bathroom faucets that come as original equipment on RVs. The holes fit standard household type fixtures. We decided to add a pull-out sprayer fixture in the kitchen and an upgraded unit in the bathroom.

While you are upgrading the bathroom fixtures, consider upgrading that original shower head. Many RVers change over to the Oxygenics brand units. They aerate the water and provide a robust shower using less water. They are especially good when you have low campground water pressure.

■ Furniture Replacement

Replacing your RV furniture is another of the more common RV upgrades. Much of the installed RV furniture is uncomfortable and sometimes just plain ugly! We replaced our booth style dinette with a custom made credenza with a pull-out Table that will seat 5 comfortably. We had it designed with 2 laptop computer drawers and 2 file drawers. The top is 18 inches deep and allows us to run our business with storage for our printer and recording equipment.

This dining credenza was made by Carl Lehman at Focal Wood Products in Nappanee, IN. He has many styles and furniture pieces and he can easily duplicate the wood stain to match what is already in your rig. http://focalwood.com/

Many folks, including us, absolutely hate the convertible sofa bed. We have few overnight guests, so we replaced it with 2 Lazy boy recliners. You should be very careful about the weight of your replacement furniture being very close to the weight of what was removed. This is especially important when replacing items in a slide out. Another important consideration with replacing sofas is loss of seatbelts. We had 2 seatbelts in our sofa. Now we only have seatbelts on the 2 front seats. If you travel with your kids, this could be a deal breaker.

Some of the best constructed and most comfortable RV chairs and sofas are made by an Amish company near Shipshewanna, IN called Lambright Comfort Chairs. They are specifically made for RV use and are available in narrow widths to fit almost anywhere. Unfortunately, they don't have a website, but they do sell to many RV refurbishing companies.

■ Changing to a residential model refrigerator

OK, you are tired of the poor performance of your RV absorption refrigerator. You are also wary of the possibility of a refrigerator fire. So you decide to replace the RV refrigerator with a residential unit. Here are the major steps.

Measure Twice, Cut Once

There are several major issues to contend with if you are contemplating changing over to a residential refrigerator. First you must very carefully measure the current refrigerator opening. Your most important measurement will be depth with the doors off. You will most likely have to look for a "Counter Depth" residential unit. You must also measure the distance from the new unit door to anything that may interfere with it. There will usually be some room to "adjust" for differences in height and width. That is why French door models are preferred. The Samsung counter depth 18 cubic foot bottom freezer unit is very popular.

While doing these measurements, take into consideration the width of the RVs door. Will the new unit fit through it? If not, you may have to remove the driver's side window assembly to both remove the old unit and receive the new one.

Go Shopping

Now that you have the measurements, it's time to shop for the new unit. You will also have to decide if you are capable of doing this work yourself. Considering the weight of refrigerators, most folks have this job done by professionals at an RV repair and refurbishment company.

Removal

The old refrigerator comes out from the inside. A small mover's dolly modified to the height of the bottom shelf helps quite a bit. First you must disconnect 12 Volts, 110 volts, Propane line (Turn Propane off), and ice maker line if so equipped. Depending on the maker of the RV, there will be more or less screws securing the refrigerator to the cabinet. Some screws may be reached from the top of the flue above the refrigerator. Then pull it into the rig. Do not remove the cooling unit on the back as caustic ammonia gas can escape. Take the doors off. That will make it thin enough to go out the door or window. You will need help with all this. Find a way to cap off the propane line. A special cap fitting for this is available at most hardware stores. Also, you must terminate the 12 volt wires with wire nuts so they do not short together.

Out with the Old and in with the New

Be sure to measure the door opening carefully. You may have to remove the door entirely as well as remove seats or other obstacles. It is possible that the door opening is just too small. Then you may have to bring the old unit out and the new one in through a window or even a windshield. Take the doors off the new refrigerator and bring it in. Again the movers dolly will be helpful. While the modifications to the opening are being made, power up the new unit and put your food in it. It may be several days before it will be moved into the opening.

Move the new unit near the hole. Connect the ice maker water line and the power cord. Lift it up and place it in the opening. Push it back as far as needed. Next, find a way to secure the unit at the top and bottom so it won't fall out when your rig is moving. Put the trim back on, and turn the unit on. Try to find a way to secure the doors during transit and you are home.

Later on you might consider connecting the refrigerator to a circuit that is on the inverter so it will run normally when moving. Some residential refrigerators will need a pure sine wave inverter to operate properly. If you have one, fine. Otherwise, you can obtain a 1000W pure sine wave inverter for around $200. Wiring should be left to professionals for this step.

Most residential units require 1.5 amps to operate, 3.5 when the defrost heaters are on, and 3 amps when the compressor cycles. If you will be boondocking, look into adding batteries to the existing battery bank.

Here are the before and after pictures of a refrigerator upgrade I helped on for my friend Nick Russell's rig. The after picture is before the trim replacement was added. This new Samsung RF 18 refrigerator came in through the front door.

▶ http://www.didelot.com/phaeton_mods/residential.html
▶ http://wheresweaver.blogspot.com/2010/09/residential-refrigerator-installation.html

■ Interior and Exterior Painting

You can make a huge difference in your RV by painting the interior and/or exterior. Interior painting can be pretty easily done with careful preparation just as at home. Even wood cabinets can be painted, but the preparation must include de-glazing the surface so the paint will adhere correctly. There are a lot of chemicals to do this with and the best advice I can give is to visit a paint store for the right material. A lighter colored interior paint job can dramatically brighten a normally dark interior. Repainting dark wood cabinets can do this as well. While you're at it, think about replacing the cabinet hardware. We did ours and just that made a big difference in the look of the interior.

Exterior painting can also dramatically change the appearance of your rig. This treatment is quite expensive starting around $10,000 and up to over $30,000. This can make an older rig with oxidized surfaces look just like new and also be easier to maintain. Make sure to get at least 2 coats of clear coat finish applied and 4 is better.

Shop around for paint jobs as there are many places that advertise this work. Get references from folks that have had it done.

Here are some I know and recommend:

▶ http://www.phoenixpaintinc.com/Pages/default.aspx Edwardsburg, MI
▶ http://www.precisionpaintingrv.com/ Bremen, IN
▶ http://mastertechrv.com/ Elkhart, IN

■ Solar installation

Many folks like to camp off the grid; can you say boondockers? There are many books and websites devoted to solar power, so I'll just give the basics.

Good planning is the key to a successful solar installation. You must decide how much power you will need for the electric appliances you need as well as the 12 volt loads you must compensate for. You should arrive at a figure in watts, which is a measure of power.

Then you decide how many and which type of solar panels can provide enough power to keep your batteries charged based on how much you will discharge them each day. If your rig has only two 12 volt batteries, consider adding at least 2 more to provide some reserve. In between the solar panels and the batteries, you must have a charge controller capable of providing for the size of the solar panel array. The best advice I can give is to contact the folks below. They are the recognized experts in this field.

▶ http://amsolar.com/

■ Adding Slide-out Rooms

This is the one of the ultimate RV upgrades to an older RV. Slide outs provide more room for living, but add to the weight of the RV. You must be sure your rig has enough gross vehicle weight rating(GVWR) to handle the added weight. Typically, this upgrade is done on older diesel rigs that can handle that weight. Figure on at least 15 to 20 thousand dollars or this upgrade. It makes sense if you will be keeping the rig and using it on a regular basis. There are several companies that will do this work, but the only one I know and trust is Master Tech RV in Elkhart, IN.

▶ http://mastertechrv.com/

■ For the tool challenged non Do-It-Yourselfer

Many of these RV upgrades can be accomplished by RVers with some knowledge of tools and some sense of adventure. If you are not one of these, here are some companies we have visited that can do many of these upgrades:

▶ http://mastertechrv.com/ Elkhart, IN
▶ http://www.rvdecor.com/pages/ Yuma, AZ
▶ http://www.braddandhall.com/productcart/pc/home.asp Elkhart, IN
▶ http://daveandljs.com/ Woodland, WA

CHAPTER 56

STORING YOUR RV

You've had a great camping season with your RV, but now it's time to store it away for the winter until next spring. There are some steps you can take to make next spring a pleasure instead of a panic.

Where will you store that rig that has given you such pleasure? The very best place is a heated barn or garage that is totally enclosed from winter weather. Unfortunately, that just isn't in the cards for most of us. Next best is a covered storage facility. The general idea here is to keep your rig from the harsh weather and ultra violet rays that can prematurely age many components of your rig.

A cover is certainly a possibility as long as it is "breathable". That way moisture will not condense under the cover and cause mildew and mold. Moisture intrusion is probably the biggest cause of damage to stored RVs. Set a container or two of Damp Rid or Dri-Z-Air inside your rig to absorb any moisture that does intrude. It is possible to run a de-humidifier, but it must be emptied of accumulated water and must be powered for months on end. Commercially available desiccants like those already mentioned should do the job.

Another issue with covers is that they rub on the paint where they come in contact and can possibly do damage unless the cover is firmly trapped and won't flap in those cold winter winds.

Once you decide where to store your RV, wash it thoroughly. If there is already mold, it will grow like wildfire all winter. Make sure the rig is completely dry before storing it inside or under a tarp or RV cover. Put some graphite lubricant in all the locks so they will be easy to open come spring.

Ensure your tires are pumped up to the proper pressure and lubricate wheel bearings before storage. If you store outside, consider covering your tires with light colored material to cut down on UV damage.

If you have a motorized rig, you have a little more work to do to prepare for storage. Fill the fuel tank and add a fuel stabilizer to preserve the fuel such as Sta-bil among others. Specific treatments are available for both gas and diesel engines.

It is best to change the oil and oil filter on the engine and the generator before you store for any length of time. Acid can build up in older oil and can corrode bearings. Be sure to check the antifreeze in the cooling system to be sure it can protect your engine down to any low temperatures expected. Make sure the windshield washer fluid has antifreeze in it or just drain the reservoir. This might also be a good time to do a chassis lubrication.

Batteries on both motorized rigs and trailers must be prepared for storage. If you must leave them in your rig, make sure they are fully charged and the liquid level is above the plates. Then disconnect the positive side of the battery or battery bank to keep on board systems from discharging the battery. My feeling is that the best way to care for batteries is to remove them and store them in a dry place and keep a trickle, or maintenance charger on them. Be sure to make a diagram of all the wires you disconnect so it can go back together in the spring.

Your fresh water system must also be prepared for storage, especially when freezing temperatures are likely. First, sanitize the fresh water tank with 1/4 cup bleach per 40 gallons of capacity. Then fill the tank and let it sit for a few hours. Then turn on the electric water pump and open the faucets one at a time until you smell the bleach. Don't forget the shower, toilet(s), and the outside shower if so equipped. Next drain the tank completely, fill it up again and run the water out all faucets and other openings until you cannot smell the bleach. Again drain the tank completely. Next follow the winterization procedures in Chapter 10.

Let's talk critters. Your nice big dry rig will look very inviting to all sorts of critters during the cold windy winter season. Mice, rats, raccoons, and other such critters would love to build a nest and spend the winter there. For that reason, check your RV very carefully for any possible opening. If you can poke your finger in, a mouse will enter. Along with snakes, insects and others. Squirrels are probably the worst as they can enlarge any small opening to gain entry. The damage these critters can do to your RV can cause a total loss if they are in there for any length of time.

Fill outside holes with brass or aluminum wool. It won't rust away the way steel wool will, and will block the opening. You can use a foam insulation material, like Great Stuff™ to fill smaller holes and cracks.

Put insect traps, ant bait and mouse traps around anything that touches the ground. Please do not ever place poisonous baits inside your RV. The critter will die in there and you may never get the smell out. You might even put them up on the roof if your rig is stored under trees. While you are on the roof, make sure all vent covers are securely closed and there are no cracks or other places critters can get in. You should consider having covers for your air conditioners so nothing enters there.

Be meticulous in cleaning the inside of the rig before you store it. Thoroughly clean the insides of all your cabinets and drawers. It only takes a crumb or two to attract a family of critters. You should also clean out your refrigerator of everything and scrub all the walls and shelves. Put a small box of baking soda inside to absorb any lingering odors and block the door open. I would remove all food items including canned goods. Once you get it home, check the date codes. You may be surprised how many are out of date.

Besides food items, take out all the stuff in the bathroom cabinets like toothpaste and other creams and other things that might be attractive to critters.

A stored RV is a temptation to 2 legged critters as well as those I already mentioned. Remove that flat screen TV and other easily stolen electronics. Batteries are also a tempting target for thieves, another reason to remove them and keep them maintained. If you have a trailer, purchase a good quality heavy duty hitch lock. There are locking products for 5th wheel kingpins also.

Go visit your stored rig from time to time, especially after severe weather. If you live in heavy snow country, go and brush off that heavy snow load from the rig's roof, you'll be glad you did.

At this point, your rig should be in good shape come spring and you won't find any unpleasant "surprises."

Of course, you will have to reverse most of this in the spring. That is when you must carefully check for any moisture intrusion and formation of mold. Hopefully you won't have to clean up after any critters.

CHAPTER 57

LESSONS LEARNED

Many of these lessons learned were done personally; some were learned by other folks who passed on the wisdom to us. Most of these were those "Ah Ha" moments that we remember oh so well.

■ Awnings

I love our awnings. They give us shade and privacy, and occasionally grief. Automatic wind sensors that are supposed to retract your awning when the wind reaches about twenty-five miles per hour do not always work.

It doesn't matter how many straps and hold downs you have; wind can destroy an untended awning very quickly.

The lessons learned here is to never, never leave your campsite without securing your large, expensive awning.

Always remember to check that the awnings are secure either when closed or open.

When leaving a campground in Oregon, our small awning over the left side of the rig was left out. The site was a little tight and the trees were close to the right side of the rig. So after putting the umbilical's away, John pulls out and I'm following in the car. I notice that the awning is out and I'm honking and yelling about the awning and people are pointing to it, but John just keeps rolling along. Fortunately, he had to pull over to hook up the car and we were able to store it properly.

We once saw a big rig pull out of a campground and the large, expensive, automatic awning on the passenger side was open. As he turned the corner it hit a light pole and the whole awning was ripped off of the RV. The sound was awful and, of course, everyone was looking. The expense of repair was in the thousands. Several lessons learned. Do a walk around before traveling and double check just to be sure everything is put away and stored. This includes the crank-up TV antenna, as well.

■ Cellular Phone Service

We have had a Verizon cell phone long before we started RVing. We were lucky because Verizon has had service almost everywhere we have been across the country. The other major cellular providers don't seem to have as good nationwide service. There are gaps, however, especially in sparsely populated areas in the west. We have to put up a podcast file every week, and we need reliable phone service for our Verizon air card. We once drove around Yellowstone National Park trying to get at least 2 bars of signal on our cell phone so we could upload our Podcast. Our solution was to add a Wilson wireless amplifier to boost weak signals. It works quite well, but among the lessons learned are that you can't amplify no signal at all. You may have to drive to a town to get phone service. Lessons learned: Do not trust the coverage map for your phone service, and have a backup plan.

■ Entry Steps

I don't seem to have trouble going out of the rig – it's the coming in. Twice now I have fallen into the rig, mainly because I have had too much stuff in my hands. The first time I really cut up my hand as I fell and hit the metal steps. The second time, I was on the last step and was wearing sandals, and the sandal caught on the step, and down I went, groceries and all. What a mess and not a pretty sight. Remember to have a light load coming into the rig. Lessons learned: Don't take more than you can handle into the rig. Actually, always take a little less than you think you can handle.

■ Evacuation Plan

We have never had to evacuate because of a weather event or other natural disaster. Many RVers have, however. As I write this, fires are sweeping through Utah and are causing numerous evacuations. Severe weather seems to be the biggest problem we will normally face. We have gone through several hail storms in South Dakota where we moved to a bath house to avoid broken glass from the large hail stones. There are several lessons learned from severe weather. First, have a weather radio and have it on standby at all times. Find out what county you are in when you arrive at a campground. Program it and surrounding counties into a radio equipped with Specific Area Message Encoding. When threatening weather is approaching, go to a bathhouse or clubhouse of block construction. Have a "Go" box with insurance information for your rig and car as well as a supply of required medications and a cell phone. Take the GO box with you. Find these substantial buildings as soon as you arrive at a campground, and plan how you will get to them. Do not stay in your rig during severe wind events. Straight line winds can tip even the heaviest motorhome.

■ Fueling

After having to wash diesel fuel off my hands several times, I learned to have a pair of gloves specifically for fueling in an easy to reach place.

Although many commercial truck stops have RV islands, I don't use them anymore. They tend to be a tight fit and the pumps seem to run much slower than at the truck pumps. We have also had to wait while other less considerate RVers sit at the pump while they have lunch.

■ Lessons Learned About Holding Tanks

Oh, where do I start? When you buy a used rig, be very careful the first time you dump. Start with gray water for a short time to check for leaks around the valves. If there are some, don't try to pull the black valve unless you are ready to clean up the mess that will form in the bottom of your service bay.

Next, buy the sewer hose with the thickest side-walls you can find. Pinhole leaks tend to become larger as more "stuff" flows down the line. Also stay far away from any sewer hose with a weed-eater. It just isn't pretty when you don't realize how many little slices you just took into that thick walled hose.

The first accessory you should buy and place immediately after the valve assembly is a short, clear plastic section so you can see just what is flowing out of those tanks. You'll be really glad you did.

Have plenty of disposable rubber gloves as they tend to rip easily. You might even spring for a pair of heavy duty neoprene gloves. Just wash them thoroughly after you use them. For that matter, wash everything in your service bay remotely connected to dumping holding tanks at least every time you use it. This isn't funny; you can contract some very nasty infections from cross-contamination with fecal matter. Also, don't store your drinking water hose or water pressure regulator in the same compartment as your sewer hoses and accessories.

Get plastic caps for each end of every length of sewer hose you carry and use them. Even clean sewer hoses smell like, well, you know.

If your campground sewer connection is not the screw-in type, make sure you have adequate weight on the end of the hose that goes into the ground. If you don't, you may do everything right, and as soon as you pull that black tank valve, the business end of the hose will jump out of that hole like a cowboy being bucked off a horse. It's hard to describe how fast a flood of nasty, smelly, brown sludge will spread all over the ground before you can close the valve. Let me tell you, at that time, feeling helpless is the least of your problems. I filled two old sweat socks with gravel and tied them together. They do the trick, but I still keep a close eye on the ground fitting.

Here's a classic among lessons learned the hard way by someone else. When flushing your black tank with an installed tank flushing system, pay close attention to how long you leave the water turned on with the black valve closed. If you manage to fill the black tank and the toilet seal holds, the only outlet for all that pressurized sludge is up the vent pipe to the roof. If it doesn't hold, you'll see it running down your steps. I just don't even want to think about cleaning that mess up.

■ Disconnecting Fresh Water

You are all set to pack up and leave the campground and now it's time to disconnect and stow the fresh water hose. Not so fast young grasshopper. When you turn off the park fresh water supply either by a pump handle or a rotating spigot, there is still pressure in the RV water system. If it is a really hot day, you might enjoy a short, intense shower, but usually you want to stay dry and go drive your rig. I put a "Y" connector at the output side of the water pressure regulator to attach a water hose for washing or other use while in camp. Get out of the way and open the valve on the unused side and pressure will be relieved out of that port. Yes, this has happened to me twice. It's really hard to laugh at yourself when you are soaking wet and mad to boot and you write about lessons learned.

Once you roll all the water out of the hose and roll it up, connect the ends together to keep it clean. Next lesson learned is to remember to unscrew the water pressure regulator. It is quite expensive to ship these around the country. Be sure and store it with the hose in a compartment without sewer hoses.

■ Hooking Up Your Toad

Lessons learned here are: Practice, practice, practice. There are a number of steps that must be performed to successfully hook up a towed car to a motorhome. Almost without fail, you, the new RVer will have to do this in front of an audience at the check-in. There will also likely be someone behind you waiting to check in. They will be staring at you, too. Our recommendation is to find a church parking lot or an unoccupied large store lot and practice the unhooking and the hooking up. Do it enough times so you both can work together and get it done right every time. Avoid the embarrassing fumbling in front of the appreciative audience.

This lesson also applies to hooking up your rig once you have parked in your campsite. Practice enough so you know where everything is located, and develop a checklist for hooking up.

Whether unhooking or hooking up your toad, or setting up your campsite, there will often be well-meaning folks who either want to talk or to "help." Do not let this happen. You WILL become distracted and forget an important step in the process. Try to be tactful and explain you have a system and you will talk to them after you are finished. Imagine you are almost done hooking up and are about to put the weight on the end of your sewer hose when the next door neighbor comes over to talk. I don't have to tell you again the possible consequence of not having weight on the park connection.

■ Kitchen

I seem to have most of my lessons learned at the kitchen. I like to make a protein shake, and I have a little top heavy stick blender. So, thinking I could leave it in the container and go get some more ice... let's just say the whole floor was mopped that day more than once, and the dog was full of energy. Lesson learned: Never think you are smarter than the law of gravity

I just love our smoke detector; it makes a wonderful noise, especially when I am cooking. They seem to place the smoke detector right above the stove, so any time I cook, that noisy thing goes off. Of course, I never remembered to unplug it when I cook, so every time I would cook something on the stove, the racket would start. John, the gadget man, comes in on his white horse to rescue me. He does research on the internet and finds a smoke detector that can be disabled by a push of the button for about 10 minutes. Lesson learned: There is always an answer to the problem – you just have to find it. It's usually on the internet.

■ GPS Lies

We were on an interstate highway looking for fuel. My GPS and the Next Exit indicated a stop coming up and I saw the sign for it just ahead. Unfortunately, at the end of a pretty narrow road we ran into a barrier with "Closed" and "Out of Business" signs on it. The weeds in the road said the place had been out of business for quite some time. Well, we unhooked the car and I was able to make a fifteen point turn to go back the way we had come. Several lessons learned here, but the main one is to not get yourself in a place you can't turn around.

We were camped in a Thousand Trails park in Hershey, PA, several years ago. We took a day trip in the car and it got dark and we weren't sure how to get back. Never fear, Gertrude, our trusty GPS was there to take us home. We spent two hours driving down farm roads and country lanes and around detours with Gertrude squawking "Recalculating" constantly. To her credit, we did get back to the campground by the most convoluted route imaginable. It turns out that there were several other ways we could have gone that would have taken about forty-five minutes. We only found this out the next day in the light and with several local folks telling us. The lessons learned here is that our GPS routed us by the most direct "as the crow flies" method and Gertrude is a dummy. The detours were an added special attraction. If you can set your GPS for shortest way, try that.

■ Parking Your Rig

There are many lessons learned here. Just as in hooking up your towed car, the lesson learned here is: practice, practice, practice. No matter whether you have a motorhome or a trailer, you should practice backing into a campsite before you set out on your journey. The best way we have found is to find a large church parking lot or a closed Wal-Mart or other large store with an empty lot. Buy some rubber traffic cones; you can use them later on to mark a campsite. Set up the cones to mark the boundaries of an imaginary campsite. Then practice backing into that without knocking over the cones. This is the time for you and your partner to set up the signals you will use later in a real campground. A lesson I learned from this was to stop and not move when you don't understand a signal. Eventually your honey will come to the window to investigate why you aren't moving. A Friday evening spectacle at many campgrounds is watching inexperienced folks try to park their rigs as the light is fading. The language can get a little rough, too. Another good lesson here is: If at all possible, plan to arrive at the campground at least two hours before sundown.

■ **Propane Appliances**

The lesson here is to leave repair or maintenance on any propane appliance or other part of the propane system to an experienced RV service technician. They have the equipment and know-how to detect pressure drops and leaks. Remember, many RV fires are caused by propane problems, especially in refrigerators. If you have a twelve volt and propane refrigerator, check to see if it is covered in the major recall by the major refrigerator manufacturers. Ours was in the group. I took the rig in to an authorized service center to have the "fix" installed. Five months later, the unit stopped working. It turned out we had a leak in the refrigerant piping that could easily have led to a fire if we didn't have the fix in place. This was a huge lesson learned for us. Check out Chapter 17 for lots of information on RV refrigerator recalls.

■ **Satellite TV**

In our time on the road, we have used both DISH Network and Direct TV for our satellite TV service. The biggest difference I can see is that Dish will work in High Definition mode with dome antennas and Direct will not. Customer service for both can be wonderful one day and almost nonexistent the next. In any case, the main lesson learned here is that roof mounted antennas can easily be blocked by trees. It's relatively simple to carry an independent portable dish you can set up on a tripod and place wherever you have a clear shot at the southern sky. High Definition antennas can be large and heavy. You will need a heavy duty tripod for them.

■ **RV Showers**

Although our shower is small, it's comfortable. However, one thing to remember is to either leave the gray tank open, or make sure there is enough room left in the tank for the shower. So I'm in the shower, enjoying the wonderful feel of getting clean, when I notice that the water is up around my ankles: I think, "Oh boy, the drain is plugged." Well, in a very short amount of time, water was starting to over flow the shower stall and John is nowhere in sight or sound! I'm yelling his name – he is not answering me, I'm without clothes and water is going everywhere. Let's just say that I spent the rest of the afternoon cleaning the bathroom and not talking to John until I calmed down (it really wasn't his fault) and took another shower. Lesson learned: It is good to keep water in the gray tank to clean your sewer hose, but check the level in the gray tank (if the tank is closed) before taking a shower.

This might be a good place to talk about how much fun it is taking a shower in a campground with low water pressure. I do not like dancing around the shower head trying to get wet all over. One of the lessons learned here is to have enough water in your fresh water tank that you can use your water pump, if it has enough flow to be better than the wimpy pressure from the campground. We have found that the best solution is an Oxygenics Shower head. It mixes air with the water and seems to produce a strong spray even with low incoming pressure. It's a winner folks. Lessons learned are fun, aren't they?

■ Wal-Mart Stops or Wallydocking

There will be occasions where you may stop for the night in a Wal-Mart parking lot. The lesson here is to immediately go inside to get permission to park overnight from a manager. Unless local ordinances prevent it, the manager will likely agree and even direct you to an area of the lot where you should park. If you ignore this advice, do not be surprised to get a knock on your door at 2:00 AM and find the local constabulary directing you to leave immediately.

Among other lessons learned the hard way is to park with a clear lane to depart in the morning. You may be parked in what you think is a good spot and when you wake up, ten more rigs are parked all around you. Plan ahead.

This is a good place to talk about RVers' etiquette in parking lots as developed by the Escapees RV Club, and now endorsed by most other RV groups.

■ Industry-Sanctioned Code of Conduct

(RVers' Good Neighbor Policy)

1. Stay one night only!
2. Obtain permission from a qualified individual.
3. Obey posted regulations.
4. No awnings, chairs, or barbecue grills.
5. Do not use hydraulic jacks on soft surfaces (including asphalt).
6. Always leave an area cleaner than you found it.
7. Purchase gas, food, or supplies as a form of thank you, when feasible.
8. Be safe! Always be aware of your surroundings, and leave if you feel unsafe.

■ Water Leaks

If you detect water leaking into your rig, investigate immediately before the repair costs are out of sight. Water will run in the most direct path of gravity and this can be sideways. Our lesson learned was a leak in our slide-out roof that eventually caused the cabinets underneath to loosen and sag. If you can't find the leak source, have it checked out by a qualified RV service technician as soon as possible.

■ Weight and Overloading

Your rig and tow vehicle or towed car should be weighed when you purchase it and periodically after that. Weighing should be done on each end of each axel. You will want to know if you are overweight front to back as well as side to side. Shift cargo around as much as possible to even the load. If you exceed the Gross Vehicle Weight (GVW), you are looking at tire failure, front end suspension damage (on motorhomes), and frame damage (on towables). All of these can cost thousands of dollars to repair. Pay attention, because if your insurance company weighs the rig after a claim, they can, and probably will, deny a claim on an overweight rig. Once you know the weight, you can consult your tire manufacturer's charts for correct tire pressure to support that weight. The lessons learned here is those manufacturer's specifications are important. If you pay attention, you might save your life or at least a lot of money.

■ Windshield Wipers

I really don't mind driving in the rain – I just slow down and take my time. It is important, however, to remove the windshield wiper covers before moving down the road and needing to turn them on. Traveling in the south, you can get some real frog stranglers of rain. So, here I am driving and enjoying the beautiful day and thinking nothing could go wrong. Don't ever think those thoughts; it started to pour, and when I turned on the wipers, this big mess appeared on the windshield. With every swish more and more gunk was left on the window. Trying to pull over in traffic was a nightmare, but we managed, and poor John had to run out in the pouring rain to remove the covers. Let's just say he was not happy... I thought he looked really cute all wet. Lesson learned: Double check to make sure everything is stowed for travel.

RV TERMS

120 AC/12 DC/LP-gas – refers to the power sources on which RV refrigerators operate; 120 AC is 120-volt alternating current (same as in houses); 12 DC is 12-volt direct current (same as in motor vehicles); LP-gas. Some RV refrigerators can operate on two of the three sources, others on all three.

Adjustable Ball Mount – An adjustable ball mount allows the ball to be raised, lowered and tilted in small increments to allow fine tuning of the spring bar setup and to compensate for tow vehicle "squat," which occurs after the trailer coupler is lowered onto the ball.

Airbag – In RV terms, a sort of shock absorber positioned at the forward and rear axles of a motorhome.

Airstreaming – Using an Airstream travel trailer as RV of preference. Towing an Airstream travel trailer.

Anode Rod – An anode rod, when used in a water heater, attracts corrosion causing products in the water. These products attack the anode rod instead of the metal tank itself. The anode rod should be inspected yearly and changed when it is reduced to about 1/4 of its original size. The rods are used in steel water heater tanks – an aluminum tank has an inner layer of anode metal to accomplish the same thing. Anode rods should not be installed in an aluminum tank!

Arctic Pack – - Also spelled Arctic Pac and Arctic Pak, an optional kit to insulate RVs for winter camping.

Auxiliary battery – Extra battery to run 12-volt equipment.

Axle Ratio – The final drive gear ratio created by the relationship between the ring and pinion gears and the rotation of the driveshaft. In a 4.10:1 axle ratio, for example, the driveshaft will rotate 4.1 times for each rotation of the axle shaft (wheel).

Back-up monitor – Video camera mounted on rear of motorhome to assist the driver visually with backing up the motorhome, via a monitor mounted in the driver's compartment or in a central area of the cab where it can be viewed by the driver from the driver's seat. These monitors are usually left in the 'on' position to also assist the driver with the flow of traffic behind the motorhome and in watching a "towed" vehicle.

Ball Mount – The part of the hitch system that supports the hitch ball and connects it to the trailer coupler. Ball mounts are available in load-carrying and weight-distributing configurations.

Basement Model – An RV that incorporates large storage areas underneath a raised chassis.

Black Water – Waste (sewage) from the toilet that is flushed into a black water holding tank, usually located beneath the main floor of the RV.

Blueboy/Blue-Boy – Term for portable waste holding tank, often this plastic tank comes in a bright shade of blue, hence the term.

Boondocking – Camping in an RV without benefit of electricity, fresh water, and sewer utilities.

Bowtie – Reference to Chevrolet because of the "bowtie" trademark.

Box – Reference to motorhome's "living space" on a class A, built from the chassis up.

Brake Actuator – a device mounted under the dash of a towing vehicle to control the braking system of the trailer. Most brake actuators are based on a time delay, the more time the tow vehicle brakes are applied the "harder" the trailer brakes are applied.

Brake Controller – A control unit mounted inside the vehicle that allows electric trailer brakes to become activated in harmony with the braking of the tow vehicle. This device can be used to adjust trailer brake intensity, or to manually activate the trailer brakes.

Breakaway Switch – is a safety device that activates the trailer brakes in the event the trailer becomes accidentally disconnected from the hitch while traveling.

BTU – British thermal unit – A measurement of heat that is the quantity required to raise the temperature of one pound of water 1-degree F. RV air-conditioners and furnaces are BTU-rated.

Bubble – Loose term for defining a variety of conditions; such as when describing the level of RV sitting. (For example: my RV is 'off-level' a half bubble; referring to a 'bubble-leveler' tool). This can also be used to describe a delamination condition.

Bump Steer – A term used to describe a condition where the front axle feels to be rapidly bottoming out on the jounce bumpers and transferred back through the steering column and steering wheel. There can be several different causes to the problem with different cures for each condition. Sometimes a simple fix such as shocks or a steering stabilizer; sometimes more detailed corrections needed for correcting serious manufacturing oversights.

Bumper-Mount Hitch – This type of hitch is available in two configurations: A bracket with a ball mounted to the bumper or a ball is attached to the bumper (typically on pickup trucks). These hitches have very limited RV applications.

Bumper-Pull – Slang term regarding the hitch or towing method for a conventional travel trailer or popup; receiver and ball-mount type hitch.

Bunkhouse – An RV area containing bunk beds instead of regular beds.

Cabover – The part of a type C mini-motorhome that overlaps the top of the vehicle's cab, and usually contains a sleeping or storage unit.

Camber – Wheel alignment – Camber is the number of degrees each wheel is off of vertical. Looking from the front, if the tops of wheels are farther apart than bottoms, it means "positive camber". As the load pushes the front end down, or the springs get weak, camber would go from positive to none to negative (bottoms of wheels farther apart than tops).

Camper Shell – is a removable unit to go over the bed of a pickup truck.

Campground – Any kind of park that allows overnight stays in an outdoor sleeping area. It can be accessible only by foot, by hikers or backpackers, or can be a well developed RV Resort Park.

Caravan – A group of RVers traveling together with their various RVs. Large caravans often space RVs five minutes or so apart with CB radios used for communication between the various RVers. The end vehicle is sometimes called the "tailgunner" and it's the occupants watch out for a caravan member that may have had road trouble in order to assist, however possible.

Cassette Toilet – Toilet with a small holding tank that can be removed from outside the vehicle in order to empty it.

Castor – Wheel alignment – The steering wheels' desire to return to center after you turn a corner.

Chassis Battery – Battery in motorhome for operating 12 volt components of drive train.

Class A Motorhome – An RV with the living accommodations built on or as an integral part of a self-propelled motor vehicle. Models range from 24 to 40 feet long.

Class B Motorhome – is also known as a camping van conversion. These RVs are built within the dimensions of a van, but with a raised roof to provide additional headroom. Basic living accommodations inside are ideal for short vacations or weekend trips. Models usually range from 16 to 21 feet.

Class C Motorhome – An RV with the living accommodations built on a cutaway van chassis. A full-size bed in the cabover section allows for ample seating, galley and bathroom facilities in the coach. It is also called a "mini-motorhome" or "mini." Lengths range from approximately 16 to 32 feet.

Coach – Another name for a motorhome

Cockpit – The front of a motorized RV where the pilot (driver) and co-pilot (navigator) sit.

Condensation – Condensation is a result of warm moisture-laden air contacting the cold window glass. Keeping a roof vent open will help to reduce the humidity levels. Those added roof vents help to prevent cold air from dropping down through the vent while still allowing moist air to escape. Using the roof vent fan when showering or the stove vent fan when cooking also helps prevent excess moisture buildup.

Converter – An electrical device for converting 120-volt AC power into 12-volt DC power. Most RVs with electrical hookups will have a converter, since many of the lights and some other accessories run on 12-volt DC.

Covered Camper Wagons/Tepees – are canvas-covered wagons with or without electricity. Typically accommodates four or more people.

Coupler – The part of a trailer A-frame that attaches to the hitch ball.

Crosswise – A piece of furniture arranged across the RV from side to side rather than front to rear.

Curb Weight – The weight of a basic RV unit without fresh or waste water in the holding tanks but with automotive fluids such as fuel, oil, and radiator coolant.

Curbside – The side of the RV that would be at the curb when parked.

Detonation – Also known as "knock" or "ping," this is a condition in which some of the unburned air/fuel in the combustion chamber explodes at the wrong time in the ignition cycle, increasing mechanical and thermal stress on the engine.

Diesel Puller – Term for front engine diesel motorhome.

Diesel Pusher – is a motorhome with a rear diesel engine.

Dinette – booth-like dining area. Table usually drops to convert unit into a bed at night.

Dinghy – A vehicle towed behind a motorhome, sometimes with two wheels on a special trailer called a tow dolly, but often with all four wheels on the ground.

Dry Camping/Boondocking – camping in a recreational vehicle with no hookups and no utilities.

DSI Ignition – direct spark ignition – this term refers to the method of igniting the main burner on a propane fired appliance. The burner is lit with an electric spark and the flame is monitored by an electronic circuit board. This ignition system is used in refrigerators, furnaces and water heaters. There is now a version of stove tops that light the burners with a DSI ignition.

Dual Electrical System – RV equipped with lights, appliances which operate on 12-volt battery power when self-contained, and with a converter, on 110 AC current when in campgrounds or with an onboard generator.

Dually – A pickup truck, or light-duty tow vehicle, with four tires on one rear axle.

Ducted AC – is air conditioning supplied through a ducting system in the ceiling. This supplies cooling air at various vents located throughout the RV.

Ducted HEAT – is warm air from the furnace supplied to various locations in the RV through a ducting system located in the floor. (Similar to house heating systems)

Dump station – Usually a concrete pad with an inlet opening connected to an underground sewage system at a campground or other facility offering dumping service to RV travelers.

DW – Dry weight. The manufacturer's listing of the approximate weight of the RV with no supplies, water, fuel or passengers.

Engine Oil Cooler – A heat exchanger, similar to a small radiator, through which engine oil passes and is cooled by airflow.

Equalizing Hitch – is a hitch that utilizes spring bars that are placed under tension to distribute a portion of the trailer's hitch weight to the tow vehicle's front axle and the trailer's axles. The hitch is also known as a weight-distributing hitch.

Extended Stay Site – Sites allotted for RVers to stay for an extended period of time, like a month or a season. Often times, parks that allow extended stays have restrictions against RVs that are more than 5 or 10 years old.

Federal Parks – Parks run by the National Forest Service (NFS) or the National Park Service (NPS). These parks often offer work programs for reduced rate camping.

Fifth-Wheel Trailers – Fifth-wheel trailers are designed to be coupled to a special hitch that is mounted over the rear axle in the bed of a pickup truck. These trailers can have one, two or three axles and are the largest type of trailer built. Because of their special hitch requirements, fifth-wheel trailers can only be towed by trucks or specialized vehicles prepared for fifth-wheel trailer compatibility.

Final Drive Ratio – is the reduction ratio found in the gear set that is located farthest from the engine. This is the same as the axle ratio.

Fiver – Other name for fifth wheel.

FMCA – Abbreviation for Family Motor Coach Association.

Frame-Mount Hitch – Class II and higher hitches are designed to be bolted to the vehicle frame or cross members. This type of hitch may have a permanent ball mount, or may have a square-tube receiver into which a removable hitch bar or shank is installed.

Fresh water – Water suitable for human consumption.

Full hookup – Term for campground accommodations offering water, sewer/septic and electricity; also refers to a RV with the abilities to use 'full-hookups'.

Full-timing – Living in one's RV all year long. These RVers are known as full-timers.

Galley – The kitchen of an RV.

Gas Pusher – Slang for rear gasoline engine mounted chassis on motorhome.

Gaucho – Sofa/dinette bench that converts into a sleeping unit; a term less used now than formerly.

GAWR (Gross Axle Weight Rating) – The manufacturer's rating for the maximum allowable weight that an axle is designed to carry. GAWR applies to tow vehicle, trailer, and fifth-wheel and motorhome axles.

GCWR (Gross Combination Weight Rating) – is the maximum allowable weight of the combination of tow vehicle and trailer/ fifth-wheel, or motorhome and dinghy. It includes the weight of the vehicle, trailer/fifth-wheel (or dinghy), cargo, passengers and a full load of fluids (fresh water, propane, fuel, etc.).

Gear Vendor – Brand name for an auxiliary transmission designed to give the driver control of the vehicle's gear ratio and being able to split gears for peak performance and at the same time have an overdrive.

Generator – An electrical device powered by gasoline or diesel fuel, and sometimes propane, for generating 120-volt AC power.

Genset – Abbreviation for generator set.

Gooseneck – A colloquial name for fifth-wheel travel trailers.

Gray water – is used water that drains from the kitchen and bathroom sinks and the shower into a holding tank, called a gray water holding tank that is located under the main floor of the RV.

Group Camping Areas – Camping areas at a campground that accommodate larger groups of twenty or more. Typically, group camping areas have a fire ring and/or other central location for group activities.

GTWR (Gross Trailer Weight Rating) – Maximum allowable weight of a trailer, fully loaded with cargo and fluids.

GVWR (Gross Vehicle Weight Rating) – is the total allowable weight of a vehicle, including passengers, cargo, fluids and hitch weight.

Hard-sided – RV walls made of aluminum or other hard surface.

Heat Exchanger – A heat exchanger is a device that transfers heat from one source to another. For example, there is a heat exchanger in your furnace – the propane flame and combustion products are contained inside the heat exchanger that is sealed from the inside area. Inside air is blown over the surface of the exchanger, where it is warmed and the blown through the ducting system for room heating. The combustion gases are vented to the outside air.

Heat Strip – A heat strip is an electric heating element located in the air conditioning system with the warm air distributed by the air conditioner fan and ducting system. They are typically 1500 watt elements (about the same wattage as an electric hair dryer) and have limited function. Basically they "take the chill off"

High Profile – is a fifth-wheel trailer with a higher-than-normal front to allow more than 6 feet of standing room inside the raised area.

Historic sites — These are sites of national cultural importance. They include buildings, objects, monuments and landscapes. Historic sites are generally open to visitors.

Hitch – The fastening unit that joins a movable vehicle to the vehicle that pulls it.

Hitch Weight – The amount of weight imposed on the hitch when the trailer/fifth-wheel is coupled. Sometimes it is referred to as conventional trailer "tongue weight." Hitch weight for a travel trailer can be 10-15 percent of overall weight; fifth-wheel hitch weight is usually 18 to 20 percent of the overall weight.

Holding Tanks – Tanks that retain waste water when the RV unit is not connected to a sewer. The gray water tank holds wastewater from the sinks and shower; the black water tank holds sewage from the toilet.

Hookups – The ability of connecting to a campground's facilities. The major types of hookups are electrical, water and sewer. If all three of these hookups are available, it is termed full hookup. Hookups may also include telephone and cable TV in some campgrounds.

House Battery – Battery or batteries in motorhome for operating the 12-volt system within the motorhome, separate from the chassis.

HP – Abbreviation for "horse power".

HR – Abbreviation for Holiday Rambler, a well-known RV manufacturer.

Hula skirt – Term used for a type of dirt skirt accessory some RVers use on the back of their motorhome to aid in the protection from debris thrown from their rear wheels to the vehicles directly behind them or being towed behind them. This dirt skirt is usually the length of the rear bumper and resembles a 'short' version of a Hawaiian 'hula-skirt', hence the term.

Inverter – A unit that changes 12-volt direct current to 110-volt alternating current to allow operation of computers, TV sets, and such when an RV is not hooked up to electricity.

Island Queen – is a queen-sized bed with walking space on both sides.

Jackknife – 90% angle obtained from turning/backing fifth wheel or travel trailer with tow vehicle. Jackknifing a short bed truck towing a fifth wheel without the use of a slider hitch or extended fifth wheel pin box can result in damage to the truck cab or breaking out the back window of the truck cab from the truck and fifth wheel "colliding".

KOA – Kampgrounds of America, a franchise chain of RV parks in North America that offers camping facilities to vacationers and overnighters.

Laminate – sandwich of structural frame members, wall paneling, insulation and exterior covering, adhesive-bonded under pressure and/or heat to form the RVs walls, floor and/or roof.

Leveling – Positioning the RV in camp so it will be level, using ramps (also called levelers) placed under the wheels, built-in scissors jacks, or power leveling jacks.

Limited-Slip Differential – A differential that is designed with a mechanism that limits the speed and torque differences between its two outputs, ensuring that torque is distributed to both drive wheels, even when one is on a slippery surface.

Livability Packages – are the items to equip a motorhome for daily living, which may be rented at nominal cost from rental firm, rather than brought from home. Include bed linens, pillows and blankets, bath towels, pots and pans, kitchen utensils, cutlery.

Log Cabins – Typically two or more rooms, and accommodates four or more people. Cabins usually have private bathrooms and a kitchen area with a refrigerator.

LP Gas – Propane; abbreviation for liquefied petroleum gas, which is a gas liquefied by compression, consisting of flammable hydrocarbons and obtained as a by-product from the refining of petroleum or natural gas. Also called bottled gas, LPG (liquid petroleum gas) and CPG (compressed petroleum gas).

Marine parks – These are unique and outstanding marine areas set aside to conserve seawater plants and animals. They're divided into zones that allow different, sustainable levels of commercial and recreational activities.

MH – Abbreviation for "motorhome".

Minnie Winnie – A brand model of Winnebago.

Motor coach – is the term for motorhome on "bus-type" chassis.

NADA – Abbreviation for National Automotive Dealers Association.

Nature reserves --These are areas of special scientific interest, set up mainly to conserve their native plant and animal communities. Few have visitor facilities.

NCC (Net Carrying Capacity) – is the maximum weight of all passengers (if applicable), personal belongings, food, fresh water, supplies – derived by subtracting the UVW from the GVWR.

Nonpotable water – Water not suitable for human consumption.

OEM – Original Equipment Manufacturer.

Park Model – Type of RV that is usually designed for permanent parking but is shorter in length than a traditional mobile home. All the amenities of a mobile home but not built for recreational travel.

Part-timers – People who use their RV for longer than normal vacation time but less than one year.

Patio mat – Carpet or woven mat for use on ground outside of RV. It may be used whether or not a concrete patio pad is available where camping.

Payload Capacity – The maximum allowable weight that can be placed in or on a vehicle, including cargo, passengers, fluids and fifth-wheel or conventional hitch loads.

Pilot – a pilot is a small standby flame that is used to light the main burner of a propane fired appliance when the thermostat calls for heat. Pilots can be used in furnaces, water heaters, refrigerators, ovens and stove tops.

Pitch-in – Term for a RV campground "get-together", usually means "pitching-in" a covered dish or casserole.

PO – Abbreviation for "pop-up" camper.

Pop-out – Term for room or area that 'pops-out' for additional living space in RV. This type of expanded living area was more common before the technology of slide-out rooms became popular and available.

Popup/Pop-Up – Folding camping trailer.

Porpoising – A term used to define an up and down motion with a RV.

Primitive camping – Also known as "dry camping", boondocking. Camping without the modern convenience of full-hookup facilities of city/well water, sewer/septic and electricity. Primitive campers rely on 'on-board' systems for these conveniences; generator, batteries, stored water, etc.

Propane – LPG, or liquefied petroleum gas, used in RVs for heating, cooking and refrigeration. Also called bottle gas, for manner in which it is sold and stored.

Puller – slang for front engine motorhome. Term most often used to refer to front mounted diesel engine motorhomes.

Pull-through – A campsite that allows the driver to pull into the site to park, then pull out the other side when leaving, without ever having to back up.

Pusher – Slang for rear engine motorhome. Term most often used to refer to diesel engine motor homes.

Receiver – The portion of a hitch that permits a hitch bar or shank to be inserted. The receiver may be either 11/2-, 15/8- or 2-inch square; the smallest being termed a mini-hitch.

Reefer – Slang for "refrigerator". Refrigerators are often found in either a "two way" or "three way" operating mode. Two way: has a gas mode and an AC mode. Three way: has a gas mode, AC mode, and 12v DC mode. The coolant used in RV refrigeration is ammonia. The two most common manufacturers of RV refrigerators are Norcold and Dometic.

Regional parks – Near large population centers, these parks offer open space and recreational and cultural opportunities for urban residents.

RIG – what many RVers call their units.

Road Wander – Term used to describe a lack of ability to maintain the motorhome in a straight, forward travel without constant back and forth motion of the steering wheel.

Roof Air Conditioning – For most RVs, the air conditioning unit is mounted on the roof. Some RVs have "bus a/c" that is contained in a basement storage area.

RV – short for Recreation Vehicle, a generic term for all pleasure vehicles which contain living accommodations. Multiple units are RVs and persons using them are RVers.

RVDA – Abbreviation for Recreational Vehicle Dealer's Association.

RVIA – Abbreviation for Recreational Vehicle Industry Association.

RV Park – Almost always privately owned, caters to overnight or seasonal guests who have recreational vehicles.

RV Resort Park – Almost always privately owned, caters to overnight or seasonal guests who have recreational vehicles. RV Resort is often an indication of a well developed, higher end park, but since any RV Park can call itself an RV Resort; this is not always the case.

Safety Chains – A set of chains that are attached to the trailer A-frame and must be connected to the tow vehicle while towing. Safety chains are intended to keep the trailer attached to the tow vehicle in the event of hitch failure, preventing the trailer from complete separation. They should be installed using an X-pattern, so the coupler is held off the road in the event of a separation.

Screen room – Term for screen enclosure that attaches to the exterior of a RV for a "bug free" outside sitting area. Some screen rooms have a canvas type roof for rain protection as well.

Self-contained – An RV that needs no external connections to provide short-term cooking, bathing, and heating functions and could park overnight anywhere.

Shank – Also called a hitch bar or stinger, the shank is a removable portion of the hitch system that carries the ball or adjustable ball mount, and slides into the receiver.

Shore cord – The external electrical cord that connects the vehicle to a campground electrical hookup.

Shore Power – Electricity provided to the RV by an external source other than the RV battery.

Slide-in – Term for a type of camper that mounts on a truck bed, because often this type of camper "slides-in" to the truck bed.

Slide-out – Additional living space that "slides-out" either by hydraulics, electricity or manually, when the RV is setup for camping.

Slider – Slang for slider-hitch.

Slider-hitch – Refers to a sliding hitch used on short bed trucks for enabling them to tow fifth wheels, allowing them sufficient clearance to jack-knife the trailer.

Snowbird – Term for someone in a northern climate that heads "south" in winter months.

Soft-sides – Telescoping side panels on an RV that can be raised or lowered usually constructed of canvas or vinyl and mesh netting.

Spring Bar – Component parts of a weight-distributing hitch system, the spring bars are installed and tensioned in such a manner as to distribute a portion of the trailer's hitch weight to the front axle of the tow vehicle and to the axles of the trailer.

State Park – These parks, run by state facilities, have many recreation opportunities and/or visitor centers. They are set within an extensive scenic setting.

State Wayside – Rest stops providing parking areas and restroom facilities with limited or no recreational opportunities.

State conservation areas – These are parks, often containing important natural environments, which have been set aside mainly for outdoor recreation.

Stinger – See shank.

Street side – The part of the vehicle on the street side when parked.

Sway – Fishtailing action of the trailer caused by external forces that set the trailer's mass into a lateral (side-to-side) motion. The trailer's wheels serve as the axis or pivot point. This is also known as "yaw."

Sway Control – Devices designed to damp the swaying action of a trailer, either through a friction system or a "cam action" system that slows and absorbs the pivotal articulating action between tow vehicle and trailer.

Tail Swing – Motorhomes built on chassis with short wheelbases and long overhangs behind the rear axle are susceptible to tail swing when turning sharply. As the motorhome moves in reverse or turns a corner, the extreme rear of the coach can move horizontally and strike objects nearby (typically road signs and walls). Drivers need to be aware of the amount of tail swing in order to prevent accidents.

Tail gunner – is the end RV or vehicle in a caravan. This driver is usually on the caravan staff.

Telescoping – Compacting from front to back and/or top to bottom to make the living unit smaller for towing and storage.

Tent Sites – no utilities, allows tent campers only.

Thermocouple – a thermocouple is a device that monitors the pilot flame of a pilot model propane appliance. If the pilot flame is extinguished the thermocouple causes the gas valve to shut off the flow of gas to both the pilot flame and the main burner.

Three-way refrigerators – These are appliances that can operate on a 12-volt battery, propane, or 110-volt electrical power.

Tip-out – Term for room (generally in older RVs) that "tipped-out" for additional living space once RV was parked. Newer RVs mainly use 'slide-out' rooms.

Toad – Another name for the towed vehicle.

Toe – Wheel alignment – Toe is the measure of whether the front of the wheels (looking down from the top) are closer (toe-in) or farther (toe-out) than the back of the wheels.

Tongue Weight – The amount of weight imposed on the hitch when the trailer is coupled. See "hitch weight."

Tow Bar – A device used for connecting a dinghy vehicle to the motorhome when it's towed with all four wheels on the ground.

Tow Rating – The manufacturer's rating of the maximum weight limit that can safely be towed by a particular vehicle. Tow ratings are related to overall trailer weight, not trailer size, in most cases. However, some tow ratings impose limits as to frontal area of the trailer and overall length. The vehicle manufacturer according to several criteria, including engine size, transmission, axle ratio, brakes, chassis, cooling systems and other special equipment, determines tow ratings.

Tow car – A car towed by an RV to be used as transportation when the RV is parked in a campground.

Toy-hauler – Term for fifth wheel, travel trailer or motorhome with built-in interior cargo space for motorcycles, bikes, etc.

Trailer Brakes – Brakes that are built into the trailer axle systems and are activated either by electric impulse or by a surge mechanism. The overwhelming majority of RVs utilize electric trailer brakes that are actuated when the tow vehicle's brakes are operated, or when a brake controller is manually activated. Surge brakes utilize a mechanism that is positioned at the coupler that detects when the tow vehicle is slowing or stopping, and activates the trailer brakes via a hydraulic system (typically used on boats).

Transmission Cooler – A heat exchanger similar to a small radiator through which automatic transmission fluid passes and is cooled by airflow.

Travel Trailer – Also referred to as "conventional trailers," these types of rigs have an A-frame and coupler and are attached to a ball mount on the tow vehicle. Travel trailers are available with one, two or three axles. Depending upon tow ratings, conventional trailers can be towed by trucks, cars or sport-utility vehicles.

Triple towing – Term for three vehicles attached together. This is usually a tow vehicle pulling a fifth wheel and the fifth wheel pulling a boat.

TV – Abbreviation for "tow vehicle".

Umbilical Cord – The wiring harness that connects the tow vehicle to the trailer, supplying electricity to the trailer's clearance and brake lights, electric brakes and a 12-volt DC power line to charge the trailer's batteries. An umbilical cord can also be the power cable that is used to connect to campground 120-volt AC electrical hookups.

Underbelly – The RVs under floor surface, which is protected by a weatherproofed material.

UTQGL (Uniform Tire Quality Grade Labeling) – A program that is directed by the government to provide consumers with information about three characteristics of the tire: tread wear, traction and temperature. Following government prescribed test procedures, tire manufacturers perform their own evaluations for these characteristics. Each manufacturer then labels the tire, according to grade.

UVW (Unloaded Vehicle Weight) – Weight of the vehicle without manufacturer's or dealer-installed options and before adding fuel, water or supplies.

Wagonmaster – A leader, either hired or chosen, who guides a caravan of recreational vehicles on a trip. The wagonmaster usually makes advance reservations for campgrounds, shows, cruises, sightseeing and group meals.

Wally World – Slang term used by RVers to describe a Wal-Mart.

Weekender's – People who own their RVs for weekend and vacation use.

Weight-Carrying Hitch – Also known as a "dead-weight" hitch, this category includes any system that accepts the entire hitch weight of the trailer. In the strictest sense, even a weight-distributing hitch can act as a load-carrying hitch if the spring bars are not installed and placed under tension.

Weight-Distributing Hitch – Also known as an "equalizing" hitch, this category includes hitch systems that utilize spring bars that can be placed under tension to distribute a portion of the trailer's hitch weight to the tow vehicle's front axle and the trailer's axles.

Weights: – water (weight): 8.3 lbs. per gallon; LP gas (weight): 4.5 lbs. per gallon; Gasoline: weighs 6.3 pounds per gallon; Diesel fuel: weighs 6.6 pounds per gallon; Propane: weighs 4.25 pounds per gallon.

Wet Weight – Term used by RVers to describe the weight of a RV with all storage and holding tanks full. i.e., water, propane, etc.

Wheelbase – Distance between center lines of the primary axles of a vehicle. If a motorhome includes a tag axle, the distance is measured from the front axle to the center point between the drive and tag axles.

Wide body – Designs that stretch RVs from the traditional 96-inch width to 100 or 102 inches.

Wilderness – Wilderness is usually an 'overlay' on national parks or reserves. Wilderness areas are large, remote and essentially unchanged by modern human activity. They are managed so that native plant and animal communities are disturbed as little as possible.

Winnie – Nickname for Winnebago, a well-known RV manufacturer.

Winterize – To prepare the RV for winter use or storage.

World Heritage-listed areas – The globally recognized World Heritage list contains some of the most important examples of natural and cultural heritage in the world. More than 600 precious places are on the list, from the Great Barrier Reef to the pyramids of Egypt.

Yaw – Fishtailing action of the trailer caused by external forces that set the trailer's mass into a lateral (side-to-side) motion. The trailer's wheels serve as the axis or pivot point. This is also known as "sway."

Yurts – circular, domed tent-like structures with wood floors, electricity, heating, lockable doors and sleeping accommodations for typically for four or more people.

ABOUT THE AUTHORS

Kathy and I are really just plain folks like you, but we live in a forty-foot RV instead of a house. Maybe we lost our minds a bit; but we're happy we did. I am retired from the US Navy as well as a retired manufacturing Quality Manager. Kathy has worked extensively in the medical administrative field. We had travelled worldwide due to my naval service as well as locations on both coasts of our beautiful country. We would see the big bus conversions and Winnebago RV's on the interstates and we both said, "one day that will be us". We started dreaming in earnest in 2003, a year before my job was out sourced. We went to shows and visited dealerships just to see if we could really do this. We could. We took the plunge two years later after we sold our house in Florida and bought "The Dream Machine", our 2004 Fleetwood Expedition diesel motor home. Since then we have travelled extensively through the states we used to fly over and discovered a unique and awesomely beautiful land that pictures do not give justice to.

We have been volunteers, workampers, podcasters, and now authors. Our Podcast, or internet radio show is titled Living the RV Dream and we discuss everything about the RV lifestyle. Check it out on iTunes in the podcast section or on our website. Our blog is also available on our website on the Podcast and blog page.

We have written 2 books. The first is "So, You Want to be an RVer?" Next came "So, You Want to be a Workamper?" Both are available on-line I hope you enjoy our books; and if you see us on the road, honk and wave.

We have a very extensive website with much information about every kind of RVing. Check it out at:

▶ http://www.livingthervdream.com.

Visit our huge Facebook group at:

▶ https://www.facebook.com/groups/livingthervdream/

Email us at: johnandkathyhuggins@yahoo.com